Coherent Stress Testing

Dr Riccardo Rebonato (London, UK), is Head of Front Office Risk Management and Head of the Clients Analytics team at GBM RBS. He is visiting lecturer at Oxford University (Mathematical Finance) and adjunct professor at Imperial College (Tanaka Business School). He sits on the Board of Directors of ISDA and on the Board of Trustees for GARP. He is an editor for the International Journal of Theoretical and Applied Finance, Applied Mathematical Finance, Journal of Risk, and the Journal of Risk Management in Financial Institutions. He holds doctorates in Nuclear Engineering and in Science of Materials/Solid State Physics. He was a research fellow in Physics at Corpus Christi College, Oxford, UK.

Coherent Stress Testing

A Bayesian Approach to the Analysis of Financial Stress

Riccardo Rebonato

A John Wiley and Sons, Ltd., Publication

Registered office
John Wiley & Sons Ltd, The Atrium, Southern Gate, Chichester, West Sussex, PO19 8SQ, United Kingdom

For details of our global editorial offices, for customer services and for information about how to apply for permission to reuse the copyright material in this book please see our website at www.wiley.com.

Library of Congress Cataloging-in-Publication Data

Rebonato, Riccardo.
  Coherent stress testing : a Bayesian approach / Riccardo Rebonato.
     p. cm.
  ISBN 978-0-470-66601-2
  1.   Risk management. 2.   Probabilities. 3.   Bayesian statistical decision theory.   I. Title.
  HD61.R42 2010
  658.15′501519542 – dc22

                                                                    2010005778

A catalogue record for this book is available from the British Library.

ISBN 978-0-470-66601-2

Typeset in 10/12 Times-Roman by Laserwords Private Limited, Chennai, India

To my parents
To my wife
To my son

Contents

Acknowledgements

It gives me great pleasure to acknowledge the support I received while writing this book.

Dr Keating provided very insightful comments and pointed out some 'loose thinking'. I am very grateful for that.

Many of my colleagues have helped me a lot, by challenging my thoughts, pointing out what did and did not work, and suggesting how I could improve the approach. I am sure that I will forget many, but I certainly extend my thanks to Dr Gary Dunn, Dr Ron Keating, Dr Ronnie Barnes, Mr Daniel Burns, Dr Michael Smith, Mr Paul Fairhurst, Dr Jeremy Broughton, Dr Ed Hayes, Mr Craig Schor, Dr Tom Connor and, for his unflinching criticism, Dr Stephen Laughton. Above all, however, I thank Dr Jan Kwiatkowski, who proposed an earlier version of the Linear Programming approach that I describe in Chapter 10. His contribution has extended well beyond this technical suggestion, as over the years he has become my Bayesian mentor.

I have greatly benefited from discussions that I have had with regulators, at the Boston Fed, at the FSA and at the MSA. I am grateful for the time they spent discussing my ideas on stress testing.

I have presented parts of the material in this book at several conferences in the US and in Europe, and therefore I have received extremely useful and insightful comments from many delegates. The book would be much the poorer without their suggestions: thank you.

At John Wiley & Sons, Ltd, Caitlin Cornish first and then Pete Baker have shown from the start great enthusiasm for the project. I am very grateful for this.

Last but not least, my wife and my parents have given me continuous support and encouragement. In a way, it is to them that I owe my greatest debt of gratitude.

Despite all this help, I am sure that there are still many mistakes and imperfections in the book. I am fully and solely responsible for these.

Chapter 1

Introduction

[Under uncertainty] there is no scientific basis on which to form any calculable probability whatever. We simply don't know. Nevertheless, the necessity for action and for decision compels us as practical men to do our best to overlook this awkward fact and to behave exactly as we should if we had behind us [...] a series of prospective advantages and disadvantages, each multiplied by its appropriate probability waiting to be summed....

Robertson (1936)

1.1 Why We Need Stress Testing

Why a book about stress testing? And why a book about stress testing *now*? Stress testing has been part of the risk manager's toolkit for decades.[1] What justifies the renewed interest from practitioners and regulators[2] for a risk management tool that, truth be told, has always been the poor relation in the family of analytical techniques to control risk?[3] And why has stress testing so far been regarded as a second-class citizen?

Understanding the reason for the renewed interest is simple: the financial crisis of 2007–2008–2009 has shown with painful clarity the limitations of the purely statistical techniques (such as Value at Risk (VaR) or Economic Capital) that were supposed to provide the cornerstones of the financial edifice. In the year and a half starting with July 2007, events of once-in-many-thousand-years rarity kept on occurring with disconcerting regularity. Only a risk manager of Stalinist dogmatism could have lived through these events and 'kept the faith'. Clearly, something more – or, rather, something *different* – had to be done. But what? And what analytical tools should we employ to fix the problem?

---

[1] See, e.g., Sorge (2004) for a review of stress testing methodologies put together before the sub-prime crisis, or Alexander and Sheedy (2008) for a recent approach firmly rooted in the statistical analysis of past data.

Stress testing is dealt with, often in a rather cursory manner, in most standard texts on risk management. I assume in this book that the reader is broadly familiar with current stress-testing practice. By quoting from the work of Aragones, Blanco and Dowd (2001), I explain in this chapter a common shortcoming of these approaches. Indeed, this shortcoming is one of the motivations of the approach I propose.

[2] See, e.g., BIS (2009).

[3] "Those who can, do, and those who can't, do stress testing", a proud risk quant told me less than two years ago.

'Stress testing' has become the stock answer to these questions. But the unease and suspicion with which this technique has been regarded has not melted away. The frog has not been kissed (yet) into a handsome prince. The current attitude seems one of resigned acceptance of a *faute-de-mieux* measure of risk: a far cry from an enthusiastic embrace of a new and powerful analytical tool. Two cheers, the mood seems to be, for stress testing. Can we do better? And why has stress testing been regarded as such an ungainly frog in the first place?

If by stress testing we mean the assessment of very severe financial losses arrived at without heavy reliance on statistical techniques, but by deploying instead a large dose of subjective judgement, some answers to the latter question are not difficult to see. Rather than paraphrasing, I would like to quote extensively from an article by Aragones, Blanco and Dowd (2001), who put their fingers exactly on the problem:

> ... traditional stress testing is done on a stand-alone basis, and the results of stress tests are evaluated side-by-side with the results of traditional market risk (or VaR) models. This creates problems for risk managers, who then have to choose which set of risk exposures to 'believe'. [R]isk managers often don't know whether to believe their stress test results, because the stress tests exercises give them no idea of how likely or unlikely stress-test scenarios might be....

And again:

> A related problem is that the results of stress tests are difficult to interpret because they give us no idea of the probabilities of the events concerned, and in the absence of such information we often don't know what to do with them. Suppose for instance that stress testing reveals that our firm will go bust under a particular scenario. Should we act on this information? The only answer is that we can't say. If the scenario is very likely, we would be very unwise not to act on it. But if the scenario was extremely unlikely, then it becomes almost irrelevant, because we would not usually expect management to take expensive precautions against events that may be too improbable to worry about. So the extent to which our results matter or not depends on unknown probabilities. As Berkowitz [1999] nicely puts it, this absence of probabilities puts 'stress testing in a statistical purgatory. We have some loss numbers, but who is to say whether we should be concerned about them?'

The result of this state of affairs is not pretty: we are left with

> ... two sets of separate risk estimates – probabilistic estimates (e.g., such as VaR), and the loss estimates produced by stress tests – and no way of combining them. How can we combine a probabilistic risk estimate with an estimate that such-and-such a loss will occur if such-and-such happens? The answer, of course, is that we can't. We therefore have to work with these estimates more or less independently of each other, and the best we can do is use one set of estimates to check for prospective losses that the other might have underrated or missed...

In modern finance, risk and reward are supposed to be two sides of the same coin. Risk is 'priced' in terms of expected return by assigning probabilities[4] to outcomes. But when

---

[4]Note that I did not say 'assigning objective probabilities known and agreed upon by all the market participants'. See Shefrin (2008) for a discussion of asset pricing under heterogeneous beliefs about probabilities. See also the discussion in Chapter 3.

it comes to extreme events, absent of any probabilistic assessment, we don't know how to 'price' the outcomes of stress testing. And if our confidence in assigning a probability to extremely rare events has been terminally shaken by the recent market events,[5] the state of impasse seems inescapable.

Perhaps there is hope – and it is exactly this ray of hope that this book pursues. First of all, 'probabilistic statement' need not be equated with 'frequentist (i.e., purely data-driven) probabilistic statement'. As I discuss in Chapter 4, there is a different way of looking at probability that takes into account, but is not limited to, the pure analysis of data. I maintain (and I have argued at length elsewhere[6]) that the subjective view of probability is every bit as 'respectable' as the purely-data-driven (frequentist) one. I also believe that it is much better suited to the needs of risk management.

This view, while not mainstream, is not particularly new, especially in the context of financial risk management – see, e.g., Berkowitz (1999). However, the subjective approach brings about an insidious problem. It is all well and good to assign subjective probabilities to stand-alone events. But, if we want to escape from Berkowitz's purgatory, we will have to do more. We will have to combine different stress scenarios, with different subjective probabilities, into an overall coherent, albeit approximate, stress loss number at a given confidence level (or, perhaps, into a whole stress loss distribution). How is one to do that? How is one to provide *subjectively* these co-dependences – and *tail* co-dependences to boot? How is one to ensure that the subjectively-assigned probabilities are reasonable, let alone feasible (i.e., mathematically possible and self-consistent)?

This book offers two routes to escape this purgatorial dilemma. The first is the acknowledgement that the risk manager can only make sense of data on the basis of a model (or of competing models) of reality. A risk manager, for instance, should have a conception of the direction of causation between different events: does a dramatic fall in equity prices 'cause' an increase in equity implied volatilities? Or is it an increase in implied volatility that 'causes' a dramatic fall in equity prices? The answer, at least in this case, may seem obvious. Unfortunately, correlations, and even conditional probabilities, contain no information about the direction of causation. Yet, this information about causation, even if imperfect, is powerful. It is ignored in the frequentist approach at a great loss for the risk manager. Speaking about the sciences in general, Pearl (2009) points out that there is 'no greater impediment to scientific progress than the prevailing practice of focusing all of our mathematical resources on statistical and probabilistic inferences'. I believe that exactly the same applies in the area of quantitative risk management.

If one is prepared to 'stick one's neck out' and make some reasonable assumptions about the direction of the arrow of causation, just like Dante one can begin to glimpse some light filtering through the thick trees of the *selva oscura*. In the case of stress testing, the route to salvation is via the provision of information that is not 'contained in the data'.

Sure enough, even if one can provide this extra information not all is plain sailing. Organizing one's understanding about how the world might work into a coherent and tractable analytical probabilistic framework is not an easy task. Fortunately, if one is prepared to make some reasonable approximations, there are powerful *and intuitive* techniques that can offer great help in building plausible and mathematically self-consistent joint distributions

---

[5]Of course, there are techniques such as Extreme Value Theory (EVT) that promise to give us a quantitative probabilistic glimpse of extremely rare events. I discuss in Chapter 4 my reservations about this and related techniques.

[6]See Rebonato (2007).

of the stress losses that have been identified. These technical tools (Bayesian networks and Linear Programming) have been well known for a long time, but their application to risk management problems, and to stress testing in particular, has been hesitant at best. This is a pity, because I believe that they are not only powerful and particularly well suited to the problem at hand, but also extremely intuitively appealing. And in Section 2.2 of the next chapter I will highlight how important appeal to intuition can be if the recommendations of the risk managers are to be acted upon (as opposed to 'confined to a stress report').

Once we accept that we can, approximately but meaningfully, associate stress events with a probabilistic assessment of their likelihood, the questions that opened this chapter begin to find a compelling answer. We need stress testing, and we need stress testing *now*, because the purely-data-based statistical techniques we have been using have proven unequal to the task when it really mattered. Perhaps the real question should have been instead: 'How can we do *without* stress testing?'

Of course, there is a lot more to risk management than predicting the probability of losses large and small. But, even if we look at the management of financial risk through the highly reductive prism of analysing the likelihood of losses, there still is no one single goal for the risk manager. For instance, estimating the kind of profit-and-loss variability that can be expected on a weekly or monthly basis has value and importance. Ensuring that a business line or trading desk effectively 'diversifies' the revenue stream from other existing lines of activity *under normal market conditions* is also obviously important. So is estimating the income variability or the degree of diversification that can be expected from a portfolio of businesses over a business cycle. And recent events have shown the importance of ensuring that a set of business activities do not endanger the survival of a financial institution even under exceptional market conditions. These are all important goals for a risk manager. But it would be extraordinary if the same analytical tools could allow the risk manager to handle all these problems – problems, that is, whose solution hinges on the estimation of probabilities of events that should occur, on average, from once every few weeks to once in several decades. This is where stress testing comes in. Stress testing picks up the baton from VaR and other data-driven statistical techniques as the time horizons become longer and longer and the risk manager wants to explore the impact of events that are not present in her dataset – or, perhaps, that have never occurred before.[7]

As I explain in Chapter 4, stress testing, by its very nature, can rely much less on a frequentist concept of probability, and almost *has* to interpret probability in a subjective sense. In Bayesian terms, as the time horizon lengthens and the severity of the events increases, the 'prior' acquires a greater and greater weight, and the likelihood function a smaller and smaller one.[8] In my opinion, this is a strength, not a weakness, of stress testing. It is also, however, the aspect of the project I propose that requires most careful handling. Frequentist probability may make little sense when it comes to stress testing, but this does not mean that probability *tout court* has no place in stress testing. If anything, it is stress testing without *any* notion of probability that, as Aragones, Blanco and Dowd remind us, is of limited use. The challenge taken up in this book is to provide the missing link between

---

[7]Is Extreme Value Theory not supposed to provide information about the far tails of a distribution? It may, but only if the underlying phenomenon is time-stationary over sufficiently long time periods (decades if we try to estimate once-in-a-decade events). Also, EVT is silent about the causal mechanism that produces the tail events. There is no way of telling whether, conditional on today's state of the world, the probability of the tail event predicted by the EVT applies. See Chapter 4 and Sections 4.2 to 4.4 in particular.

[8]For readers not familiar with Bayesian analysis, I shall explain what I mean by this in Chapter 4.

stress events and their approximate likelihood – as explained, an essential prerequisite for action[9] – without inappropriately resorting to purely frequentist methods.

The enterprise I have briefly sketched therefore gives us some hope of bringing stress losses within the same conceptual framework as the more mundane losses analysed by VaR-like techniques. The approach I suggest in this book bridges the gap between the probabilities that a risk manager *can*, with some effort, provide (marginal, and simple conditioned probabilities) and the probabilities that she requires (the joint probabilities). It does so by exploiting to the fullest the risk manager's understanding of the causal links between the individual stress events. By employing the causal, rather than associative, language, it resonates with our intuition and works with, not against, our cognitive grain.

The approach I suggest is therefore intended to give us guidance as to whether and when we should really worry, and to suggest how to act accordingly. It gives, in short, tools to ensure that the stress losses are approximately but consistently 'priced'. Hopefully, all of this might give us a tool for managing financial risk more effectively than we have been able to do so far.

This is what this book is about, and this is why, I think, it is important.

1.2 Plan of the Book

This book is structured in four parts. The first, which contains virtually no equations, puts stress testing and probabilistic assessments of rare financial events in their context. The second part presents the quantitative ideas and techniques required for the task. Here lots of formulae will be found. The third part deals with the quantitative applications of the concepts introduced in Part II. The fourth and last part deals with practical implementation issues, and equations therefore disappear from sight again.

Let me explain in some detail what is covered in these four parts.

After the optimistic note with which I closed the previous section, in Chapter 2 I move swiftly to dampen the reader's enthusiasm, by arguing that stress testing is not the solution to all our risk management problems. In particular, I make the important distinction, too often forgotten, between risk and uncertainty and explain what this entails for stress analysis.

With these caveats out of the way, I argue that the expert knowledge of the risk manager is essential in constructing, using and associating probabilities to stress events. This expert knowledge (and the 'models of reality' that underpin it) constitutes the link between the past data and the possible future outcomes. In Chapter 3 I therefore try to explain the role played by competing interpretative models of reality in helping the risk manager to 'conceive of the unconceivable'. Chapter 3 is therefore intended to put into context the specific suggestions about stress testing that I provide in the rest of the book.

In Chapter 4 I describe the different types of probability (frequentist and subjective) that can be used for risk management, and discuss which 'type of probability' is better suited to different analytical tasks. The chapter closes with an important distinction between associative and causal descriptions. This distinction is at the basis of the efficient elicitation of conditional probabilities, and of the Bayesian-net approach described later in the book.

In Part II I lay the quantitative foundations required for the applications presented in the rest of the book. Some of the concepts are elementary, others are less well-known. In

---

[9] 'Some of the things I vaguely apprehend are, like the end of the world, uninsurable risks, and it's useless to worry about them' – Keynes, quoted in Skidelsky (2009), page 71.

order to give a unified treatment I deal with both the elementary concepts (Chapter 5) and the somewhat-more-advanced ones (Chapter 6) using the same conceptual framework and formalism. Venn diagrams will play a major role throughout the book. Chapter 7 shows how very useful bounds on joint probabilities can be obtained by specifying marginals and (some) singly-conditioned probabilities. Chapter 8 introduces Bayesian nets, and Chapter 9 explains how to build the conditional probability tables required to use them. This concludes the tool-gathering part of the book. (A simple introduction to Linear Programming can be found in Appendix Chapter 15.)

Part III is then devoted to the application of the conceptual tools and techniques presented in Part II. This is achieved by introducing two different possible systematic approaches to stress testing, of different ambition and scope, which are described in Chapters 10 and 11.

Finally, in Part IV I address more practical questions: how we can try to overcome the difficulties and the cognitive biases that stand in the way of providing reasonable conditional probabilities (Chapter 12); how we can structure our chain of stress events (Chapter 13); and how we can embed the suggestions of the book into a viable approach in a real financial institution (as opposed to a classroom exercise). Doing so requires taking into account the reality of its governance structure, its reporting lines and the need for independence of a well-functioning risk-management function (Chapter 14).

I have prepared Parts II and III with exercises. I have done so not because I see this book necessarily as a text for a formal course, but because I firmly believe that, in order to really understand new quantitative techniques, there is no substitute for getting one's hands dirty and actually working out some problems in full.

1.3   Suggestions for Further Reading

Stress testing is the subject of a seemingly endless number of white, grey and variously-coloured consultation papers by the BIS and other international bodies. At the time of writing, the latest such paper I am aware of is BIS (2009), but, no doubt, by the time this book reaches the shelves many new versions will have appeared. Good sources of up-to-date references are the publication sites of the BIS, the IIF and the IMF.

Part I

Data, Models and Reality

Chapter 2

Risk and Uncertainty – or, Why Stress Testing is *Not* Enough

In the introductory chapter I made my pitch as to why stress testing is important and why I believe that the approach I propose can show us the way out of Berkowitz's (1999) purgatory. I don't want to convey the impression, however, that stress testing can be the answer to all our risk management questions. The problem, I think, does not lie with the specific approach I suggest in this book – flawed as this may be – but is of a fundamental nature. To present a balanced picture, I must therefore share two important reservations.

2.1 The Limits of Quantitative Risk Analysis

The first reservation is that the quantitative assessment of risk (and I include stress testing in this category) is an important part of risk management, but it is far from being its beginning and end. Many commentators and risk 'gurus' have stressed the inadequacies of the current quantitative techniques. The point is taken. But even if the best quantitative assessment of risk were available, a lot more would be required to translate this insight into effective risk management. The purpose of analysis is to inform action. Within a complex organization, effective action can only take place in what I call a favourable institutional environment.[1] So, in a favourable institutional environment the output of the quantitative analysis is first escalated, and then understood and challenged by senior management. This is now well accepted. But there is a lot more, and this 'a lot more' has very little to do with quantitative risk analysis. The organizational set-up, for instance, must be such that conflicts of interest are minimized (in the real world they can never be totally eliminated). Or, the agency problems that bedevil any large organization, and financial institutions *in primis*, must be understood and addressed in a satisfactory manner. And again: an effective way must be found to align the interests of the private decision makers of a systemically-relevant institution such as a large

---

[1] A strong governance structure is a common expression with a similar meaning. I prefer to speak of institutional environment, which encompasses such intangibles as a 'robust risk management culture', because even the strongest governance structure can fail if it does not dovetail constructively with the underlying culture of the organization.

bank with those of the regulators – and, more to the point, of society at large. And the list can go on.

VaR & Co have received so much criticism that it sometimes seems that if we had the right analytical tools, all our risk management problems would be solved. If only that were true! The institutional environment in which the risk management decisions are made is where the heart of risk management lies. Yes, the quantitative analysis of risk is part of this 'institutional environment' – and perhaps an important one – but it remains, at best, a start.

2.2   Risk or Uncertainty?

My second reservation is about our ability to specify probabilities (frequentist, subjective or otherwise) for extremely rare events when the underlying phenomenon is the behaviour of markets and of the economy. As the reader will appreciate, I make in this book 'minimal' probabilistic requirements, often asking the risk manager to estimate no more than the order of magnitude of the likelihood of an event. Nowhere in my book will the reader find the demand to estimate the 99.975th percentile of the loss distribution at a one-year horizon.[2] But even my more limited and modest task may be asking too much. Let me explain why I think this may be the case.

One of the applications of stress testing that has been recently put forth is for regulatory capital. Regulatory capital has to do with the viability of a bank as a going concern – the time horizon is, effectively, 'forever'. I do not know what 'forever' means in finance, but certainly it must mean more than two, four or even ten years. When the horizon of required survivability becomes so long, I am not sure that, for matters financial, we truly have the ability to associate probabilities, however approximate, to future events. Perhaps Keynesian (or Knightian) uncertainty provides a better conceptual framework.

What is the difference? 'Risk' and 'uncertainty' are today used interchangeably in the risk-management literature, but a careful distinction used to be drawn between the two concepts: the word 'risk' should be used in those situations where we know for sure the probabilities attaching to future events (and, needless to say, we know exactly what the possible future events may be). We should instead speak of uncertainty when we have no such probabilistic knowledge (but we still know what may hit us tomorrow). Indeed, as far back as in the early 1920s Knight (1921) was writing

> ...the practical difference between [...] risk and uncertainty, is that in the former the distribution of the outcome in a group of instances is known (either through calculation *a priori* or from the statistics of past experience), while in the case of uncertainty, this is not true, the reason being in general that it is impossible to form a group of instances, because the situation dealt with is in a high degree unique....

This distinction was kept alive for several decades. For instance, as game theory became in the post-war years an increasingly important technique in the economist's toolkit, Luce and Raiffa (1957) were still clearly pointing out that the two concepts yield very different

---

[2]This is the mythical percentile that appears in the most uncompromising versions of the Economic Capital Project. See Rebonato (2007) for a discussion. I do not use the word 'mythical' lightly, because the 99.975th percentile of the one-year loss distribution brings into play losses of such magnitude that should, on average, have been incurred only once since the days of Homer.

types of results and 'solutions' and devote in their textbook on game theory different chapters to the two categories. Yet, the boundaries between the two concepts have become increasingly blurred, and the two words are now frequently used interchangeably. So much so that the current prevailing view in economics has become that all probabilities are known (or at least knowable), and that the economy therefore becomes 'computable', in the sense that there are no 'unknown unknowns'. Current mainstream economics firmly endorses a risk-based, not uncertainty-based, view of the world. In the neo-classical synthesis 'uncertainty plays a minimal role in the decision making of economic agents, since rational utility-maximizing individuals are [assumed] capable of virtually eliminating uncertainty with the historical information at hand'.[3]

The consequences of this distinction are well presented by Skidelsky (2009) in his discussion of the Keynesian view of probability:

> Classical economists believe implicitly, and Neoclassical economists explicitly, that market participants have complete knowledge of all probability distributions over future events. This is equivalent to say that they face only measurable risk...

In basing the calculation of regulatory (or economic) capital on the full knowledge – down to the highest percentiles – of 'all probability distributions over future events', the regulators have implicitly embraced the neo-classical view: that is, that when it comes to matters financial, human beings are always faced with risk, not with uncertainty, even when they are dealing with events of such rarity and magnitude that they could bring a bank to its knees.

Why has the concept of risk prevailed over uncertainty, despite the rather extreme assumptions about human cognitive abilities (and the world itself!) that it implies? From an academic perspective, unfortunately, dealing with uncertainty brings about rather 'unexciting' analytical results, often based on minimax solutions: we disregard probability completely, and we arrange our actions so as to minimize the damage if the worst (however unlikely) materializes. There is no great edifice of economic thought that can be built on such dull foundations. Succinctly put, 'in conditions of uncertainty, economic reasoning would be of no value'.[4] This is not a good recipe for exciting papers or for getting a tenure-track position at a prestigious university.

Matters are different when it comes to risk – i.e., when we assume that we can know the probabilities of future events perfectly. Dealing with risk rather than uncertainty allows us to speak about trade-offs and non-trivial optimality,[5] and opens the door to much more exciting analytical results, such as expected utility maximization, portfolio diversification, rational expectations, the efficient-markets hypothesis, etc. – in short, to modern finance. No wonder risk has won hands down over uncertainty.

In addition, from a practical perspective, speaking of risk provides an illusion of quantifiability and precision that regulators like because of the supposed 'objectivity' of the rules it brings about.

---

[3]Greer (2000), page 33, quoted in Davidson (2009). To be fair, there is still active research in the area of uncertainty–such as, for instance, Kreps, Epstein, Wang and others. One of their more interesting results is that under uncertainty prices need not be unique. I am grateful to Dr Keating for pointing this out.

[4]Lucas (1977, page 15), quoted in Davidson (2009, page 35).

[5]Minimax solutions are, of course, also optimal, but in a rather uninteresting manner.

But the fact that one set of results is more 'sexy', more fun to obtain and more handy to use than the other does not necessarily make that set more true – or more useful. The real question should be: leaving aside which approach is more fun to work with, is the problem at hand better described by a risk- or an uncertainty-based approach? If we are talking about the magnitude of weekly, monthly and perhaps even yearly losses, I believe that the risk (i.e., the known-probability-based) framework can yield very useful results. Traditional (frequentist) statistical techniques such as VaR do provide, in this domain, useful information. But what about much rarer events?

Stress testing tries to graft onto this substratum of frequentist information a less precise, but still probabilistic, assessment of risk. I think that this is useful, but I truly do not know how 'far in the tail' even the subjective approach can be pushed. When we deal with the cataclysmic events that can put at risk the whole financial system, I do harbour serious doubts as to whether stress testing – and stress testing for capital allocation purposes in particular – may not be already trying to stretch well into the Knightian-uncertainty domain. Would an intelligent risk manager have been able in late 2006 to give even an order-of-magnitude assessment of the probabilities attaching to the events that were to unfold in the next 24 months? As an attempt to help the risk manager with such a difficult task, I suggest in the next chapter a conceptual approach that may give some guidance in 'conceiving the unconceivable'. But the task remains daunting.

These considerations notwithstanding, I have taken a leaf out of Keynes' book and, as the quote that opens this work recommends, I have decided to follow a pragmatic approach, and to make use of a pared-down probabilistic approach. This is because, if private financial institutions and regulators want to associate capital to stress events – and this appears to be the choice of the moment – under the current conceptual framework *some* form of probabilistic assessment of losses is unavoidable. Indeed, imposing a link between capital and probability of losses constitutes one of the cornerstones of the current regulatory paradigm. I have some doubts about the wisdom of this approach,[6] but, on the other hand, I have no better suggestions. I have therefore taken the approach that, given the present probability-related way of looking at capital, some link between large losses and the probability of their occurrence should be provided. We should therefore ask the risk manager to make use of those types of probabilities (frequentist or subjective) that are better suited to the problem at hand. And we should then set the terms of the problem in such a way that the 'difficult' probabilities (the joint distributions) are obtained or approximated from more cognitively resonant quantities (such as marginal or conditional probabilities) using as much information as possible about 'how the world works'.

The approach I propose is therefore radically different from the frequentist VaR and Economic Capital methods, which 'go for the jugular' and attempt instead the direct estimation of the king probabilistic quantity, i.e., of the joint distribution. I have taken the approach, in short, that one should use different tools for different problems (on the basis that 'when your only tool is a hammer, every problem begins to look like a nail'), and that it is better to be approximately right than precisely wrong.

---

[6]One might wonder, for instance, whether regulators, rather than private firms, should apply a minimax approach to regulation.

2.3 Suggested Reading

For a clear and very readable discussion of the difference between uncertainty and risk in decision making, a good starting point is Luce and Raiffa (1957). An explanation of what uncertainty (rather than risk) implies for asset prices and economic prediction can be found in Skidelsky (2009), who discusses the issue in the context of Keynes' views on the matter.

Chapter 3

The Role of Models in Risk Management and Stress Testing

Experience brings out the impossibility of learning anything from facts till they are examined and interpreted by reason; and teaches that the most reckless and treacherous of theorists is he who professes to let fact and figures speak for themselves.

Alfred Marshall quoted in Friedman and Jacobson Schwartz (1963 [2008])

In this chapter I deal with two distinct but related topics that have a direct bearing on stress testing.[1] These topics are of a more general and abstract nature than the material covered in the rest of the book. They are, however, every bit as important.

The first topic deals with the role of models in arriving at an understanding of financial phenomena and attempting to predict future financial events. A crucial distinction I will make is between reduced-form and micro-specified (structural) models. My claim is that, when it comes to stress testing, micro-specified models are much better suited to the task. Indeed, I will try to explain why the much more commonly used reduced-form models can be particularly misleading in the case of stress testing.

The second topic deals with coordination and positive feedback mechanisms in financial markets. I believe this feature is very important, and helps our understanding of why, in some important circumstances, prices appear to move away from any reasonable understanding of 'fundamentals'. The relevance of this 'run-away behaviour' for stress testing is self-evident. Important as it is, however, the understanding of coordination and feedback mechanisms is not as crucial to my overall argument as the understanding of the role played by models in financial predictions. So, if the reader is not convinced by my second thesis presented in this chapter, but accepts the first, the overall gist of the book will remain valid. If I fail to convince the reader of the validity of the first argument, however, then I will be unlikely to make a convincing case for the main approach proposed in this book.

---

[1] Some parts of this chapter have been adapted from Rebonato (2009) and Rebonato (2010).

3.1   How Did We Get Here?

As the saying goes, we learn from our mistakes. If this is true, after the events that unfolded during the 2007–2009 financial crisis the risk management profession should be comprised of some of the wisest individuals on the planet. How did we end up becoming so wise? And what have we learnt? More concretely: if any of the numerous new risk management ideas that are now been touted as the 'new best practice' had been put in place in, say, late 2005, would things have turned out any better? If not, what should we do instead?

Great upheavals urge a radical rethink of the way we make sense of reality. Finance and economics are no exceptions. The Great Depression of the 1930s gave impetus to the transition from classical to Keynesian economics. The economic woes of the late 1960s and of the 1970s urged the switch from Keynesianism to neo-classical economics. Similarly, the events of the late 2000s are bringing to the fore a radical rethinking of the neo-classical economics orthodoxy – its reliance, for instance, on the ability of rational investors and private-sector firms to self-regulate economic activities.[2]

As a consequence, the economic profession is in a state of 'restlessness', and vigorous criticism to the orthodox way of thinking is now coming not from mavericks 'out on the fringes' or from conspiracy theorists, but from mainstream, establishment economists and central bankers:

> The modern risk management paradigm held sway for decades. The whole intellectual edifice, however, collapsed in the summer of last year [2007].[3]

Change is in the air. For this reason it is particularly important to put the current thinking about quantitative risk management in its intellectual context.

We did not get where we are by accident or 'from scratch', i.e., by thinking in the abstract: 'how should we analyse financial risk?' The logical underpinning of quantitative risk management as it has been practised in the run-up to the crisis is intimately enmeshed with the prevailing (neo-classical) conceptual framework of financial economics. Take, for instance, one of the cornerstones of the neo-classical finance edifice, Markowitz's portfolio diversification. It shares obvious conceptual similarities with the risk management statistics, such as VaR or Economic Capital, that underpin the estimation of regulatory capital: indeed, 'diversification' is a key word both in Markowitz's portfolio theory and in contemporary risk management. But efficient asset allocation and modern risk management share a far deeper intellectual legacy: the idea, that is, that Rational Man, equipped with a Perfect Computing Machine, is supposed to be able to estimate all the statistical properties of return distributions (in the case of Economic Capital down to the highest percentiles), and to use this information to make financial decisions under risk.

As the quote above reminds us, this way of looking at financial risk has held sway for decades. But if we are at a juncture when the very foundations of the edifice of neo-classical finance are being questioned – and I believe we are – then our way of looking at the management of financial risk must be revisited as well. That we are at such a turning

---

[2]See, e.g., Skidelsky (2009), Introduction.
[3]Former Chairman Alan Greenspan, Congressional testimony, 23 October 2008.

point is perhaps most clearly shown (again) by the words of the chastened high priest of the Rational Investor school, Chairman Alan Greenspan (2009):

> The extraordinary risk-management discipline that developed out of the writings of the University of Chicago's Harry Markowitz in the 1950s produced insights that won several Nobel prizes in economics. It was widely embraced not only by academia but also by a large majority of finance professionals and global regulators. But in August 2007, the risk management structure cracked. All the sophisticated mathematics and computer wizardy essentially rested on one central premise: that the enlightened self-interest of owners and managers of financial institutions would lead them to maintain a sufficient buffer against insolvency by actively monitoring their forms' capital and risk positions.

It is silly to claim that we got where we are because the assumptions that underpin this way of looking at financial problems are 'wrong'. Model assumptions are always wrong, and to use McKenzie's (2006) metaphor, a model is not a passive mirror of an external reality. When it comes to neo-classical finance, perhaps we have all been beguiled by the elegance of the construction, and we have begun taking the scaffolding (i.e., the assumptions) too seriously and literally. But, in the end, it is far too simplistic to claim that the root of all evil were 'unrealistic assumptions' or 'the blind faith in the normal distribution' – whose failure to describe returns is, by the way, one of the most uncontroversial and universally accepted facts in mainstream financial econometrics. When it comes to quantitative risk analysis, something more fundamental is at play. We do not need another model. What is required is a richer way of thinking about how models interact with financial reality.

3.2 Statement of the Two Theses of this Chapter

What does it mean that we require a new way of thinking about how models interact with financial reality? As I mentioned in the opening paragraphs of this chapter, I present two distinct arguments. Each argument can, in turn, be split into sub-theses, which for clarity I present below.

Argument 1: *Centrality of Models*

1. We must recognize that data (e.g., empirical return distributions) do not speak by themselves, but only make sense in the context of models of reality. Without a plausible (not necessarily a 'true') generative model, data analysis is blind.

2. This does not mean, however, that we should look for the Holy Grail of *the* correct interpretative model of reality. *Especially when it comes to quantitative risk analysis*, the search for a unique 'true' model (i.e., a unique 'correct' mapping from new information to price changes) may be misguided, futile and, at times, even harmful.

3. It is instead more fruitful to entertain the possibility of the coexistence of a plurality of plausible interpretative models of reality, ranging from the fully fledged, rigorously articulated, mathematically formalized and microstructurally founded models of the neo-classical synthesis, to the glorified rules of thumb used by traders.

4. Each of these models can be, and is, adopted or abandoned by market participants and analysts in an unpredictable fashion.[4]

The second argument requires the validity of the first, and builds on it as follows.

Argument 2: *Importance of Coordination*

1. Given the simultaneous coexistence of a variety of interpretative models of reality, and given the inability by traders to maintain a 'conviction' position for very long – the more so, the more turbulent the market conditions – market participants often find it advantageous to engage in a game of coordination.

2. In this game of coordination traders often adjust their positions not so much on the basis of their independent analysis of fundamentals, but by taking into account what other market players will do.

3. The coordinated actions of many traders can give rise to positive-feedback mechanisms, which can cause 'wild' price moves.

4. These coordination and feedback mechanisms may be active at several levels in the market and in the economy at large: from private investors to proprietary traders, from institutional investors to central banks, etc.

3.3   Defence of the First Thesis (Centrality of Models)

I now handle in order the points into which I sub-divided Argument 1.

3.3.1   Models as Indispensable Interpretative Tools

Quantitative risk management in general, and stress testing in particular, are nowadays typically approached as an exercise in statistical analysis of return distributions. These, in turn, are derived from historical records (time series) of risk factors. The assumption behind this approach is that the answers to all our quantitative risk management questions can be found just by 'looking at the data'. Non-parametric approaches to Extreme Value Theory are the logical conclusion of this approach, and constitute its natural extension to the domain of stress testing.

Now, much too much has been written about whether the normal distribution provides an adequate description of financial returns (for many applications, it clearly does not), and about which alternative statistical distributions may be up to the task. Let us leave aside the fact that, given a finite amount of relevant data, choosing among various distributional alternatives is a statistically very difficult task.[5] My claim is that, *in itself*, knowledge that our existing data are better fitted by, say, a Stretched Exponential or a Power Law than by a Gaussian distribution is of little help, *especially when dealing with tail behaviour*. When it comes to the real 'black swans', i.e., to the events that can create havoc of systemic dimension, I maintain that this type of analysis is of very little use.

---

[4]McKenzie's (2006) engine is particularly apposite here, as a changed model implies a change in causality.
[5]See, for instance, the discussion in Malvergne and Sornette (2006), Chapter 2.

This is a bold claim, because these more exotic distributions are often invoked as *the* solution to the quantitative analysis of the extremely rare event. To see how I can justify my assertion I must explain the difference between reduced-form and micro-structural models.

In general, reduced-form models abstract from the detailed mechanisms that generate the phenomenon at hand, and rely on observed regularities to fit to the data the model 'free parameters'. In physics, for instance, the very complex quantum interactions among the electrons and between the electrons and the nuclei in a solid can be 'reduced' to a simple model of balls linked by harmonic springs. The strength of the spring is then fitted to some observable properties of the material (for instance, its elastic properties, or the slope at the origin of the phonon dispersion curve).

The fitting part of this approach is crucial to our discussion: physicists know that the springs do not really give a true micro-description of the solid, but force a link with physical reality by imposing the correspondence between a certain property of the idealized 'toy model' and the real solid under study. To go beyond this level of model reduction physicists then attempt to *explain* the strength of the spring on the basis of a theory of electron interactions. This is where *ab initio* band structure calculations take over from empirical potentials. When they engage in band-structure calculations physicists give a micro-specified description of the spring. Sure enough, band structure calculations (despite the grand-sounding *ab initio* label) also conceal their own reduced-form models (for instance, the pseudo-potentials that describe the electron-nucleon interactions).

The important point here is not that micro-specified models are necessarily 'better' than reduced-form ones (the elastic properties of a solid, for instance, are often better *accounted for* by the simpler spring model). What micro-specified models do is that they try to explain what reduced-form models only describe. They therefore provide a level of understanding that the often-better-fitting reduced-form models cannot provide. And, above all, micro-specified models give a clear indication of when the validity of a certain toy model stops.

As a result, reduced-form models are loved by engineers, who have to deal with challenging but well-defined and 'within-the-paradigm' problems, and superciliously regarded by pure physicists, who strive for explanation rather than description.

One more observation: in physics – and, indeed, in many of the social sciences such as economics[6] – the interaction between micro-specified and reduced-form models is very much like a series of Russian matryoshka dolls: a new structural model will typically introduce higher-level reduced-form models in its formulation. A structural model explains, that is, the exogenous features of the reduced-form model 'underneath' (the 'springs'), but does so by introducing a higher-level reduced-form description of reality. This is in turn phenomenologically fitted to some finer observable quantities of the phenomenon under study. So, the spring model is a structural model with respect to continuum mechanics (which dispenses altogether with the concept of atoms), and is a reduced-form model with respect to *ab initio* band structure calculations.

The real question, therefore, is not so much whether a model is micro-structurally founded or 'reduced-form' in the absolute, but at what level we stop explaining and we begin describing.

When we look at current quantitative risk management in this light, its most extraordinary feature is where it locates itself in this spectrum between full model reduction and

---

[6]In economics there has been in the post-war years a concerted effort to provide micro-foundations to earlier economic descriptions that made use of 'macro' quantities. For instance, the domain of macroeconomics has progressively been eroded in the process – how profitably and successfully is a different story.

complete micro-specification: it is the most hard-core reduced-form model that we can possibly conceive! The only superstructure we allow to be built on data is the distribution of returns, with its coefficients as the free-fitting parameters of the reduced-form model (i.e., the equivalent of the strength of the springs in the model of solid). To pursue the metaphor of the study of solids, it is as if, in order to understand the elastic properties of materials, we simply recorded the mechanical behaviour of glass, wood, steel, diamond, grass and molybdenum under tension, looked for a suitable statistical distribution able to fit these disparate behaviours *and we stopped there*.

When the implicit assumption is made that we should fit very accurately the existing data to very sophisticated distributions, without concerning ourselves at all with the generative mechanisms of the distributions themselves, we have given up any attempt to explain.[7] We claim that pure description is enough. Dispensing in such a radical way with any explanation is, in a way, the ultimate reduced-form model.

Unfortunately when one uses reduced-form models (just because they bypass a specification of how the data were generated in the first place), one has no way of telling when yesterday's parametrization ceases to be of use. The fitting of statistical distributions (no matter how sophisticated) to past data therefore shares all the advantages and the unavoidable shortcomings of reduced-form models: without an understanding of how the exceptional returns in the beautifully-fitted fat tail have been generated, there is no way of telling if yesterday's parametrization is still valid today. And, when it matters, it invariably is not.

This is well echoed in the words of Allison and Zelikow (1999) in their seminal *Essence of Decision*:

> Our first proposition is that [...] bundles of [...] related assumptions constitute basic frames of references or conceptual models in terms of which analysts and ordinary lay persons ask and answer the questions: What happened? Why did it happen? What will happen? Assumptions like these are central to the activities of explanation and prediction.[8]

In passing, believing that the history of price changes 'speaks by itself' and does not require any underlying model of reality shares the same intellectual foundations and credibility as chartism.[9] I fear that it is just as useful. Once again, imperfect, but plausible, micro-specified ('structural') models are infinitely more powerful in making financial

---

[7]There is an even closer parallel to the interatomic potentials in solids. Once the limitations of the simple (but powerful) spring-like model became apparent, one line of research became focused on creating more complex, but still reduced-form, models based on less-and-less-elegant variations on the simple spring theme. By and large, this proved to be a dead-alley: the improvement in understanding was marginal, and the increase in complexity substantial.

The parallel with quantitative risk management here is remaining wedded to the same level of model reduction (all the information is in *some* return distribution), but tinkering with the exact shape of the distribution (say, Levy rather than Gaussian), without trying to explain why and under which circumstances a Levy distribution may emerge.

[8]Introduction, page 4.

[9]An obvious distinction must be made here: chartism attempts to predict the first moment of the return distribution ('where prices go'). Risk management concerns itself with the second (or higher) moments. The first task is immensely more difficult, and, with the possible exception of high-frequency data, there is virtually no evidence that this prediction can be successful. Estimating the second moment, on the other hand, can be done much more successfully. The second moment of a distribution, however, does not contain all the information we may want to know from a risk persective. If our interest is in extreme events, reliance on past data alone without a model to tell us when the data are relevant has little chance to fare any better than chartism.

decisions because they give a possible explanation of why we should worry *today*. As we shall see, these simple explanatory models of reality play a pivotal role in the approach I propose in this book.

There is another reason why relying on the fit to an unconditional return distribution, no matter how accurate, does not help us very much. Even if we had ascertained beyond reasonable statistical doubt that, say, a Levy distribution with a characteristic exponent of exactly 1.75 gave the best description of our data, *in itself* this would be of little practical use. Yes, with this piece of information the probabilities of occurrence of extreme events would certainly be much higher (and probably more realistically accounted for) than if we had used a more 'tame' distribution. But, even if it were attainable and 'true', such an *unconditional* estimate (an estimate, that is, unrelated to *present* market conditions) would be of very little use to the risk manager. This is because, absent a model of reality, there is no way of telling whether the same information is *conditionally* relevant – i.e., is relevant to today's world. Systematically buying insurance against extreme adverse events is far too expensive to be contemplated as an everyday strategy. And as any trader knows well, buying insurance *on an ongoing basis* against tail events will (more than) negate the excess return she expects to reap from entering into the risky trades in the first place.

What we need, again, are perhaps imperfect, but plausible, models of reality that tell us when it may be worthwhile to 'use our silver bullets' and spend money on protection, or simply to reduce the size of our exposure. What a useful quantitative risk analysis should provide is the *conditional* assessment that today, given the particular market conditions we are in and *given our understanding of how the world works*, certain extreme events are more or less likely to occur than they normally are. A risk manager can only carry out this analysis if she has at her disposal an imperfect but plausible structural model that links market information to outcomes.

In the preceding paragraphs I have repeatedly mentioned 'models' (in the plural). This naturally brings me to my second point.

3.3.2   The Plurality-of-Models View

I stated in points 2 and 3 of Argument 1 that a plurality of interpretative models coexist 'in the market'. This statement may seem commonsensical and uncontroversial, but it is not part of the economics orthodoxy (the rational-expectations and efficient-market hypotheses in particular). If we accept the neo-classical view of rationality, in fact, according to Muth (1961) in the presence of risk

> [rational] expectations are formed on the basis of all the available information concerning the variable being predicted. Furthermore [...] individuals use available information intelligently; that is, they understand the way in which the variables they observe will affect the variable they are going to predict.

As a consequence 'expectations are essentially the same as the predictions of the relevant economic theory' (Muth, 1961). There is, in effect, a 'communism of models', whereby 'all agents inside the model, the econometrician and God all share the same model'.[10]

---

[10]Interview with Thomas Sargent by Evans and Honkapohja (2005) quoted in Frydman and Goldberg (2007). It is worthwhile noting in passing that a strand of criticism of this view of rationality does not bring into play the

The logical inflexibility of some aspects of the neo-classical paradigm is difficult to fathom for the educated layperson, or, indeed, for academics in other disciplines. For instance, most people would find it only natural that, even if presented with the same information, different intelligent and educated individuals – indeed, even different experts in the field – will in general reach different conclusions in matters of economic relevance (say, 'Is the economy about to enter a recession?'). Yet heterogeneity of prior beliefs given the same background information is difficult to reconcile with the hyper-rational, super-Bayesian view of *Homo Economicus*. Consider the following quote by Bernard Dumas, Professor of Finance at the University of Lausanne, in his review of Shefrin (2008):

> Judging from the large volume of trade in the financial markets and the astounding volatility of prices, one has to accept the idea that investors hold divergent and fast fluctuating beliefs. For this to make sense, I see only two possible hypothesis. [Either] both individual and professional investors receive a lot of information – some of it public *but a lot more private* – on which they act. Or they all receive similar information, but each one interprets this information somewhat differently.[11]

Let us pause to consider the full meaning of this quote. The suggestions that different individuals, given the same information, may process it somewhat differently, and reach somewhat different conclusions does not strike the average educated person as unreasonable. Perhaps what most would consider outlandish is actually maintaining the opposite. And even staunch market critics would consider heterogeneity of opinions more plausible than a degree of insider trading so pervasive as to constitute, effectively, the backbone of financial markets (as the expression 'some of it public *but a lot more private*' implies). Yet, this is not the prevailing model of neo-classical financial economics, according to which, for instance, the volume of trading remains a puzzle ('Why trading at all, if everyone adjusts prices in the same manner?', to paraphrase the argument in Bookstaber (2008)). So, the view that rational individuals may have different beliefs and reach different conclusions can be taken to be an 'arresting, although by no means mainstream, hypothesis' (Dumas, 2008). And Hersh Shefrin, the Mario L. Bellotti Professor of Finance at the Leavy School of Business, Santa Clara University, is hailed by Dumas for proposing such an apparently commonsensical view as a 'maverick and a pioneer'.

This hyper-rational view can be, and has been, criticized,[12] but at least it has an impeccable, if slightly otherworldly, logical coherence. The same cannot be said of current quantitative risk management, which has borrowed freely but haphazardly from the neo-classical toolkit. In common with finance theory, the statistical distribution of returns has for instance become central to quantitative risk management – if anything it has assumed a status of almost religious idolatry. However, the debatable (but at least logically coherent) link between these returns distributions and decisions via expected utility maximization has been forgotten, or bastardized beyond recognition, in risk management practice. Somewhere along the line, the implicit assumption has been smuggled in that, once obtained, impossibly accurate statistical distributions of returns would, effectively, 'speak by themselves'

---

cognitive limitations of human beings, but questions the ability to project into the future firm knowledge about preferences, technological advances, etc. This school of thought is referred to as Imperfect Knowledge Economics.

Cognitive biases do enter the description – see, e.g., Frydman and Goldberg (2007), Chapter 5 – but the over-extension of 'perfect knowledge' economics would apply even in the absence of these cognitive biases.

[11]Bernard Dumas, endorsing Shefrin (2008), my emphasis.

[12]See, e.g., Frydman and Goldberg (2007), Shefrin (2000), Shefrin (2008) and Shleifer (2000).

and self-evidently point to the correct risk management choice. At best, crude, ad hoc, logically dubious and cognitively unappealing rules of thumb have been offered as crutches to justify the decision-making process. Magic percentiles – the higher the better – were supposed to constitute the be-all-and-end-all of risk management. (See Rebonato (2007) for a non-technical discussion of these points.)

Lack of logical coherence is regrettable. However, I am not at all advocating that the way to improve quantitative risk management is to integrate the statistical data analysis with *a* single correct model of reality (be it the neo-classical one or any of the many alternatives that are being, and have been, proposed). Quite the opposite: I maintain that *for risk analysis purposes* what is more productive is the awareness of the different plausible interpretative models of reality, and of how different agents, by embracing these different plausible models, may react to new information. The relevance of this approach to risk management stems from the observation that – *pace* the neo-classical picture of *Homo Economicus* – market participants do freely and eclectically move between different explanatory paradigms, and adjust their actions accordingly. Risk managers can only hope to keep track of this ever-shifting explanatory landscape if they themselves display a similar degree of mental flexibility and eclecticism. Again, the words of Allison and Zelikow (1999) are particularly appropriate:

> Concepts and theories, especially ones that do real work, become accepted, conventional and efficient for communicating answers. [...] [W]hen one family of simplifications becomes convenient and compelling, it is even more essential to have at hand one or more simple but competitive conceptual frameworks to help remind the questioner and the answerer what is omitted. They open minds a little wider and keep them open a little longer. Alternative conceptual frameworks [...] are essential as a reminder of the distortions and limitation of whatever conceptual framework one employs.[13]

3.4   Defence of the Second Thesis (Coordination)

In my first thesis I argued that models are indispensable tools, not a luxury, if we want to make sense of reality. And that, at any one time, a number of models will in general offer themselves as plausible explanations of a given state of affairs. If correct, the second part of my first thesis has a direct bearing on the argument about coordination that I present below.

3.4.1   Traders as Agents

What is the link between a plurality of models and coordination?

If only one model of reality were the correct one (and if it were known to all the perfectly rational agents in the economy), a need for coordination would not arise.[14] Yes, everybody would analyse data in the same way and reach the same conclusions about economic events. But coordination (indeed, identity) of action would be a necessary by-product of this communism of models (shared, remember, by the market agent, the econometrician and God), not a conscious goal.

---

[13] Allison and Zelikow (1999), Introduction, page 8.
[14] Admittedly, for the result to hold, everyone should share not only the same model and information, but also the same endowment and the same risk aversion.

Matters immediately look very different if many models can be considered to be a plausible description of reality by reasonable and well-informed market agents. In the presence of this model uncertainty, perhaps the greatest danger for any one trader is not so much to be 'wrong' (whatever that may mean), but to be out of step with the way fellow traders will interpret reality. This is because most market participants are agents and not principals, and their 'staying power' (i.e., the length of time over which they will be able to convince the ultimate providers of capital or liquidity not to worry about the 'temporary mark-to-market losses') is very short.[15]

This is poorly accounted for by financial economics, which typically looks at market participants as principals who invest their own money with a clear understanding of fundamental value and an Olympic disregard for the temporary vagaries of prices. Such a picture, however, does not chime well even with casual observation of market dynamics. In times of severe market turmoil even a 'conviction trade' – put in place by an agent whose principal does not share the same knowledge[16] *and the same payoff profile* – can last much less than a week. In these days of balance sheet and capital constraints, of skittish risk managers and of worried regulators, the life of a pseudo-arbitrageur caught on the wrong side of the consensus interpretation of a market event may not be brutish and nasty, but is certainly short.

As a suggestive example of a recent event that fits well with this interpretation, consider what happened to the Bear Stern share price in the immediate wake of the 'Thursday rescue' by the Fed. Recall that on 14 March 2007, the investment bank Bear Sterns was running out of cash, and the possibility of a systemically disastrous bankruptcy was looming. To avert this occurrence the Fed's first course of action was to make funding available to Bear Sterns through JP Morgan. The measure was complex, unprecedented and the press releases that accompanied it far from crystal clear.[17]

Now, we must remember that there was no precedent for the rescue plan, and that there was a high degree of uncertainty about its mechanics and about the validity and enforceability of the various guarantees. Under these circumstances, it would be reasonable to expect that different traders would interpret the scant available information in a variety of possible ways. If these interpretations were translated into 'independent' trades one would expect that, after the netting off of the bullish and bearish trades, a relatively modest movement up or down in the share price due to the residual un-netted views would result. But, given the complexity of the matter and the lack of any precedents one would have expected that 'wait-and-see' would have been the better part of valour.

So, unless the extraordinary news of the day lent themselves to an unequivocal interpretation by the vast majority of market participants (which they obviously did not), a view of the independent, uncoordinated traders would not suggest an opening price move shooting up or down in the first half hour of the trading day. Plausibly, one could expect *some* initial price movement (due to the predominance of positive or negative interpretations of the ambiguous facts). And one would also not be surprised to see this initial price change during the day, as more and more traders began to look at the information in a different light.

But this is not at all what happened. The stock price action on Friday morning saw an initial euphoria and relief rally that brought the share price up by 10% in less than an hour. So, despite the uncertainty of the situation, at the opening of the trading day a vast majority

---

[15] See Shleifer (2000).

[16] This is what Shleifer (2000) calls the unfortunate divorce of 'brawn and brains'. This is one of the explanations put forth by critics of unfettered market efficiency for the observed existence of limits to (pseudo)-arbitrage.

[17] For a detailed and illuminating account, see Cohen (2009), Chapter 6, page 70 and *passim* in particular.

of traders seemed to analyse the scant available information by giving the same positive interpretation to the actions of the Fed. But just a few hours later *on the same day* the share price was down 50%.[18]

The interesting fact throughout these roller-coaster price gyrations is that no meaningful piece of information regarding Bear Sterns materialized during the course of the 60% peak-to-trough price drop. The price action, with a sudden rise at the opening, a brief period of range trading and a rapid decline to a completely different equilibrium is difficult to reconcile with a view of different market agents independently expressing their views on the basis of their competing models of reality. An explanation, instead, that invokes coordination among traders can account for these price moves, and many similar events, much more naturally and convincingly. It is to this explanation that I therefore turn.

3.4.2   Agency Brings About Coordination

Leaving this example aside, the view of trading that I propose is consistent with a coordination game played by the market participants. A thumb-nail sketch of what I suggest would start from the observation that these market participants are predominantly agents. This agency position reduces their 'staying power', and can force them out of a position (at great loss) before they can be proven right. *This* (i.e., a premature forced termination of a trade) is the state of affairs an agent trader will try most to avoid. Hence the desire to coordinate.

Let us look at this in a bit more detail. As information arrives, traders have to analyse it and process it in a very short time. As a first step they will tend to categorize this information in one of the 'market modes' they recognize – the 'inflationary story', the 'repeat-of-the-Great-Depression story', the 'emerging-market-decoupling story', etc. Now, a principal investor should just try to pick the right 'story' – this is trading based on fundamentals. But we have seen that the worst situation for an individual agent trader is not so much to be 'wrong', but to give a *dissonant* categorization of the new piece of information. As a consequence, she will have interest in coordinating her categorization with that of the other market participants.[19] This coordination becomes more important, the greater the state of turmoil of the market – and, therefore, the smaller the 'leeway' providers of capital and liquidity are prepared to give to the traders who invest money on their behalf.

A view that has a lot in common with the one I have sketched above (but that focuses on a similar coordination enacted by principals – i.e., ultimate investors – rather than agents) has been recently formalized by Ozdenoren and Yuan (2008),[20] who point out that

> ...investors have an incentive to coordinate, which may generate self-fulfilling beliefs and multiple equilibria. Using insights from global games, we pin down investors' beliefs, analyze equilibrium prices, and *show that strong feedback leads to higher excess volatility*....[21]

---

[18]The [i]nitial reaction seemed to be very positive [...] Why it went south I don't know. I can tell you I had analysts calling me on Friday morning. They couldn't figure out why the stock was getting pummeled this way, because they were saying, 'I don't get it. It seems like a good thing. Why is the market reacting like this? It seems like a good thing ...' (Mr Molinaro reported in Cohen (2009), page 71).

[19]The second safest thing for a trader, the saying goes, after being right on one's own, is to be wrong with everyone else.

[20]Agency relationships, of course, only exacerbate the dynamics highlighted by Ozdenoren and Yuan (2008).

[21]My emphasis.

And of course, Keynes wrote about this as far back as the 1930s, when he compared investment decisions to a competition run at the time by a newspaper. In those political-correctness-unaware days, a parade of pretty faces was shown in an evening paper (Akelrof and Shiller, 2009), and a prize was promised to the readers who would pick *not the most attractive face*, but the one *chosen by the majority of readers as the most attractive*. In my reading of what happened, the equity traders on the fateful Thursday of the attempted Bear rescue were doing exactly this: they were not trying to choose the prettiest face, but the face that the majority of other traders would vote as the prettiest. I believe that, especially in situations of market turmoil, the beauty-parade-of-models metaphor is more relevant today than ever.

Another comment about coordination: different agents (hedge fund managers, proprietary traders of banks, asset managers, pension fund trustees, etc.) have different horizons. Here by horizon I do not necessarily mean the investment horizon. Rather, I am referring to the time frame over which a losing trading position or investment can be allowed to run before the ultimate providers of capital pull out the money, stop-loss limits are breached, lenders sell collateral or regulators require defensive actions. In general, the quieter and more benign the market conditions, the longer this horizon will be. In periods of market turmoil, however, when uncertainty about value quickly increases, fewer and fewer agents are trusted with running a 'fundamentally sound' but losing position, and even the ultimate principals with the longest staying power throw in the towel.

When this happens the need for coordination ceases to be limited to the speculative fringes of the investment landscape, but becomes a pervasive feature of the economy. During the winter of 2007 and throughout the first half 2008, for instance, many traders felt that the prices of some securities had fallen 'too much' with respect to any plausible fundamental,[22] but were reluctant to try to 'catch a falling knife'. In these situations of generalized uncertainty nothing is more lethal than being a contrarian too soon, and coordination becomes an imperative.

3.4.3   From Coordination to Positive Feedback

Why is coordination so important from the point of view of risk analysis in general, and of stress testing in particular? Because it can produce positive feedback mechanisms, herding behaviour, cascades and, ultimately, even bubbles (see, e.g., Chamley, (2004)). Coordination, and feedback in particular, can bring about 'the emergent properties of interacting systems – for want of a better term, organized complexity' (Miller and Page, 2007). As Miller and Page point out

> [w]e often see unanticipated statistical regularities emerging in complex systems. These regularities go beyond the usual bounds covered by the Central Limit Theorem [...] Agent intention can [...] alter the patterns that emerge in complex systems. [...] As we give the agents even more strategic ability, we often see elaborate dances of strategies, with good and bad epochs, cycles, and crashes. [...] *In systems characterized by the Central Limit Theorem, interactions cancel each other out and result in a smooth bell*

---

[22]At one point, for instance, the prices of some highly structured securities implied mortgage default rates for Alt-A borrowers of 75%.

> *curve. In complex systems, interactions reinforce one another and result in behaviour that is very different from the norm.*[23]

These behavioural features may therefore leave their signature in the distribution of asset prices in the shape of fat tails even if the statistical distribution of new information were perfectly Gaussian – which, in all probability, it is not in the first place. Furthermore, all these dynamics are clearly exacerbated by the presence of leverage in the financial system.

Coordination plus leverage can therefore produce cumulative price moves of magnitudes that are well in excess of what would apply if every agent acted independently using her own 'model'. When this happens the distribution of returns can easily become populated by the 'ten-standard-deviation' events at whose occurrence newspapers never cease to marvel. In neo-classical finance the existence of irrational bubbles is difficult to explain.[24] And certainly, one must resist the temptation to see bubble-creating mechanisms in every aspect of market dynamics. After all, the 'market' is made up of a variety of players, each with different goals, institutional constraints, horizons and, yes, 'models'. In most circumstances, the occurrence of a sequence of coordination-driven run-away price moves can be broken by the springing into action of a different class of traders, investors or hedgers. However, as discussed above, there are situations when this may not happen. It is when these natural circuit breakers fail that danger looms.

3.5 The Role of Stress and Scenario Analysis

If these views are correct, how should we carry out the quantitative analysis of financial risk? To go back to the Keynes beauty parade, one profitable approach is to try to gauge which of today's 'pretty faces' are in the running to be chosen by most readers tomorrow – or, to abandon the metaphor, to be aware of today's plausible interpretative models of reality, so as to be prepared when the one that will prevail tomorrow will assert itself as the 'winner', and when possible, to ask the question: what is today's 'dominant story'?

The relevance of this to stress testing is clear.

First, we must recognize that thinking the improbable-but-plausible is at the core of the art of stress testing. Being too wedded to one view of the world – in a way, being too 'logically coherent' – can make us blind to very plausible alternatives. During periods of turmoil, events impossible according to one view of the world can happen twice a week. And neglecting the possible effect of coordination can make us underestimate the magnitude – and sometimes the suddenness – of price swings.

Second, an understanding of the reason for the coordination of traders' actions and of when and where this coordination might occur is essential if the risk manager wants to be able to identify the 'vulnerabilities' of the portfolio under her watch. And as we shall see in Chapter 13, being cognizant of the 'pressure points' of a portfolio is extremely important, especially if a bottom-up approach to stress testing is adopted.

My analysis therefore calls for a very important role for expert subjective judgement. Stress testing and scenario analysis become two of the practical tools to translate these

---

[23]Chapter 4, pages 49–50, my emphasis.
[24]Leyland and Gennote's work, quoted in McKenzie (2006), posits rational investors who know or do not know the re-hedging plan of portfolio insurers.

subjective inputs into a coherent representation of the vulnerabilities of a portfolio. Scenario analyses and combinations of stress events provide us with a tool to describe and, when appropriate, quantify our uncertainty about how future events will unfold (their likely magnitude, whether they are plausible or not, whether they are likely to occur together). They therefore become the natural tools to take into account the multiplicity of possible interpretative models of reality that I have discussed above, and to express the risk managers' understanding of the feedback dynamics that may apply to her portfolio.

This is all well and good at a very abstract level. But how do my suggestions fit with the organizational reality of a financial institution, and of a regulated one in particular? To be of practical relevance, any suggestion as to how we may control financial risk must lend itself to being embedded in the organizational and governance structure of a financial institution, of which risk management is only one part, and often far from the most important one.

One important aspect of what I called above the organizational structure is the creation and dissemination of risk management information: who gets to see what and at what point in time. Inevitably, as information percolates up the organizational chain, it becomes more and more condensed, synthetic and stylized. Key risk indicators tend to take the place of discursive narrative. Once we are at Management Committee level or above we are fully in PowerPoint land. If any suggestion about stress testing is to be taken seriously, it must take this reality into account. It must, for instance, lend itself to the preservation of intuitive and cognitively appealing information even after the successive distillations that produce a board report have been carried out. The approach that I suggest in this book takes full account of these needs, and its outputs can be not only presented, but also challenged and discussed, at all levels in the organization. See in this respect my discussion in Chapter 14.

Admittedly, introducing competing models and the need for expert judgement in the risk analysis takes away 'objectivity' from the process (even if this objectivity was probably never there in the first place). And formula-based approaches, for all their limitations, do have the positive features of allowing standardization, reproducibility and comparability across firms. So, even as they recognize the limitations of traditional quantitative measures of risk, neither private firms nor regulators can afford to do away with them. But it is the balance between the quantitative and the subjective that could be profitably altered. This, of course, will require greater engagement, by regulators and by senior managers, with the more subjective aspects of risk management. This is certainly a very demanding process. I will discuss in Chapter 14 if (and, if so, how) this may be done in practice.

Luckily, not everything becomes more difficult when one shifts the weight away from statistical measures of risk towards 'expert judgement'. Many of the senior decision-makers of financial institutions have neither the technical ability nor the inclination to challenge the mathematical assumptions of a statistical model. They are, however, both perfectly capable *and, given their likely professional background, often naturally inclined* to question the subjective reasoning process that leads to a well-thought-out stress scenario. Unlike the statistical assessment of a probability or a percentile, a stress scenario is ultimately a 'story', with its resonance in our understanding of what has happened in the past and of whether and *why* it may or may not happen again today. Ultimately it has a 'narrative'. And when it comes to influencing decisions and prompting action, the power of a 'story' should never be underestimated. A 'plausible model of reality' is exactly that, a 'story' that connects a variety of visible and readily understandable inputs to more or less extreme outcomes. The cognitive resonance of this approach may make a big difference when it comes to informing behaviour and, perhaps, to deciding to use the silver bullets of protection I referred to above.

I think it is useful to present in this context an extended passage from Casebeer (2008):

> A research program by Mark Johnson, George Lakoff, (Lakoff and Johnson, 1980), Giles
> Fauconnier and Mark Turner (2002) has explored reasoning by metaphor and analogy in
> a rich research program; they and others conclude that our most complex mental tasks
> are usually carried out not by 'classical mechanics' of rational actor theory (where stories
> really have no place in the details) but rather by a set of abilities that enable us to make
> analogies and map metaphors, which forms the core of human cognition. Exploration
> into the 'storytelling man' is a research program that combines metaphor and analogy
> into an examination of the powerful grip narrative has on human cognition; narratives
> can restructure our mental spaces in ways that profoundly affect our reasoning ability.

I would not want to overemphasize the 'emotional' and 'meta-logical' aspects of a well-designed stress testing programme. After all, I intend to present in this book tools for a sober and rational analysis of financial risk, not for an 'intuitive approach to risk management'. And indeed, I will stress the importance of strict logical coherence in our stress assessments. However, the ultimate goal of a risk manager is not to produce risk reports, but to influence the behaviour of the decision-makers in a financial institution and to 'obtain results'. If this is the goal, assuming that the recipients of the information are hyper-rational agents capable of digesting and analysing reams of data irrespective of the way they are presented is not a very useful starting point. If 'stories' have the power to influence behaviour more than the dry presentation of information, this should not be ignored. And if stress-based analysis shares some important features of 'story telling', so much the better.

The regulators have become aware of the need to think outside the narrow statistical, model-based approach that they had until recently so strongly emphasized, and are engaging with the financial industry in a far-reaching re-thinking of their stress-testing and scenario-analysis framework.[25] As I have had the privilege of being personally involved in this process, I can confidently say that the regulators are genuinely open to new ways of looking at risk – including more subjective ones. As their remit requires, they will not dictate how individual firms will carry out these new tasks, but they will opine on the quality and acceptability of the outcomes. My suggestion is that, in their assessments of the industry efforts, they may want to consider the quality of the process by which the 'stressful outcomes' produced by the banks have been arrived at. Have these results been obtained by looking at financial reality via the narrow prism of a single 'best model'? Or have they taken into account the plurality of plausible models of reality and the coordination among market players that this can generate. Just as importantly, they may want to consider how these initiatives fit in practice in the organizational structure of the regulated institutions: who gets to see these results, what kind of challenge and questioning they generate, what actions are prompted.

I believe that the approach I describe in this book can be so implemented as to satisfy these complex requirements.

3.6 Suggestions for Further Reading

Some of the themes developed in this chapter can be found in Rebonato (2009). A very good reference about coordination and herding behaviour in general, and with specific references

---

[25]See, e.g., BIS (2009).

to finance, is Chamley (2004). Two recent articles that cover topics of coordination in financial markets are Guarino and Cipriani (2008) and Ozdenoren and Yuan (2008).

The emergence of complex coordination from the actions of agents is the subject of the trendy discipline of 'complexity studies'. The grandfather of the approach is probably Nobel-prize winner Thomas Shelling, whose *Micromotives and Macrobehaviour* (1978) remains a classic. The reader should then approach the more recent literature with some circumspection, because the quality is rather uneven. Miller and Page (2007) provide a sober, non-technical introduction.

Heterogeneity of beliefs and its impact on asset prices are treated very well in Shefrin (2008), who uses concepts from behavioural finance to recast the traditional asset pricing paradigm. Of particular interest is the treatment of the stochastic discount factor in the presence of heterogeneous beliefs. The treatment by Shefrin is to be commended for its clarity. Buraschi (quoted in Rebonato (2009)) provides another interesting perspective on the importance of heterogeneous beliefs in the case of derivatives markets.

A cogent critique of the neo-classical view that market agents can identify precisely the set of variables that drive financial outcomes is given by the Imperfect-Knowledge Economics (IKE) school. The book by Frydman and Goldberg (2007) is excellent and thought-provoking. Also see Frydman and Goldberg (2009) for a perspective on the implications for the scope of optimal regulation.

For a discussion of the limits of arbitrage in the presence of principal/agent relationships, and of the consequences of this 'divorce of brawn and brains' for asset pricing, Shleifer (2000) provides an excellent discussion.

Soros (1987) and Soros (2008) offer a perspective about feedback mechanisms in financial markets that is related to the one presented in this chapter. Not surprisingly, the insights about the workings of financial markets afforded by George Soros deserve very careful reading.

Chapter 4

What Kind of Probability Do We Need in Risk Management?

...between one out of three and even...

The odds of nuclear confrontation between Russia and the USA, as stated by President J. F. Kennedy during the Cuban missile crisis, quoted in Allison and Zelikow (1999) – certainly not a frequentist statement, and yet one of which President Kennedy was able to make very profitable use.

4.1 Frequentist versus Subjective Probability

In common speech we use the same word 'probability' to cover a variety of meanings. Take for instance the following three sentences:

> The probability of this coin landing 'heads' is 50%.
> There is a high probability that Mr Burns killed his wife.
> The probability of a woman becoming President of the United States within ten years is less than 10%.

The same word ('probability') has been used in the three sentences, but clearly we do not really mean quite the same 'thing' in the three instances. For instance, try to modify the first and last sentences as follows:

> The probability of this coin landing 'heads' is $50.002 \pm 0.001\%$.
> The probability of a woman becoming President of the United States within ten years is less than $10.034 \pm 0.001\%$.

In the first case the sentence makes perfect sense. The statement may be correct or not, and we may want to ask a lot of questions about how carefully the experiment was designed – for instance, how many times the coin was tossed, how we ensured that the conditions were exactly the same, how we established the confidence interval, etc. But in principle there is nothing in the first sentence that offends our common sense.

The second sentence, however, leaves us at best perplexed. Perhaps we even find it nonsensical. We are not sure how anybody could possibly have arrived at this statement. And even if we were told that the statement is exactly true (whatever 'true' in this context means), we would not quite know what use to make of all that incredible precision.[1]

The coin-tossing probability represents a text-book case of frequentist probability. The President-of-the-US probability is a classical example of subjective probability. It is related to, and sometimes interchangeably referred to as, probability as degree of (rational) belief.

The philosophical debate on frequentist versus subjective probability has been raging for almost a century, and I will not even begin to address it.[2] Much as I will try to remain as 'impartial' as possible, I must however admit up-front that I find the subjective (Bayesian) view of probability much more convincing than the frequentist one. To be more precise, I like to think in terms of a continuum of settings, from almost perfectly frequentist to almost completely subjective. In Bayesian terms, the exact positioning on this spectrum depends on the relative importance of the prior and the likelihood functions – where by 'importance' I mean how peaked these functions are. If you are familiar with Bayesian probability you may agree or disagree with my view, but it will at least make perfect sense to you. If you are not, I will not try to introduce the terms of the debate. Should anybody be interested in my views on the matter, Rebonato (2007) has an extensive but non-technical discussion of the topic.

For the purpose of our discussion, this definition of frequentist probability, or rather of its domain of applicability, will serve us well (Jaynes, 2003):

> The traditional frequentist methods [...] are usable and useful in many particularly simple, idealized problems; but they represent the most proscribed special case of probability theory, because they presuppose conditions (independent repetition of a 'random experiment' but no relevant prior information) that are hardly ever met in real problems. This approach is quite inadequate for the current needs of science.

In my opinion the frequentist approach is unfortunately just as inadequate for the current needs of quantitative risk analysis. Yet, whenever we employ statistical techniques such as VaR, we implicitly endorse a purely frequentist view of probability. We assume that all the information of relevance is 'in the data' (in the likelihood function). We imply that we have no knowledge whatsoever about how the world works (leaving aside technical details, we assume that our prior is infinitely diffuse). We believe, in short, that we are tossing coins, and not making informed guesses about the gender of the next President of the United States.

---

[1]For instance, if someone told you that the probability of this coin landing heads is truly $50.002 \pm 0.001\%$, leaving aside your moral scruples, you would immediately know how to make a lot of money setting up a casino table called flip-the-coin. Your precise knowledge, if not shared by the rest of the population, could allow you to reap untold riches. But what extra profit could you make from the knowledge that the probability that the next President of the United States will be a woman is $10.034 \pm 0.001\%$, rather than 10%, given that the event will happen only once?

[2]I do take sides in this debate, but in this very charged topic I try always to keep in mind the following quote by Ted Rosencrantz (in Rebonato, 2008):

> Here's one useful rule of thumb: there are very few fields in which every single practitioner is an idiot. If your understanding of a field is such that all practitioners of it must be idiots, then probably you're not understanding it correctly.

Is this reasonable? If we cast our minds to real-life risk management problems, when can we expect coin-tossing-like probabilities to be appropriate? First of all, for the frequentist approach to make sense we must be dealing with repeated draws under identical conditions from exactly the same price distribution – see again the quote above by Jaynes. To have access to this distribution we must have 'relevant' data, i.e., data that pertain to the same market conditions and institutional arrangements that we encounter today. And if we want to make very precise statements about the underlying distribution – e.g., if we want to say something about very high percentiles – we must also have *lots* of relevant data.

By the way, when we use statistical tool such as VaR, we proclaim ourselves innocent of any knowledge about how the world works (the ultimate *hypotheses-non-fingo* approach), but, as we choose the length of our dataset, we claim that we know exactly which portion of the past is relevant to predicting the future. Very often, for instance, we claim that, say, the last 200 days are perfectly and equally relevant to predicting what will happen tomorrow, but that what happened 201 days ago bears no relevance whatsoever to our predictions.[3] Sometimes our weighting scheme is not so 'digital', but how do we decide about weights and 'decay constants' without a prior understanding of the relevance of past events? I do not really understand how this is possible, but let me gloss over this point.

Let us rejoin the main thrust of the argument. First, as we have seen, for the frequentist approach to be valid, I must draw from the same distribution under identical conditions – the world must not have changed a bit over my sampling period and the projection horizon. Second, if I want to talk about rare events, I need lots of relevant data. But these two joint requirements impose a limit on the horizon over which I can project my forecast. This is simply because, in an environment as dynamic and ever-changing as financial markets, I do not have many independent draws obtained under the same conditions as the ones prevailing today. So, with data collected in the last few months or years I can perhaps estimate with some degree of confidence the tails of daily or weekly, monthly and perhaps yearly distributions of price changes. But I cannot reasonably expect to say anything reasonable about the 99.975th percentile of the one-year distribution (as a 'fundamentalist' interpretation of the Economic Capital project implies).

Now, there are two routes to gathering lots of data. We can collect them at a very high frequency or we can look a long way back into the past. What about the latter option? Can this help? This may well increase the quantity of our data, but are we gathering 'relevant' data? Are we really looking at tosses of the same coin? How confident are we that data collected 50, 10, 5 or perhaps even 2 years ago are relevant to predicting what will happen tomorrow? If I want to say something about a 1-in-20-year widening in the spread of CDSs, it does not help me that 20 years ago CDSs barely existed. More generally, financial innovation – one of the hallmarks of financial markets in the last decades – has not simply added new instruments to the market place. It has greatly changed the 'workings' of the markets as well. In the 'good old days' of CDO tranche issuance, for instance, CDSs became traded in higher volumes than ever before to hedge the exposure to the various tranches retained by investment banks. This created what I have called elsewhere 'bipolar liquidity': i.e., great liquidity, and tight bid-offer spreads, in normal market conditions; and a sudden

---

[3] At the time of writing, some banks use regulatory VaR with a data window of 250 days, and others of 500 days. They both do so with the blessing of the regulators. For the former set of banks the events that followed Lehman's default have just, and very suddenly, disappeared from their risk radar screens. For the latter set, these events will remain fully relevant for one more year, and then they will also disappear into oblivion.

drying up of liquidity, with gaping bid-offer spreads, whenever a squall hits the market.[4] Clearly, information about the price movements of CDS spreads before the 'invention' of CDO tranches would be of very little use in predicting spread movements in the heyday of the synthetic CDO market. (Note again how it is non-data information that allows me to express an opinion – right or wrong as it might be – about the relevance of different patches of the past to the statistical problem at hand.)

So, going a long way back into the past may not be such a good idea, because that distant past may not be relevant to today. But what about collecting data at higher frequency? Would this give plenty of relevant (because it is recent) data?

Unfortunately, also here there are problems. To begin with, very often the frequency of data collection is beyond the control of the observer. Firms default when they want, for instance, and hurricanes arrive when they please. Sometimes we do have the ability to increase the frequency of our data collection (with FX data we can gather minute-by-minute, or even tick-by-tick, information). However, it is not obvious that the statistical properties of the distributions for the longer forecasting horizons we are probably interested in can be 'safely' obtained from the high-frequency data. Of course, if returns *were* perfectly independent, there would be well-established techniques (convolution) to obtain, in theory, one-year distributions from one-hour distributions. In principle, this would be possible exactly and not as an approximation: under independence of returns the tail of the one-hour distribution built with thousands and thousands of observations would contain all the information we need to estimate the tail of the one-day, one-week or even one-year distributions. Unfortunately, empirical analysis shows[5] that, because of the absence of serial independence of returns, this is not the case, and longer-horizon distributions cannot be 'guessed' simply by collecting lots of high-frequency data.[6]

So, when we try to estimate the probability of occurrence of very rare events, we are caught between the rock of the relevance of very ancient data and the hard place of the frequency of data collection: look too far back in the past, and the data may refer to an altogether different world; collect data too frequently (assuming that you can), and you may be uncovering the microstructure of short-scale phenomena that, as a risk manager, you are unlikely to be interested in.

This places some hard limits on the applicability of frequentist statistical methods to the estimation of the probability of rare events in general, and of high percentiles in particular. Let us look at the different aspects of the problem one by one:

- Whenever I speak of the probability of, say, a given price move I must always specify over which time period this move applies. A move in long-term yields by 200 basis points may be extraordinary for a one-day horizon, but commonplace over a year.

- The longer this projection horizon (the 'holding period'), the fewer the independent (non-overlapping) segments of history of the same length I have at my disposal. With four years' worth of (relevant) data, I have about 1000 independent observations of daily returns; but only 16 observations of quarterly returns.

---

[4] See Rebonato (2009, 2010).

[5] See, e.g., Figure 2.2 in Malvergne and Sornette (2006), and the discussion that accompanies the figure.

[6] '[A]ssessing extreme risks at large timescales (1 or 10 days) by simple convolution of the distribution of returns at time scales of 1 or 5 minutes leads to crude approximations and to dramatic underestimation of the amount of risk really incurred' (Malvergne and Sornette, 2006, page 36).

- Even if I can increase the quantity of data by looking farther back in the past, as I do so I become less and less confident that what I have gathered is relevant to today's conditions.

- If I try to gather data at higher frequency than the prediction horizon I am interested in – assuming that I can – I have no confidence that the results from the high-frequency data can be extrapolated to the regime I am interested in. The more so, the more I am interested in the tails.

- The number of independent and relevant pieces of information therefore gives me an idea of the 'rarity' of events I can say something meaningful about from a frequentist point of view: with the 1000 daily relevant data points mentioned above, I can hope to say something (*very* imprecisely) about the 99.9th percentile of the underlying distribution of *daily* returns. But I will only be able to talk (again *very* imprecisely) about the 93.75th percentile of the distribution of *quarterly* returns – and about the 75th percentile of the distribution of *yearly* returns.

This information is meaningful and useful. Unfortunately, it does not even begin to address the needs of capital allocation: what I can measure has little direct relevance to prudential capital; what has relevance for prudential capital, I cannot measure (at least within a frequentist framework).

What can we do then? Are we lost in the mist of Knightian uncertainty? Perhaps by making use of a subjective approach we can push our boat one or two more orders of probabilistic magnitude beyond the safe frequentist shores. As I said in Chapter 1, I believe that beyond that there is a domain of extremely severe events for which no probabilistic assessment (subjective or frequentist) makes sense. But between the mundane losses for which frequentist techniques work reasonably well and Armageddon the hope is that perhaps we can patch together some reasonable additional probabilistic information.

In my opinion this must come from the subjective input of market participants. This subjective input is, of course, informed by what happened in the past – where else can our beliefs be grounded in? But our understanding of how the world works could make us think, for instance, that events in 1930–1931 may be more relevant to the economic climate of 2009–2010 than, say, what happened in the 1960s, or even in 2006. Or, again, I don't know whether the 'money glut' or the 'savings glut' explanation of what went wrong in 2007 (and of what we need to get out of the mess) is more correct. As a risk manager my task is not to take sides between neo-classical and neo-Keynesian economists, but to acknowledge that both views are plausible, and that the outcome produced by both views of the world (say, about future inflation, or the occurrence of more banking failures) should be given a non-negligible subjective probability in my scenarios. See the discussion in Chapter 3 about competing models of reality.

Sometimes markets provide their own subjective assessment of the likelihood of future events. Implied volatilities, for instance, can sometimes respond to new events much more quickly and intelligently than the best GARCH model is able to. Indeed, if you believe in efficient markets, market prices provide the *best* estimate of future everything. Now, in the wake of the recent crisis few theories have taken more serious knocks than the efficient-market hypothesis. However, only a fool would totally neglect the 'implied' information contained in spreads, volatilities, prices, etc. Disentangling the risk premium from expectations – say, in credit spreads – is, of course, not easy; but, again, when spreads move from 200 to 1200 basis points, the question of whether risk aversion accounts for 40%, 50% or 60% of the increase is really neither here nor there.

In short, asking for 'expert judgement' means asking the risk manager to quote the odds for a bet for which she does not know whether she will be the bookie or the punter. If the nature of the bet is such that frequentist methods are appropriate (if the bet is of the coin-tossing variety), it would be crazy for the risk manager *not* to make large use of frequentist techniques. If, however, the bet is of the President-of-the-US variety, and I were forced to advertise my odds, I would look at many sources of information, but not at the frequency of past women Presidents in the US.

Providing 'expert judgement' is not easy, and there is a large literature that highlights the systematic biases we make when we make forecasts. I deal with this topic (i.e., how to be aware of human decisional biases and how to try to correct for them) in Chapter 12. But, again, we should not be discouraged by the difficulty and the unfamiliarity of the task. After all, if our probabilistic assessments turn out to be within the correct order of magnitude, given the rarity of the events at hand, it would still be a great feat.

4.2   Tail Co-dependence

All I have said so far pertains to the estimation of the probability of occurrence of a single rare event. However, the events we are interested in when we deal with stress testing arise from the interaction of a series of concomitant factors. Say 'interaction' and 'stochastic variables', and correlation is the word that springs to mind. Indeed, the concept of correlation is very popular, but it has very strong limitations. For our purposes, its greatest shortcoming is that it is in no way synonymous with co-dependence. (By the way, even co-dependence is not the be-all-and-end-all of our understanding of how different variables interact, because it is still ultimately rooted in an associative, rather than causal, description of complex phenomena.) Let us take matters in order, however, and try to understand first why correlation is so popular.

Let us start from its nicest features. Correlation is one of the few measures of dependence that can be nicely decomposed into a simple pairwise statistic. When we are dealing with many variables and we talk about correlation we are implicitly saying that each variable influences, and is influenced by, each of the other variables in a simple pairwise fashion. This is computationally, and cognitively, great, but it should not make us believe for a second that the mathematical structure we are imposing on the phenomenon at hand should be reflected in the way the world actually works. Whether A is positively or negatively correlated with B will often depend on what C does: so, for instance, a loosening of monetary policy may or may not have an effect on inflation depending on the level of unemployment or the demanding for borrowing.

Even when a pairwise dependence does an adequate job at describing the phenomenon at hand, there is no *a priori* reason to believe that the strength of this pairwise co-dependence should be independent of the magnitude of the moves in the two risk factors. We can see why this may be the case by means of a little toy model that, for all its simplicity, contains in a nutshell some very interesting implications.

As everybody remembers during a financial shock, and forgets shortly thereafter, in periods of extreme market turbulence correlations among assets become more 'polarized', tending towards $+1$ or -1. We can take this as a descriptive *datum*, to store in our data bank of curious pieces of information about the financial markets. Or we may try to create a simple structural model to explain this phenomenon. The simple model may go a bit like this.

We assume that the observed changes in asset prices are produced by the changes in a relatively small number of driving factors – plus the usual idiosyncratic component. Let us call 'loadings' the sensitivities of the price return processes to the various factors (say, news about company earnings, GDP growth, etc.) that determine the changes in the vector of stock prices.

Now, suppose that there is a common factor (say, liquidity) that affects the returns on asset prices alongside all the other factors. In this toy model normal liquidity times are characterized by run-of-the mill realizations of the liquidity shock, and liquidity crises correspond to much larger draws from the liquidity shock distribution. For instance, we could model this by allowing the liquidity shock to be drawn from a jump-diffusion process, or from a more general and interesting Levy process, but nothing essential hangs on this.

Depending on the relative magnitude of the 'loadings' on the various factors on the one hand and of the idiosyncratic terms on the other, the correlation among assets due to the common liquidity factor could be very small when liquidity times are normal – i.e., when the draws of the liquidity stochastic process are of non-exceptional size. However, periods of liquidity crisis are characterized by exceptionally large shocks to this common liquidity factor. When this happens the liquidity factor can account for the lion's share of the moves of all the assets. The assets become much more correlated then in normal times. This is the first feature that our little model can explain.

Let us see what else we could do. It would also be plausible to build into the model the feature that different assets should have negative or positive loadings onto the liquidity factor (think, for instance, of Treasuries and emerging market bonds). These modelling choices would then cause risky assets to move together (south), and risk-less or safe assets (e.g., Treasury bonds and highly-rated supranational paper) to appreciate. This could give rise to the observed 'close to $+1$ or -1 correlations' in extreme market conditions. We have explained another feature.

One can be a little cleverer. The market perception of what constitutes a liquid asset can change with the severity of the liquidity crisis. As the events of 1998 show, for instance, in periods of extreme stress on-the-run Treasuries can become noticeably more in demand than almost identical off-the-run issues. So, the magnitude, and perhaps even the sign, of the loadings onto the liquidity factor could themselves be a function of the magnitude of the liquidity shock. We have managed to explain why co-dependence may be a function of the magnitude of the liquidity shock. Imagine what an interesting and complex empirical copula the data produced by this little model could generate.[7]

For all this simplicity, this example already shows that a very complex co-dependence structure can be easily 'implied' by a very simple structural model. Suppose now that we examine the data produced by this toy model, but with no knowledge of how they had been generated. If our analysis were purely descriptive and relied exclusively on looking at the data,[8] we could still, of course, calculate a correlation matrix from the output generated by this model, but the number we would come up with would not be particularly meaningful. Indeed, no single correlation number, large or small, would be adequate – and the interesting

---

[7]Keep in mind this simple example, and its last 'twist' in particular, for when we come to the associative-versus-causal description of phenomena presented in the last section of this chapter.

[8]In Section 4.4, I describe a purely-data-driven approach as 'associative'.

one, i.e., the correlation that applies during periods of stress, will be present in our dataset only in a handful of points. The vast majority of the data will then refer to the 'uninteresting' (tame) correlation, and our overall estimate will be close to meaningless.

The discussion above suggests that correlations allow us to move from marginal to joint distributions only for one very special (and tame) class of distributions, namely the elliptical ones. Elliptical distributions are nice to work with. Unfortunately, computational expediency has a very limited impact on the way the world actually works, especially in the tails. If what we are interested in are joint probabilities, the 'correct' way to go from marginal to joint distribution is, of course, via copulas (see, e.g., Nelsen (1999) or McNeil, Frey and Embrechts (2005)). But the interesting differences between most copulas are in the tail behaviour, where, again, the relevant data points are rare, and often (when 'ancient') of dubious relevance to today's conditions.[9]

There is more. As we have seen, correlations do not allow us in general to go from marginal to joint probabilities. And as for copulas, theoretically they provide the 'correct' solution to this problem, but in the tails they give rise to some pretty fundamental calibration problems. But let us leave all these *caveats* aside and assume that, somehow, we have managed to conjoin our marginals in the cleverest possible way and have gained access to the joint probabilities. I will argue below that, devoid of a model 'of how things work', even these supposedly all-informative joint probabilities fall short of providing a cognitively resonant tool for risk management and stress testing. This brings me to the distinction between associative and causal descriptions of reality that I deal with in Section 4.4.

4.3   From Structural Models to Co-dependence

I have argued in the first part of this chapter that a frequentist view of probability – a view, that is, that purely relies on data and makes little or no use of an underlying structural model (however simple) – is unlikely to be of much use in assessing the (marginal) probability of stand-alone extreme events. This does not mean, however, that nothing can be done: and this is exactly where subjective probabilities come in.

Subjective marginal (stand-alone) probabilities for stress events can profitably combine data information with our models of how the world works. If we try to ascertain probabilities of events that are too rare, the task remains near impossible – this is the Keynesian uncertainty domain. But there is a useful range of still-remote-but-not-so-extremely-rare events about whose stand-alone probability of occurrence something *can* be said. Yes, I argue in this book that it pays to be humble and modest in our approach. Humility and modesty, however, should not prevent us from providing some order-of-magnitude estimates for the probability of their occurrence. Doing much more may just be unrealistic (or even hubristic). But doing less may mean throwing away some very useful pieces of information. In the approach I propose I will therefore often ask the risk manager to estimate as best she can at least the order of magnitude of the marginal probabilities.

---

[9]Indeed, I employed copulas a few years ago with a student of mine (Shamrakov, 2006) in order to explore the dependence between credit spreads and equity prices for a large number of firms, of different initial credit ratings. As we were interested in tail co-dependence I recall that, if we had had to rely purely on the data, the choice of one copula over another would have been close to arbitrary. Once again, what provided great help was supplementing the raw data with a simple, Merton-like structural model. The choice of this model, needless to say, introduced an important subjective element to our data analysis.

What can we do then? I believe that we may be able to go a long way by integrating stand-alone probabilities with simple models of reality, such as, for instance, the liquidity toy model sketched above. The point of the rather lengthy description given above of this little model was not its specifics, but the realization that a simple understanding of how the world may work can take us a long way towards *implying* a co-dependence structure when its estimation from the raw data, for any of the reasons above, is not feasible. This is why I will present in the rest of the book ways to integrate some carefully chosen (marginal or conditional) probabilities for the stand-alone events with our 'world models'.

As a by-product I will obtain joint probabilities (or bounds for them). These probabilities will allow us to escape Berkowitz's purgatory, and to treat the output of stress testing on a comparable basis with the output from VaR & Co. If we want to use stress testing to calculate capital, having an idea of the order of magnitude of the various stress losses will prove invaluable. However, obtaining joint probabilities should not be seen as our end result. Building, using, refining and, when necessary, throwing away a causal structure between the variables at play (a model) will provide a much more powerful tool for risk management action.

Of course, this means that, in Bayesian language, I advocate a far greater role in my approach for my prior than is allowed for by the statistical analysis typically used in a risk management context. A greater relevance of the prior in turn means that we have to resort to a (more) subjective interpretation of probability. Yes, this does also mean a departure from 'objectivity', but this should be welcomed and not regretted, as pure objectivity in any scientific endeavour is, in my opinion, a pious myth.[10]

The rest of this book will therefore unapologetically require the risk manager to provide her subjective probabilities where appropriate – but, far more importantly, her tentative understanding of how the world works. Doing so in a logically coherent manner is not easy. Bayesian nets will provide my tool of choice in carrying out this programme.

Bayesian nets are often interpreted as computational devices to obtain in a parsimonious and 'frugal' manner a difficult set of quantities (the joint probabilities), from simpler building blocks (marginal and conditional probabilities). However, looking at Bayesian nets simply as a handy book-keeping device to obtain joint probabilities would be a missed opportunity. Such a reductive view neglects the distinction between associative and causal descriptions of a complex phenomenon. It is to the discussion of this important aspect that I therefore now turn.

4.4 Association or Causation?

A purely probabilistic approach to risk management (and, for that matter, to the analysis of any complex phenomenon) places all the emphasis on the association among variables, rather than on the causal links among them. This is unsatisfactory on several accounts.

First, assigning links among variables on a causal rather than associative basis is cognitively much easier and more 'natural'. To see what this means, consider the following example, modified from Pearl (2009). Suppose that the variable in whose prediction we are interested is whether a garden pavement will be slippery or not. The other variables in

---

[10]In *Plight of the Fortune Tellers* (2007) I describe a case where lack of one's prior would induce a Martian to make a grossly wrong guess about the biasedness of a coin even in a simple coin-tossing experiment. So important is this example that I toyed with the idea of calling that book *Coin-Tossing Martians and the Next President of the United States*. Fortunately, everyone, from my editor to my wife, disabused me of the idea.

this baby problem are the season, whether it rained or not, whether the pavement is wet and whether a sprinkler was on or off. We could take a purely associative approach, and build all the probability tables required. As we shall see in Chapters 8 and 9, these would require the specification of stand-alone probabilities (such as probability of rain tomorrow), and conditional probabilities. These, in turn, could be very simple and 'natural' (such as the probability of rain tomorrow, given that it is autumn), or very complex and 'awkward' ones (such as the probability that the sprinkler is off, given that it is autumn, that the pavement is not slippery and that it has been raining). Assigning some of these probabilities can in some cases feel like answering a well-posed question, but in other cases we seem to be 'working against the cognitive grain', and we are faced with difficult, puzzling or even paradoxical probabilistic assignments.

From the point of view of associational relationships, there is nothing wrong with what we are trying to do (filling the conditional probability tables) – in particular, there is nothing to distinguish the 'natural' from the 'awkward' assignments. Now, if we are using a purely frequentist approach, we just collect data and calculate all the conditional probabilities from our dataset. But what if we have to provide *subjective* probabilities? If this is the task at hand, our cognitive aptitude at dealing with some questions rather than others does make a big difference. What is happening here? Why are we finding some questions easier to answer than others?

The root of the problem lies in the fact some of the assignments we are requested to make invoke a causal link among variables, and others are linked by a subtler ('diagnostic') kind of relationship. It so happens that our mind works much more effectively in a causal rather in an associative mode.[11] When we try to answer difficult questions by taking a purely probabilistic (associative) approach we are therefore not doing ourselves any favours. The results of this analysis will also be cognitively very difficult to use.

'Awkward' and 'natural' conditional probabilities do not only make a difference when we assign them subjectively. The associative link between variables 'contained' in a purely probabilistic description can make our interpretation difficult, and this can be true even when we have plentiful and relevant data. If *understanding*, rather than just analysing, the output of complicated analysis is our final goal, this cannot be satisfactory.

Fortunately, an associative approach is not the only possible one. In the sprinkler example, we can follow a different approach and create a simple causal model of 'garden reality', whereby

- the season of the year affects the probability of rain and of the sprinkler being on or off (but is not affected by either);[12]

- the status of the sprinkler (on or off) and whether it rained or not affects the probability of the pavement being wet (but sprinkler status and occurrence of rain are not caused by the wetness of the pavement);

- the wetness of the pavement affects its slipperiness (but the slipperiness does not 'cause' wetness).

---

[11] See Pearl (2009), Chapter 1, and references therein on this point.

[12] Of course, whether it is summer or autumn is not affected by the pavement being wet or not. However, knowledge that the pavement is wet *does* change my probability assessment of the season being autumn. When we work from the season (autumn) to the probability of the pavement being wet we are working in a causal mode. When we work backwards from the state of the pavement we are working in a diagnostic mode. See the discussion in Chapter 12.

All of a sudden, *given this model*, certain conditional probabilities make a lot more sense, and appear a lot more 'natural' than others. For instance, the conditional probability of the pavement being wet given the season of the year (via the mediated 'causes' of rain and sprinkler) appears 'natural' and cognitively sensible to assign. In particular, it appears natural and sensible in a sense that the conditional probability of the season being springtime, given that the pavement is slippery but not wet, is not. Yet, if we take a purely associational approach, there is nothing to distinguish between the two probabilities – there is nothing to indicate, that is, that the former probability naturally falls out from a causal appreciation of how the world works, while the latter requires our mind to work 'backwards'.[13] As Pearl (2009) eloquently puts it:

> [I]f conditional independence judgements are by-products of stored causal relationships, then tapping and representing those relationships directly [is] a more natural and more reliable way of expressing what we know or believe about the world. This is indeed the philosophy behind causal Bayesian nets.

The second reason why causal models (and causal interpretations of Bayesian nets) are more powerful than associative ones is that simple modifications of the causal link among variables can give rise to large and 'mysterious' changes in association (and in measures of association, such as correlation) and in joint probabilities. Suppose, for instance, that the world changes a little (and, by the way, when it comes to the financial world, it tends to change a lot rather than a little). In our small garden world, suppose that we have installed a clever sprinkler, which does not come on if it is already raining.

It is very easy to encode this change in our chain of causal links among variables (we shall see how to do it with Bayesian nets in Chapter 8, but the reader can go with the flow and imagine the gist of the construction). However, if we look at the problem from a purely associative point of view, i.e., just by looking at the changes in marginal, conditional and joint probabilities before and after the installation of the clever sprinkler, we can be very puzzled. After the installation of the clever sprinkler, we would observe, for instance, that some of these probabilities have changed a lot, and others not at all. But why these and not those? In general we will observe that the probabilities have changed in a way that, if we do not know what caused what, can be both complex and difficult to make sense of – this is what I meant above when I used the term 'mysterious'.

Pearl (2009) addresses a closely related point when he writes:

> [C]ausal models (assuming they are correct) are much more informative than probability models. A joint probability tells us how probable events and how probabilities would change with subsequent observations, but a causal model also tells us how these probabilities would change as a result of *external interventions*.[14]

All of this is of great relevance when it comes to our attempts to understand the financial world for risk management purposes in general, and for stress testing in particular. The frequentist approach that has been at the core of the reigning paradigm has studiously eschewed all causal information. Association without causes has been the modelling structure

---

[13]As we shall see, 'backwards' in this context means in a diagnostic rather than a causal mode. See Chapter 12.

[14]Pearl (2009), page 32, my emphasis.

of choice: think, for instance, of how the calculation of the VaR statistics works when the historical simulation method is employed. Pure juxtaposition (association) without any overarching structure lies at the core of its *modus operandi*. This is the price that has been paid in the pursuit of objectivity – and a very high price indeed it has been.

Now, when the relationships among variables are stable and we can observe them for a long time,[15] the associative approach can be inefficient, but we can still have some hope of saying something about the variables of interest (in our garden world, whether the pavement is slippery). But when it comes to stress testing, the paucity of the relevant observations and the mutability of the causal relationship between them makes an approach based on association (i.e., on probabilities without causal links) close to hopeless. This is why the provision of causal information is so fundamentally important for stress testing.

The link between causal descriptions and the interpretative models of reality discussed in the previous chapter should be evident. From Chapter 3 to Chapter 4 my argument has begun to 'rotate' from a purely discursive and qualitative approach to the somewhat more precise observations about the differences between the causal and probabilistic relationships I have just presented. In the rest of the book the 'rotation' of my argument from the discursive and qualitative to the quantitative will gather pace in Part II. This is because some mathematical formalization and a reasonable degree of precision are indispensable to turning a 'good idea' into an operative blueprint for action. However, the importance of a qualitative understanding of the issues at play should never be underestimated, and should remain with the reader throughout the book.

So, for instance, a lot of effort will be devoted to showing how to go from conditional and marginal probabilities to the joint distribution. Indeed, I will often refer to this latter quantity as the probabilistic Holy Grail. However, one should never lose sight of the fact that causal links are primary, richer, more flexible and more informative than probabilities (joint or otherwise). And that joint probabilities may well be 'king', but only from a purely associative perspective.

4.5   Suggestions for Further Reading

So vast is the literature on the Bayesian versus frequentist debate, that it is virtually impossible to give a comprehensive list of 'essential readings'. For an eloquent, impassioned and uncompromising defence of the Bayesian view of the world the reader can refer to Jaynes (2003). A reviewer hailed the book as 'the most important contribution to the problem of induction since Aristotle'. As another book in my list of suggested readings (Williamson, 2005) has been given a virtually identical accolade, we must be living in a particularly productive decade. Hyperbole aside, Jaynes' book is very clear and certainly inspiring, but, at times, almost strident. For a more balanced view, see Poirier (1995).

Moving to more technical topics, see Malvergne and Sornette (2006) for a good discussion of the difficulty in fitting tail distributions. An excellent and concise introduction to Extreme Value Theory and copula theory can be found in McNeil, Frey and Embrechts (2005). For its combination of concision, clarity and precision this is probably the best book I am aware of about quantitative risk management. A good discussion of parametric, non-parametric

---

[15]In the language of the previous sections, this means when the data are relevant and plentiful.

and semi-parametric approaches to Extreme Value Theory can be found in Malvergne and Sornette (2006), especially in their Chapter 2.

The important distinction between association and causation is discussed very well in Pearl (2009).

Finally, I deal in more detail, but still in a non-technical manner, with some of the topics of this chapter in Rebonato (2007).

Part II

The Probabilistic Tools and Concepts

Chapter 5

Probability with Boolean Variables I: Marginal and Conditional Probabilities

5.1 The Set-up and What We are Trying to Achieve

This chapter does not attempt to provide a systematic introduction to probability theory. The reader is expected to be already familiar with the fundamentals.[1] My tasks are to explain in the simplest possible way a selected number of topics and ideas – some elementary, some slightly more advanced – that we shall use in Part III; to present the notation that will be used in the rest of the book; to introduce some graphical tools (Venn diagrams) that are very useful for thinking about conditional probabilities; and to give the simplest self-consistent framework that can allow the reader to think coherently about marginal, conditional and joint probabilities. I have made no attempt to either rigour or generality.[2]

After reading this and the next chapter the reader should be able to understand why, if she had the joint probability distribution among n variables, she would know everything she can probabilistically say about them; and also why obtaining this quantity is so difficult. Readers who have followed the qualitative discussion about co-dependence that closed the previous chapter should already have an idea of why that is the case. This difficulty will motivate the topic of Chapters 6 to 8, which can be summarized as follows: under what conditions can we make the task of obtaining the joint distribution more tractable – and, more specifically, sufficiently tractable to be of use in stress testing.

---

[1] See Section 4.5 (Suggestions for Further Reading) for some recommendations about introductory and intermediate-level texts in probability theory well suited to my treatment.

[2] For instance, I will only deal with a finite number of variables, and I will allow them to assume only one of two possible values. Some of the extensions (such as allowing for more than two possible realizations) would be simple enough others would take us on a long detour.

When it comes to scenarios, very often a very important question is: what is the probability of this scenario happening? Let me make the question a bit more meaningful.[3] Consider first a precise scenario (e.g., an upward move of a yield curve by 50 basis points or more).[4] I call this scenario event E. I can then ask the question: 'What is the probability that this event will happen over the next week?' After the observation period has elapsed (in this case, one week) we will know for sure whether the event happened or not, but 'today' there is some degree of uncertainty – however small – about the outcome. If this is the case, E is a two-valued Boolean random variable, where 'Boolean' means that it can assume values 'true' (T) or 'false' (F), and two-valued means just what it says. It is important to understand that the random variable we are talking about does not assume a numerical value (say, 50 basis points), only a logical value (T or F). Strictly speaking, if the move in the yield curve turned out to be 49 or 51 basis points, then event E did not occur. That is why we will have to be careful when defining the events. More about this later.

A large part of this book will deal with assigning probabilities (marginal, conditional, joint) to events, that is, to two-valued Boolean variables (or, more shortly, Boolean variables or even variables when no ambiguity can arise). The treatment below is tailored to this task.

Before getting started it is useful to have a map of the road ahead for the present and the next chapter. As I said, the probabilistic Holy Grail is gaining access to the joint distribution. Unfortunately, even all the marginal and (singly-conditioned) probabilities do not allow us in general to gain access to this quantity. They will not allow us, that is, to answer some questions such as: 'What is the probability of the first two scenarios materializing but the third and fourth not coming true?' Ideally, this would be just the information we would like to have because Nature will not produce scenarios (if she does) one at a time, but in a combination of her liking. If we want to associate some capital to these *joint* events, or more simply, if we want to have an idea as to whether we should worry or not, we would like to have at least an order-of-magnitude idea of the probability of occurrence of the *joint* scenarios Nature will put in front of us. Being able to answer – even in an approximate manner – questions such as the one above requires knowledge of quantities informationally much richer, but correspondingly more difficult to obtain, than marginal or singly-conditional probabilities, that is, of the full joint distribution.

I cannot stress how difficult it is to estimate a joint distribution when the events we are looking at are very rare. Even estimating the stand-alone probability of one scenario in isolation is a daunting task, which for truly 'stress' events, I do not believe can be accomplished with better-than-order-of-magnitude precision. But what is a well-nigh impossible task is estimating purely from financial time series information about tail co-dependencies. In Chapter 4 I explained why this is the case. Only the knowledge of these tail co-dependencies (not correlations![5]) would allow us to go from the marginal to the joint distribution.

Should we throw up our hands in despair then? Perhaps not. If we are prepared to add to the purely frequentist information our understanding of how the world works (or might work) we can turn an impossible task into a very difficult one. Where can this 'extra information'

---

[3]We will have to be a lot more precise than this (see Section 9.2).

[4]Note that saying 'an upward move of a yield curve by 50 basis points' does not make a lot of sense, or is not what we probably meant in the first place. If we think of '50' as a real number, the probability of 'an upward move of a yield curve by *exactly* 50 basis points' is zero. Even if we recognize that basis points move in discrete increments, a move by exactly 50 basis points (rather than 49 or 51) is not what we probably had in mind. Specifying clearly the event is important. For the moment, however, we just go with the flow.

[5]As I pointed out in Chapter 4, correlations allow us to go from the marginals to the joint distribution only in the case of elliptical distributions. In general, there is no reason to believe that, especially in the tails, the dependence among n variables should neatly decompose into pairwise dependencies.

come from? Correlations (and, for that matter, also conditional probabilities) convey no information about causal relationship.[6] But surely we often have some ideas of what causes what. A dramatic fall in the S&P is more likely to cause an increase of equity volatility than the other way around. (Of course, some other cause, such as the default of a major bank counterparty, may cause both the S&P to fall and equity volatility to increase – but also in this case we have an idea of what caused what).

Bayesian nets (or Bayesian networks, or acyclical directed graphs if you prefer difficult words) are a very powerful and intuitive technique to systematize our knowledge about causal relationships among variables and translate it directly into probabilistic information. It may all sound very abstract now, but I will show in Part III how to turn these lofty words into a concrete action plan.

So, here is the game plan:

- Our final goal is to gain access to the joint distribution.

- Getting there directly is too hard.

- Therefore we start from marginal (stand-alone) probabilities and conditional probabilities of very low order.[7]

- We realize that these are in general not enough to get us what we want (the joint distribution).

- We therefore inject information about how we expect the world to work.

- Given this extra information, the tool that gives us hope to get from what we can laboriously estimate to the joint distribution we truly need are Bayesian nets.

- The simpler the structure we allow for our Bayesian net, the fewer (and simpler[8]) the conditional probabilities we will have to supply.

- When we feel that providing some conditional probabilities is too difficult, and our causal structure does not pin down the joint probabilities uniquely, there still are some very useful bounds that can be found.

---

[6]One may say that same-time across-asset correlations convey no information about causal relationships, but time lagged time series do. Indeed, there is a whole field of econometrics (Granger causality) devoted to uncovering causality from lagged time series. See, e.g., Granger (1969) and Hacker and Hatemi-J (2006) for an extension to non-normal variates and for a more modern treatment that uses the unit-root approach to time series analysis. In principle, the idea is simple: suppose we have two time series of changes, Δx and Δy, and that we want to explore whether x Granger-causes y. First, we do a regression of Δy on lagged values of Δy. If some lag values are found to be significant, we carry out further regressions on various lags of Δx. These lags are added to the regression if they are significant on a stand-alone basis, and if they increase the explanatory power of the model.

There are two problems with this, one of a practical and one of a theoretical nature. The practical problem is that financial markets tend to adjust so quickly that, unless one deals with high-frequency data, it is difficult to find stable, robust and convincingly non-zero time-lagged correlations.

The second problem is that, even if we could detect such a lagged correlation, without a model of reality there would be no telling whether some other cause (not captured in our data series) might not have caused the leading variable, and so, indirectly, caused both the leading and the lagged indicator.

[7]The probability of A given that I know that B has happened (denoted by $P(A|B)$) is a *singly*-conditioned probability, because I am availing myself of the knowledge that only one event (B in this case) has happened.

The probability of A given that I know that B and C have happened (denoted by $P(A|B, C)$) is a *doubly*-conditioned probability, because now I know that two events (in this case B and C) have happened.

I call conditional probabilities of very low order at-most-doubly-conditioned probabilities.

[8]Where by 'simpler' I mean 'of low order' in the sense explained in the footnote above.

- An example of the type of 'external information' that we will have to supply is about independence (a very strong and, in finance, very rare condition) and conditional independence. These are the scissors that will allow us to prune the branches of the Bayesian net and, hopefully, give us access to the joint distribution.

- When we have this, we have everything.

5.2   (Marginal) Probabilities

Consider an event E. Following the excellent and simple treatment by Moore (2001), I am going to define the (marginal) probability of E being true ($P(E = T)$, or more simply, $P(E)$) as the 'fraction of the possible worlds in which event E occurs'.[9] As Moore says:

> We could at this point spend two hours on the philosophy of this.
> But we won't.

I will instead give a graphical representation of this probability. Recall that E is a Boolean variable. Therefore the 'fraction of the possible worlds in which event E occurs' means the 'fraction of the possible worlds in which Boolean variable E assumes the value T'. We can visualize this as shown in Figure 5.1. There are two sets: one denoted by $E = T$, the other by $E = F$. The set $E = F$ is made up only of the cells shaded in grey. The grey cells do not 'extend under' the white cells. There is nothing to be read in the fact that the set $E = T$ is all 'inside' set $E = F$. Exactly the same information would be conveyed by Figure 5.2. The only thing that matters is the relative size of the two sets.

Recalling the definition of the probability of E (being true) given above, we can have a graphical representation of how likely E is as follows:

$$P(E) = \frac{\{E = T\}}{\{E = T \cup E = F\}} \tag{5.1}$$

In the expression above the use of curly brackets $\{A\}$ denotes the size (in some units) of a set A. If you are drawing your Venn diagrams in Excel, the size can be taken to be equal to (rather than approximated by) the number of cells in each domain.

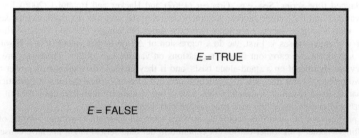

Figure 5.1   The 'fractions of the possible worlds' where event E is true.

---

[9]Why 'marginal'? Because marginal distributions are obtained by 'integrating out' the variables one is not interested in. For a two-dimensional case, where the discretized joint distribution can be represented as a table, the marginal distribution appears as a sum over rows or columns at the margin of the table – hence the name.

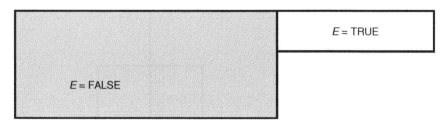

Figure 5.2 An equivalent representation of the 'fractions of the possible worlds' where event E is true.

To make things simpler, I am now going to normalize the union of set $E = T$ and set $E = F$ to 1:

$$\{E = T \cup E = F\} = 1 \tag{5.2}$$

We can simplify our notation further as follows: instead of denoting the set of 'worlds' where E is true by $E = T$, I will simply denote it by E. What shall I do with the set of 'worlds' where E is not true? I will denote this set by $\tilde{E}$.

Let us now link the size of the sets we have associated with different events with their probability of occurrence.

To start with, if we are certain that E will occur, its (*ex-ante*) probability is 1. If we are certain that it will not happen, its (*ex-ante*) probability is 0. It is then reasonable to introduce the following axioms:

Axiom 1 For any event E. $0 \le P(E) \le 1$

Axiom 2 For any event E. if $\{E = T\} = 1$, then $P(E) = 1$

Axiom 3 For any event E. if $\{E = T\} = 0$, then $P(E) = 0$

We need another axiom that involves two events, E and F. Consider Figure 5.3. To save ink, the set E now denotes what I called above set $E = T$. The two sets intersect, that is, there are possible worlds in which both E and F happen. The probability of both events happening, denoted by $P(E \cap F)$, is given by

$$P(E \cap F) = \{E \cap F\} \tag{5.3}$$

(Remember that the size of the whole set of all the possible worlds has been normalized to 1.) As we shall see, this intersection set is central to the treatment that will follow, but for the moment we still have to gather a few tools.

I can now introduce the last axiom, which relates to the probability of *either* E or F, denoted $P(E \cup F)$, happening:

Axiom 4 For any couple of events E and F, $P(E \cup F) = P(E) + P(F) - P(E \cap F)$

If we look at Figure 5.4, this is 'obvious': if I added $P(E)$ and $P(F)$ I would be double-counting the area $\{E = T \cap F = T\}$, which is therefore duly subtracted. Recall, however,

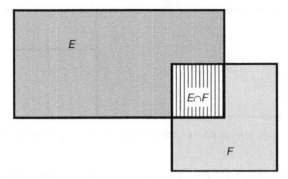

Figure 5.3   The area of overlap denotes the intersection of sets E and F.

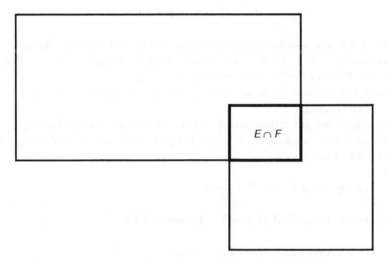

Figure 5.4   'Explaining' the axiom $P(E \cup F) = P(E) + P(F) - P(E \cap F)$.

that an axiom, however 'plausible' or 'obvious', is just that: an axiom. We must always make the graphical depiction reflect the axioms, not the other way round.

In particular, from Axiom 4 it follows that if two events E and F can never happen together – i.e., if they are incompatible – then the probability of either event happening is given by:

$$P(E \cup F) = P(E) + P(F) \quad \text{(incompatibility)} \tag{5.4}$$

But this also implies (again by Axiom 4) that

$$P(E \cap F) = \{E \cap F\} = 0 \tag{5.5}$$

Therefore the graphical representation must look something like what is shown in Figure 5.5: the two sets must have no points in common: when either event happens, the other one never does.

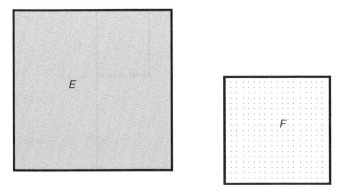

Figure 5.5 The sets E and F when the two events are incompatible.

Exercise 1 Prove using the axioms above or Venn diagrams that, for any E, $P(E) + P(\tilde{E}) = 1$.

5.3 Deterministic Causal Relationship

In order to get some familiarity with these definitions and graphical constructions, let us ask ourselves the question: how would we draw the case where there is a perfect, deterministic causal relationship[10] between E and F, in the sense that E always and invariably causes F[11]? If E deterministically causes F, then there are no possible worlds where E happened and F did not happen. Now, F may be caused by other events as well. So, to begin with, $\{E\}$ must be smaller than or equal in size to $\{F\}$. (Why?) But we can say more. The set E must be totally contained within the set F: a point of E not contained in F means a possible world where E can happen but F does not. But, if E deterministically causes F, this cannot occur. So, the picture must look something like Figure 5.6. By the way, given the way this picture has been drawn there are many more causes (although not necessarily *deterministic* causes) for F other than E. Event E may be the only deterministic cause.

A very important caveat: if E deterministically causes F, then the set E must be totally contained within the set F, but the converse is not true; that is, it is not true that if the set E

---

[10]We often say things such as: 'Smoking causes lung cancer'. But this is not an instance of deterministic causation; not because there are other causes of lung cancer, but because some smokers do not get lung cancer.

[11]I define the term 'deterministically cause' to identify the situation when the occurrence of one event is invariably associated with the occurrence of another event. The definition is a bit misleading, because perhaps A does not cause B in our intuitive undertstanding of the word 'cause', in that there may be some other event that causes both A and B. For instance, we may say that the default of a major bank counterparty 'causes' spreads to widen. But a nuclear bomb dropped on Wall Street would cause both a major counterparty to fail, *and* spreads to widen. Even if there are no states of the world where a major bank counterparty fails without spreads widening, the former event may not necessarily be the cause of the latter. Causation is an extremely complex topic, and philosophers have been at it for about 2500 years. Whenever I speak of causation in this book I steer clear of the subtle but important caveats that come with a proper treatment of causation. To make clear that I am dealing with 'causation-lite' sometimes I write 'causation'. Most of the time I do not feel this is necessary, but the reader should keep this caveat in mind.

Thinking clearly about what causes what, and about proximate and prime causes, is very important in order to organize stress tests in a coherent manner. This is one of the areas where Bayesian nets can help us. See Williamson (2005) for a treatment that deals head on with the topic of 'proper' causation, and Pearl (2009) for a good discussion of the topic.

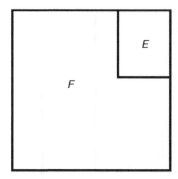

Figure 5.6   The sets E and F when E deterministically causes E.

is totally contained within the set F, then there must be deterministic causation from E to F. To see why this is the case, consider an event, G. When G happens, sometimes, but not always, F happens. But F happens, when it does, only when G happens. Then the set F is completely contained in the set G, but we would certainly not like to say that 'F caused G'.

To see more clearly what this means in terms of stress events, suppose that G represents the occurrence of a run on a major bank. Let F be the event 'The Fed takes over a major bank'. Assume, for the sake of argument, that the Fed will be moved to nationalize a major bank only if there has been a run on this bank, but will not necessarily do so. Then, clearly, the set F is a proper subset of the set G, but we would not want to say that the rescue operation by the Fed (F) has caused the run on the bank (G)! So, the condition $F \subseteq G$ is a necessary but not sufficient condition for deterministic causation.[12]

Exercise 2   How would you depict by means of Venn diagrams the situation where F has two deterministic causes, either E or G, and E and G can never happen together?

Exercise 3   How would you draw the situation where F has two deterministic causes, either E or G, and E deterministically causes G?

The two exercises above begin to give us some familiarity with the graphical tools that we will use in Parts II and III. As we shall see, these pictures will help our reasoning immensely. To see their power even more clearly, try to prove the following theorem either using the axioms 1 to 4 above, or simply by drawing a Venn diagram and putting the pieces together:

Exercise 4   For any E and F, prove that

$$P(E) = P(E \cap F) + P\left(E \cap \tilde{F}\right)$$

If in solving the exercise above you found the mental colour-and-cut-and-paste-the-sets approach easier than the algebraic one (as I do), you should be convinced that Venn diagrams will help us in situations where the reasoning can become quite subtle. They will help us,

---

[12]The notation $F \subseteq G$ indicates that the set F is a (not necessarily proper) subset of G.

that is, to think logically. This is exactly what we are going to need when we begin to deal with several scenarios.

5.4 Conditional Probabilities

Let us look again at Figure 5.3, which I have drawn again for ease of reference in Figure 5.7. The part of the drawing where most of the action takes place is in the intersection set, $E \cap F$. Its area represents the fraction of possible worlds where E and F happen together. Since the set of all possible worlds has been normalized to 1, the area of this intersection set must be smaller than or equal to 1:

$$\{E \cap F\} \le 1 \tag{5.6}$$

and, obviously,

$$\{E \cap F\} \le \{E\} \tag{5.7}$$

$$\{E \cap F\} \le \{F\} \tag{5.8}$$

Now, given the normalization of the 'size of the whole universe' to 1, the probability of both E and F happening is clearly given by

$$P(E \cap F) = \{E \cap F\} \tag{5.9}$$

But what about the probability of both E and F happening given that we know that, say, F has happened? When we ask this question, the new universe we are interested in becomes the set of possible worlds for which $F = T$. This new reference universe gives the new normalization yardstick, and in this new metric we look at the fraction of possible worlds in which E is also true. We give a special name to this ratio, namely the *conditional probability of E given F*, which we denote by $P(E|F)$:

$$P(E|F) \equiv \frac{\{E \cap F\}}{\{F\}} = \frac{P(E \cap F)}{P(F)} \tag{5.10}$$

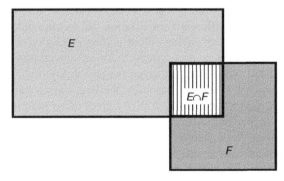

Figure 5.7 The intersection set, $E \cap F$, which must be normalized either by the size of E or by the size of F.

Conversely and symmetrically, the probability of both E and F happening given that we know that E has happened is given by

$$P(F|E) \equiv \frac{\{E \cap F\}}{\{E\}} = \frac{P(E \cap F)}{P(E)} \tag{5.11}$$

Note how the numerators ($\{E \cap F\}$, $P(E \cap F)$) do not change: it is only the 'normalization factor' in the denominator that tells us that our 'reference universe', that is, what we assume to know to have occurred, has changed.

The following table summarizes what we have defined so far:

numerator	denominator	ratio	meaning
$\{E \cap F\}$	$\{E\}$	$\dfrac{\{E \cap F\}}{\{E\}}$	$P(F|E)$
$\{E \cap F\}$	$\{F\}$	$\dfrac{\{E \cap F\}}{\{F\}}$	$P(E|F)$
$\{E \cap F\}$	$\{E \cup \tilde{E}\}$	$\dfrac{\{E \cap F\}}{1}$	$P(E \cap F)$

$$(5.12)$$

Given the definition above it is an easy task to show that

$$P(E|F) + P\left(\tilde{E}|F\right) = 1 \tag{5.13}$$

Exercise 5   Prove Equation (5.13) using Venn diagrams.

5.5   Time Ordering and Causation

One important observation is in order. There is in general no notion of causality in the concept of conditional probability, and there is no notion of temporal sequence either. In general, it is not right to think of the probability of E given F as the probability that E is caused (deterministically or otherwise) by F. Nor is it right to think that 'first F happened, and now we are going to see the probability that E might follow'. If one looks at the Venn diagram in Figure 5.7, it is clear that it contains no time information, and that the 'conditioning' only refers to a different normalization, not to time ordering or causation.

So, strictly speaking, instead of saying 'What is the probability of E happening given that F has happened?' – which leads us astray with an unwarranted whiff of temporal sequence – one should say 'What can I say about the probability of E happening *given that I know that F has happened*?' For our purposes, the best way to think about conditional probabilities is the following: the quantity $P(E|F)$ gives us an indication of whether, and by how much, we are helped in predicting E given that we know that F has happened.

Knowledge that a major bank counterparty has failed helps us (enormously) in predicting whether credit spreads have widened. Knowing that the summer–winter gas spread has widened does not help us in predicting whether a major bank counterparty has failed. In the former case, the conditional probability is (close to) 1; in the latter it is (close to) the unconditional probability (see Section 5.7).

In order to introduce causation and time ordering we need extra information that does not come from the Venn diagrams we have drawn so far. This information comes from our understanding (possibly faulty) of how the world works. This is where Bayesian nets come in. Causation and time ordering (what causes what, and what follows from what) are extremely important for stress testing. This should already give us an indication as to why probabilities (even conditional ones) – and, as we shall see, correlations – do not take us very far in this direction: marginal probabilities, conditional probabilities and correlations are the tools of the risk analyst who has no idea whatsoever of how the world works, that is, of the direction of causation. As we shall see, between a full understanding of how the world works, and no understanding whatsoever, there is the vast and useful grey area of partial and imperfect information that most humans inhabit. Again, this is where Bayesian nets come in handy – not by adding extra information that we do not have, but by helping us in thinking straight.

5.6 An Important Consequence: Bayes' Theorem

A trivial rearrangement of the above equations can give us the single most important, and useful, result in this book. From

$$P(E|F) \equiv \frac{\{E \cap F\}}{\{F\}} = \frac{P(E \cap F)}{P(F)} \tag{5.14}$$

it follows that

$$P(E|F) P(F) = P(E \cap F) \tag{5.15}$$

Of course, we must also have

$$P(F|E) \equiv \frac{\{E \cap F\}}{\{E\}} = \frac{P(E \cap F)}{P(E)} \tag{5.16}$$

and

$$P(F|E) P(E) = P(E \cap F) \tag{5.17}$$

Since the right-hand side of Equations (5.15) and (5.17) are the same (the size, $\{E \cap F\}$, of the intersection set does not change!), the same must be true of the left-hand side, and so:

$$P(E|F) P(F) = P(F|E) P(E) \quad \textbf{Bayes' theorem} \tag{5.18}$$

Simple as it is, this result is so important that it deserves a special name: Bayes' theorem.[13] In words: the probability of E given F times the probability of F must be equal to the probability of F given E times the probability of E.

---

[13] As mentioned above, there is a, shall we say, lively debate between Bayesians and frequentists about the 'correct' meaning of probability. This has nothing to do with Bayes' theorem, which even the most dyed-in-the-wool frequentist will accept as a perfectly good theorem. Frequentists and Bayesians make use of Bayes' theorem to the same degree and with the same (100%) confidence.

The theorem just established allows us to derive another relationship of which we will make extensive use. Consider the following two quantities:

$$P\left(E|F\right)P\left(F\right) = P(E \cap F) \tag{5.19}$$

and

$$P\left(E|\tilde{F}\right)P\left(\tilde{F}\right) = P(E \cap \tilde{F}) \tag{5.20}$$

A glance at a Venn diagram immediately convinces us that

$$P(E \cap F) + P(E \cap \tilde{F}) = P(E) \tag{5.21}$$

Therefore

$$P(E) = P\left(E|F\right)P\left(F\right) + P\left(E|\tilde{F}\right)P\left(\tilde{F}\right) \tag{5.22}$$

5.7   Independence

Two events, E and F, are said to be independent if[14]

$$P\left(E|F\right) = P\left(E\right) \tag{5.23}$$

Given the discussion above, this means that knowledge of whether F has happened does not help at all in assessing the probability of E happening. Think again of the failure of a major bank counterparty and the summer–winter gas spread. This way of looking at conditional probabilities is particularly helpful if we interpret probability as degree of belief (see Jaynes (2003)).

Again, paraphrasing Moore (2001), I could write a whole chapter about this. But I won't.

Let us see instead, using Bayes' theorem again, what independence implies about $P\left(F|E\right)$:

$$P\left(E|F\right)P\left(F\right) = P\left(F|E\right)P\left(E\right)$$
$$= P\left(E\right)P\left(F\right) = P\left(F|E\right)P\left(E\right)$$
$$= P\left(F\right) = P\left(F|E\right)   \text{(independence)} \tag{5.24}$$

where the second line follows from Equation (5.23), and in the last line the common term $P\left(E\right)$ has been cancelled on both sides of the equation. This tells us that, if knowledge of whether F has happened does not help us at all in assessing the probability of E happening, knowledge of whether E has happened also does not help at all in assessing the probability of F happening.

---

[14]To be meaningful, the independence condition $P\left(E|F\right) = P\left(E\right)$ also requires that $P(F) \neq 0$. I will assume that this is always the case.

Here is another simple but powerful result that holds under independence:

$$P\,(E|F) = \frac{P(E \cap F)}{P\,(F)} = P\,(E) \Longrightarrow$$

$$P(E \cap F) = P\,(E)\,P\,(F) \quad \text{(independence)} \tag{5.25}$$

In words: when E and F are independent, the probability of both E and F happening is just given by the product of the stand-alone probabilities of E and F happening.

Exercise 6 Prove that, if $P\,(E|F) = P(E)$, then $P(E = x \cap F = y) = P(E = x)$ $P\,(F = y)$ for $x, y = T, F$.

A word of caution: the concept of independence is as powerful as it is treacherous (see Williams (2001), Chapter 4, for a good discussion of the strength of the approach and of the pitfalls that can trip up the unaware).

5.8 Two Worked-Out Examples

Understanding a mathematical result is one thing (a very important one). Getting an intuitive feel for the same result is another (and every bit as important). I will present in this section two examples that highlight the subtleties involved when dealing with conditional probabilities, especially when some of the probabilities in question are very small.

5.8.1 Dangerous Running

I begin with a simple example. Let the event E be 'I'll go for a run today' and the event F be 'I'll be hit by a car today', where we can agree that 'I'll be hit by a car today' means 'I'll be hit by a car today first thing in the morning'.[15] Then Bayes' theorem says that

(the probability of my going for a run today, given that I will be hit by a car today)

times

(the probability of my being hit by a car today)

must be equal to

(the probability of my being hit by a car today, given that I have gone for a run today)

times

(the probability of my going for a run today)

---

[15]This specification simplifies the problem in that we do not have to worry about situations in which I *first* went for a run and *then* was hit by a car.

Does this make intuitive sense? With (I hope) self-explanatory notation, let us rewrite this more compactly as

$$P(run|hit)\,P(hit) = P\,(hit|run)\,P\,(run) \tag{5.26}$$

To dispel any causation and temporal fallacies, think of the following two questions

- 'If you know for sure that last Tuesday I went for a run, what would you say the probability is that I was hit by a car upon stepping out of my house that morning?'

- 'If you know for sure that last Tuesday I was hit by a car upon stepping out of my house first thing in the morning, what would you say the probability is that on that day I went for a run?'

The answers, of course, are $P\,(hit|run)$ and $P\,(run|hit)$, respectively.

At first blush one may say that $P(run|hit)$ should be about as large as $P\,(hit|run)$, and that both probabilities should be very (and similarly) low: after all, given that I have been hit by a car, it seems unlikely that I will have gone running; and given that I have gone running, it seems similarly unlikely that I had been hit by a car first thing in the morning. But is this right?

Rearranging Equation (5.26) one gets

$$\frac{P(run|hit)}{P\,(hit|run)} = \frac{P\,(run)}{P\,(hit)} \tag{5.27}$$

Now, I like to go running about twice a week. So $P(run) \simeq 2/7 \simeq 0.28$. I do not know my probability of being run over by a car today, but being since I have not been run over in my life yet, I can have a stab at estimating this probability as $P(run) \simeq 1/(50 * 365) \simeq 0.00005$, where I have massively rounded (up, of course) my age. Then the ratio $\frac{P(run)}{P(hit)}$ is given by

$$\frac{P\,(run)}{P\,(hit)} \simeq \frac{0.28}{0.00005} \simeq 5000 \tag{5.28}$$

So much for the right-hand side. But this ratio must hold also for the left-hand side:

$$\frac{P(run|hit)}{P\,(hit|run)} \simeq 5000 \tag{5.29}$$

or

$$P(run|hit) \simeq 5000\,P\,(hit|run)$$

This shows that the probability of running today given that I have been hit by a car is about 5000 times greater than the probability of being hit by a car today given that I have gone for run. Probably not what most of us would have guessed. Where does this counterintuitive result come from?

It comes from the fact that the probability of being hit by a car is so low to start with. Plausibly, I will go for a run despite being hit by a car if I have been lucky enough to sustain little damage, or if I have hurt my hand, not my legs. But the fact that I have still gone for a run only tells me something about the fact that my injury was mild or localized: the probability of being hit in the first place remains very small. The probability of running is of course affected by my having been hit by a car, but still there is a chance of, say, 5% that I will be able to run today even if I have suffered a car accident. So, the rather high probability of running today (28%) is only diminished by a factor of about 20 (1/0.05). Therefore, the probability of going for a run today given that I have been hit by a car is much, much higher than the probability of having been hit by a car first thing in the morning, given that I have gone for a run today. What I have touched upon here is the problem of representativeness (or, rather, of the neglect of baseline frequencies) in estimating probabilities. I will have a lot more to say about this in Chapter 12.

5.8.2   Rare and Even More Dangerous Diseases

This is an old story, but still worth telling. A friend of yours is afraid that she may have contracted a rare but deadly disease (Wrong-Bayesitis, WB in the following for brevity). The condition affects one person in 50 000. Your friend therefore undertakes a medical test to ascertain whether she is infected. The test has a high accuracy rate (95%). After two days of anxious waiting, the test results arrive, and they are unfortunately positive. Your friend calls you in understandable distress. Can you offer words of comfort?

Given the high accuracy of the test, the situation at first glance does not look too encouraging for your friend. However, let us see whether Bayes' theorem can help our reasoning. I denote by *WB* the event 'your friend suffers from Wrong-Bayesitis' and by *test* the event 'the test comes back positive'. From the information provided we know that the frequency of occurrence of WB in the population is $\frac{1}{50\,000} = 0.00002$. Equating in this case frequency with probability we have

$$P(WB) = \frac{1}{50\,000} = 0.00002 \tag{5.30}$$

We also know that, if a person does have WB, then the test will detect this with 95% accuracy. Therefore

$$P(test|WB) = 0.95 \tag{5.31}$$

What we need is the probability that a person is affected by WB, given that the test has come back positive: we are looking for $P(WB|test)$. So, by Bayes' theorem we have

$$P(WB|test) = \frac{P(test|WB)P(WB)}{P(test)} \tag{5.32}$$

The only quantity that we do not know is $P(test)$, but we can have a very good stab at it. Suppose that 100 people take the test. As the test is 95% accurate, 5 (almost certainly) healthy people out of 100 will receive alarming but false news from the hospital. So

$P(test) \simeq 0.05.$[16] Now we have all the information we need:

$$P(WB|test) = \frac{P(test|WB)P(WB)}{P(test)} = \frac{0.95 * 0.00002}{0.05} = 0.0038 \qquad (5.33)$$

Good news: your friend has a chance of a little more than a third of 1% of being affected by WB![17] You and your friend can open a celebratory bottle of good wine to the memory of Reverend Bayes.

Exercise 7   The result above is not quite correct, as footnote 16 suggests. Can you derive the correct result?

Where does this counterintuitive result come from? From the fact that the deadly Wrong-Bayesitis is so rare (if only!) that almost all of the positive test results are false positives. Obviously, if no-one in the world had WB any more because it has been fully eradicated, but a test with 95% accuracy were available to detect it, 5 people out of 100 would receive a positive test result in the mail, but the probability of any of them, and of your friend in particular, having WB would still be zero.

I have spent some time discussing the two examples above because they clearly make two important points. First, how easy it is to make big mistakes when thinking about very small probabilities – the type of probabilities, that is, that we are likely to encounter in stress testing. Second, how much conditional probabilities in general, and Bayes' theorem in particular, can help us to think straight in these difficult situations.

5.9   Marginal and Conditional Probabilities: A Very Important Link

This section explores a very important link between marginal and conditional probabilities. Mathematically, the results are trivial. However, I cannot stress how valuable the cognitive help provided by this link turns out to be.

One can ask the following question: given that (I know that) event E_k has happened, has the marginal probability, $P(E_i)$, of events E_i, $i \neq k$, increased or decreased? In other terms:

$$P(E_i) \lessgtr ?P(E_i|E_k) \qquad (5.34)$$

---

[16]This is not quite right, because out of the 100 people 0.002 people will actually have the disease.

[17]Needless to say, if you are a frequentist this sentence is meaningless: your friend either has the illness or she does not.

If you are a frequentist the only way for you to comfort your friend is by saying something like the following: 'My dear friend, you either have the illness, in which case the probability of you being infected is 1; or you don't, in which the case the probability is 0. Unfortunately, given the information at hand, I can't tell you which probability applies to you. I will be able to tell for sure, of course, after the incubation time has elapsed. But as for today, the only thing that I *can* tell you is that, if every person in the population were tested, the fraction who test positive and do not have the disease is $(100 - 0.38)$%. In this sense you can be 99.62% confident that you do not have the disease.'

This is probably why frequentists do not have many friends.

Bayesians, instead, who interpret probability as a degree of belief, have no problem in saying: 'Dear friend, despite the outcome of the test, the probability of you having WB is 0.38%. Tonight, go out and celebrate with a nice bottle of Amarone.'

This is probably why Bayesians are so popular and have so many friends.

And, as you can see, I am totally unbiased between a frequentist and Bayesian view of the world.

This can be expressed as a multiplier, x_i^k. So, x_i^k is defined to be

$$P(E_i|E_k) \equiv P(E_i) x_i^k \tag{5.35}$$

Exercise 8 What is the multiplier x_i^k in the case of independence?

Exercise 9 What is the multiplier x_i^k in the case of deterministic causation?

Exercise 10 What is the multiplier x_i^k in the case of incompatibility?

Now, we also know from Bayes' theorem that

$$P(E_i|E_k) P(E_k) = P(E_k|E_i) P(E_i) \tag{5.36}$$

and therefore

$$\frac{P(E_i|E_k)}{P(E_i)} = \frac{P(E_k|E_i)}{P(E_k)} \tag{5.37}$$

But, given Equation (5.35),

$$\frac{P(E_i|E_k)}{P(E_i)} = \frac{P(E_i) x_i^k}{P(E_i)} = x_i^k \tag{5.38}$$

and, from Equation (5.37),

$$x_i^k = \frac{P(E_i|E_k)}{P(E_i)} = \frac{P(E_k|E_i)}{P(E_k)} = x_k^i \tag{5.39}$$

and therefore

$$x_i^k = x_k^i \tag{5.40}$$

In words: by how much the probability of event i increases/decreases given the occurrence of event k must be equal to how much the probability of event k increases/decreases given the occurrence of event i. So, $\{x_i^k\}$ must be a real symmetric matrix.

We should pause to think about this result, which is both 'obvious' and very deep. Consider two events, such as the default of China on its internationally issued debt and a sharp widening in credit spreads for commercial mortgage-backed securities (CMBSs). How can we think about the interrelationships between these two events? More precisely, how can we assign the associated conditional probabilities?

To begin with, the stand-alone probability of China defaulting is currently much, much lower than the probability of a widening in CMBS spreads. For argument's sake, let us set $P(China) = 10^{-5}$ and $P(CMBS) = 10^{-3}$. Now, if China were to default, it would be almost certain that a generalized turmoil will hit all financial markets, and that CMBS spreads, together with all manner of different spreads, would widen. I would therefore greatly increase the marginal probability $P(CMBS)$ and set, say, $P(CMBS|China) = 10^{-1}$. This means that $x_{CMBS}^{China} = 100$.

But let us look at the problem from the opposite angle, that is, conditioning on the widening of the CMBS spreads rather than on China's default. We may be tempted to say that a widening of spreads will have very little effect, if any, on the probability of default of China, and that therefore $P(China|CMBS) \simeq P(China)$. This would imply that $x_{China}^{CMBS} \simeq 1$. But by Equation (5.40) this cannot happen: we must have

$$x_{CMBS}^{China} = x_{China}^{CMBS} \tag{5.41}$$

Therefore, it seems that we are forced to say either that the default of China has no effect on CMBS spreads (which I find difficult to believe), or that the effect of the widening of the CMBS spreads has a major effect on the probability of China's default. What went wrong?

Nothing, really – or, rather, what is wrong is the misleading use of the word 'effect'. Recall that conditional probabilities by themselves convey no causal information. So, we should not think of CMBS spreads 'causing' China's default. Rather, we should phrase the problem as follows: given that we know that CMBS spreads have widened, how would we revise our assessment of the stand-alone probability of China's default? As spreads may have widened exactly because China defaulted (besides, of course, for many other reasons) increasing our assessment of the probability that China defaulted no longer seems so unreasonable. Note that we are conditioning on the widening of the CMBS spreads, but, in this explanation, the cause of the widening was China's default. Conditioning does not mean causing. See Section 12.4 for a discussion of causal versus diagnostic interpretation of conditional probabilities.

Are we happy, however, with increasing the probability of default by as much as a factor of 100? Yes, we are, because the unconditional probability was so low to start with (10^{-5})! So, we are saying that an extremely remote event has become much more likely, but is still very remote.

The consistency check provided by Equation (5.40) is invaluable in helping us to think straight. And, as this example shows, often there is a 'direction of conditioning' that helps our reasoning (typically, but not always, the easiest direction is when we condition on the rarer event). Given the symmetry in $x_i^k = x_k^i$, the risk manager should therefore always tackle the conditional probability that she finds more 'natural' to work with. This, of course, is closely related to two topics to which I have given great emphasis in this book: one has to do with the superiority of causal as against association-based links between variables, which I discussed in Sections 3.3 and 3.4; and the other with the cognitive biases (such as the neglect of base-line frequency and the diagnostic/causal bias) that I discuss in Chapter 12.

Note also that, if all the events in question are 'stress' (and hence 'rare') events, then any conditional probability (say, $P(E_i|E_k)$) larger than about 10% must be greater than the unconditional probability $P(E_i)$. So, the conditional probabilities $P(E_i|E_k)$ fall roughly in three categories:

- Those that relate to pairs of events for which occurrence of event E_k makes little difference to the probability of observing event E_i. Then $x_i^k \simeq 1$.

- Those that relate to pairs of events for which the occurrence of stress scenario E_k makes the occurrence of event E_i significantly *less* likely. Then $x_i^k < 1$, and $P(E_i|E_k) \ll 1$

(because $P(E_i)$ was small to start with). In the limit, if the occurrence of event E_k makes the occurrence of event event E_i impossible, then $P(E_i|E_k) = 0$ and $x_i^k = 0$.

- Those that relate to pairs of events for which the occurrence of stress scenario E_k makes the occurrence of event E_i significantly *more* likely. If we truly believe that the conditional probabilities are of the order of, say, 10% to 20% or greater, then, by the same token (i.e., because every stress event E_i is rare, and $P(E_i) \ll 1$), the multiplicative factor must be much greater than 1: $x_i^k \gg 1$.

To avoid spurious precision one could therefore restrict one's attention to the following cases:[18]

- The marginal probability of event E_i is strongly increased by the occurrence of event E_k: say, $x_i^k = 10$ to 50.

- The marginal probability of event E_i is somewhat increased by the occurrence of event E_k: say, $x_i^k = 2$ to 5.

- The marginal probability of event E_i is left unchanged by the occurrence of event E_k: say, $x_i^k \simeq 1$.

- The marginal probability of event E_i is somewhat decreased by the occurrence of event E_k: say, $x_i^k = 0.5$ to 0.2.

- The marginal probability of event E_i is strongly decreased by the occurrence of event E_k: say, $x_i^k = 0.02$ to 0.1.

5.10 Interpreting and Generalizing the Factors x_i^k

Here is another interpretation and some simple generalizations of the factors x_i^k that can be of great assistance in providing conditional probabilities.
Start from

$$P(E_i, E_k) = P(E_i|E_k)P(E_k) = \underbrace{P(E_i)P(E_k)}_{\text{Independence}} x_i^k \qquad (5.42)$$

Note that $\underbrace{P(E_i)P(E_k)}_{\text{Independence}}$ is just the joint probability that would result if the two events were independent. Therefore the multiplicative factor x_i^k can be thought of as giving the 'correction from independence':

$$x_i^k = x_k^i = \frac{P(E_i, E_k)}{P(E_i)P(E_k)} \qquad (5.43)$$

We can use these factors x_i^k also to help our intuition when it comes to providing doubly-conditioned probabilities. Consider in fact the joint probability $P(E_i, E_j, E_k)$. We

---

[18]I present a different approach to assigning the factors x_i^k in Chapter 9, in Equation (9.13) and *passim*.

can always write

$$P(E_i, E_j, E_k) = P(E_i|E_j, E_k)P(E_j, E_k)$$

$$= P(E_i|E_j, E_k)P(E_j|E_k)P(E_k) \tag{5.44}$$

If we implicitly define x_i^{jk} by the relationship

$$P(E_i|E_j, E_k) = P(E_i)x_i^{jk} \tag{5.45}$$

then we obtain

$$P(E_i, E_j, E_k) = \left[\underbrace{P(E_i)P(E_j)P(E_k)}_{\text{Independence}} \right] x_i^{jk} x_j^k \tag{5.46}$$

In passing we note that the 'correction-from-independence' term is now $x_i^{jk} x_j^k$. But, more interestingly, we can repeat the same procedure for $P(E_k, E_i, E_j)$ and $P(E_j, E_i, E_k)$. Since, of course, $P(E_i, E_j, E_k) = P(E_k, E_i, E_j) = P(E_j, E_i, E_k)$, it is a simple matter to prove that

$$x_i^{jk} x_k^j = x_k^{ij} x_i^j = x_j^{ik} x_i^k \tag{5.47}$$

and therefore

$$\frac{x_i^{jk}}{x_k^{ij}} = \frac{x_i^j}{x_k^j} \tag{5.48}$$

$$\frac{x_j^{ik}}{x_k^{ij}} = \frac{x_i^j}{x_i^k} \tag{5.49}$$

$$\frac{x_j^{ik}}{x_k^{ij}} = \frac{x_i^j}{x_i^k} \tag{5.50}$$

These relationships are very useful. They tell us that, if we can specify all the marginal and *singly*-conditioned probabilities (or, equivalently, all the singly-conditioned factors x_i^j), then we can always obtain the ratios of all the doubly-conditioned probabilities. As assigning doubly-conditioned probabilities can be very difficult, we should be grateful for any help we can get along the way.

But there is (a bit) more. Define x_{ij}^k by the relationship

$$P(E_i, E_j|E_k) = P(E_i, E_j)x_{ij}^k \tag{5.51}$$

Then, by using the same decomposition of the joint probabilities, one can show that

$$x_{ik}^j = x_j^{ik} \tag{5.52}$$

This relationship directly mirrors the symmetry of the fundamental identity

$$x_k^i = x_i^k \qquad (5.53)$$

that we derived above.[19] Mathematically the result is trivial, but it can help us in assigning the probabilities because it allows us to work with and not against our 'cognitive grain'; that is, in the direction (causal rather than diagnostic) that we find more natural. For instance, the reader should ponder the implications of Equation (5.52) by assigning a concrete interpretation in terms of actual stress events to the indices i, j and k, and, again, convince herself of how obvious-yet-surprising these results are. Try, for instance, $i = \{$China defaults$\}$, $j = \{$implied equity volatilities rise by 5%$\}$, $k = \{$yield curve steepens by 50bp$\}$.

Exercise 11 Prove Equation (5.52).

We shall make more use of all these multiplicative factors in Chapter 9, where I discuss how to assign the conditional probabilities needed for the analysis. In that chapter we will also make more precise the constraint on the conditional probability imposed by the condition 'E_i is strongly increased by the occurrence of event E_k'.

5.11 Conditional Probability Maps

We can enhance our intuition further by creating a visual display of the whole set of the conditional probabilities – or, rather, of quantities related to the x_i^k factors defined above. To do so, we begin by taking logs of x_i^k and defining $b_i^k = \ln\left(x_i^k\right)$. Then the case when the probability of event E_i is left unchanged by the occurrence of event E_k corresponds to $x_i^k = 1$, and therefore to $b_i^k = \ln\left(x_i^k\right) = 0$. If we interpret 'strongly increased' as 'increased by a factor of at least 10' and 'strongly decreased' as 'decreased by a factor of at least 10', the corresponding $\ln\left(x_i^k\right)$ would be $\ln\left(x_i^k\right) \geq 2.3$ and $\ln\left(x_i^k\right) \leq -2.3$, respectively. A decrease/increase of the unconditional probability by a factor of 2 would then correspond to $\ln\left(x_i^k\right) \geq 0.69$ and $\ln\left(x_i^k\right) \leq -0.69$, respectively. See the following table:

x_i^k	$b_i^k = \ln\left(x_i^k\right)$
100	4.605
20	2.996
10	2.303
2	0.693
1	0
1/2	−0.693
1/10	−2.303
1/20	−2.996
1/100	−4.605

The quantities b_i^k range in value from $-\infty$ to $\ln \frac{1}{\max[P(E_i), P(E_j)]}$.

---

[19]In a way, once obtained, this result is 'obvious': we can always think of the joint event (i, k) as some event, say, l. Then the relationship $x_{ik}^j = x_j^{ik}$ simply restates the well-known symmetry result $x_l^j = x_j^l$.

What we would like to do is to give a graphical representation of the degree of 'stress diversification'. However, if we use the 'raw' quantities b_i^k, these can assume large positive or negative values (in the limit, all the way to $-\infty$). To give a more compact representation, we therefore define

$$\theta_i^k = \arctan\left(b_i^k\right) \tag{5.54}$$

Then each point θ_i^k will be smaller in absolute value than $\frac{\pi}{2}$. The positioning of point θ_i^k on the segment

$$\left[-\frac{\pi}{2}, \arctan\left(\ln \frac{1}{\max[P(E_i),\, P(E_j)]}\right)\right] \tag{5.55}$$

therefore gives information about how much event E_k decreases or increases (in log space) the stand-alone marginal probability $P(E_i)$: a point θ_i^k with a value close to $-\frac{\pi}{2}$ or $\arctan\left(\ln \frac{1}{\max[P(E_i), P(E_j)]}\right)$, respectively, shows that knowledge that event E_k has happened increases (decreases) a lot in our assessment of the stand-alone marginal probability $P(E_i)$. More importantly, the clustering of the points towards the upper or the lower bounds indicates the degree of event diversification relative to event E_i: clustering towards the upper bound $\left(\arctan\left(\ln \frac{1}{\max[P(E_i), P(E_j)]}\right)\right)$ indicates high concentration; clustering towards the lower bound $(-\frac{\pi}{2})$ suggests that the events are unlikely to occur together.

Figures 5.8, 5.9 and 5.10 show this graphical representation in the case of a highly concentrated, a neutral and a highly diversified set of events, given that event E_k has happened.

We can also obtain a diversification index, d_k, by summing the quantities θ_i^k over the various events E_i:

$$d_k = \sum_i \theta_i^k \tag{5.56}$$

This diversification index tells us to what extent the conditional losses from events $E_{i \neq k}$ associated with event E_k tend to 'cluster' or 'avoid each other'.

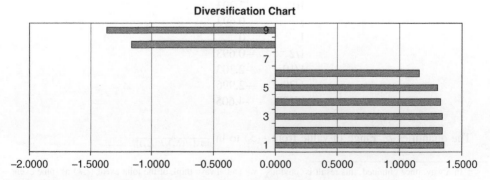

Figure 5.8   The concentration graph for a case of high concentration.

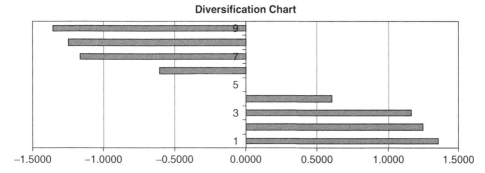

Figure 5.9   The concentration graph for a case of good diversification.

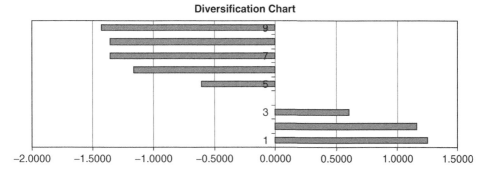

Figure 5.10   The concentration graph for a case of very high diversification.

Finally, an overall diversification index, D, for all the events can be obtained by summing over all the events E_k:

$$D = \sum_{i,k} \theta_i^k = \sum_k d_k \tag{5.57}$$

A positive, zero or negative diversification index suggests concentration, total independence or diversification, respectively.

I note in closing that as presented here the diversification index and the graphical display do not take into account the magnitude of the stress losses associated with the different events. So these indices only convey information about the relationships (clustering or avoidance) among the various events, not among the various losses. In the language of Chapters 8 and 9, they only depend on the topology of the underlying Bayesian net and on the associated conditional probability tables. They will therefore remain stable even if the exact size of positions changes over time. But we are getting ahead of ourselves.

Figure 5.9 Classification graph for a case of good diversification.

Figure 5.10 Classification graph for a case of very high diversification.

Chapter 6

Probability with Boolean Variables II: Joint Probabilities

The previous chapter dealt with the links between conditional and marginal probabilities. This chapter deals with a related topic, which is a central part of my treatment: the link between marginal and conditional probabilities on the one hand, and joint probabilities on the other. By the end of the chapter it should be clear why availability of the joint probabilities is the Holy Grail – and almost as difficult to attain.

One important remark is in order: most treatments of probability *start* from joint probabilities and *derive* from these conditional probabilities. Following Pearl (2009), I follow the opposite route, which leads from marginal and conditional to joint probabilities. This is not just a matter presentation. I believe that, as human beings, we find it very difficult to think in terms of joint probabilities, and are better suited to making cognitive use of conditional relationships. My view in this respect is unashamedly Bayesian. As Pearl (2009) points out:

> Bayesian philosophers see the conditional relationship as more basic than that of joint events – that is, *more compatible with the organization of human knowledge*. In this view, B serves as a pointer to a context or frame of knowledge, and $A|B$ stands for an event A in the context specified by B [...] Consequently, empirical knowledge invariably will be encoded in conditional probability statements, whereas belief in joint events (if it is ever needed) will be computed from those statements via the product $P(A, B) = P(A|B)P(B)$.[1]

This is exactly the approach I have taken in this book, and needless to say, there are close links between 'pointers to a frame of knowledge' and the interpretative models of reality discussed in Chapter 3.

6.1 Conditioning on More Than One Event

The treatment of the previous chapter can be easily generalized to the case where conditioning is over more than one event. For instance, if we condition on (knowledge of)

---

[1] Pearl (2009), page 4, my emphasis.

two events having happened, the conditional probability of event E_i, given events E_j and E_k, $P(E_i, |E_j \cap E_k)$, is given by

$$P(E_i, |E_j \cap E_k) = \frac{\{E_i \cap (E_j \cap E_k)\}}{\{E_j \cap E_k\}} \tag{6.1}$$

This expression will become useful when we establish the connection between the conditional and joint probabilities. As mentioned in footnote 7 of Chapter 5, I refer to a conditional probability such as the one in Equation (6.1) as a *doubly-conditioned probability*. The extension of the definition to *n*-conditioned probabilities is obvious.

Exercise 12   Convince yourself of the reasonableness of the definition above by drawing the associated Venn diagrams.

We can also easily provide an extension of Equation (5.13):

$$P(E_i, |E_j \cap E_k) + P(\tilde{E}_i, |E_j \cap E_k) = 1 \tag{6.2}$$

From Equation (6.1) we can then immediately derive

$$P(E_i \cap E_j \cap E_k) = P(E_i, |E_j \cap E_k) P(E_j \cap E_k) \tag{6.3}$$

Now, recall the definition of $P(E_j, |E_k)$:

$$P(E_j, |E_k) = \frac{P(E_j \cap E_k)}{P(E_k)} \tag{6.4}$$

Therefore

$$P(E_i \cap E_j \cap E_k) = P(E_i, |E_j \cap E_k) P(E_j, |E_k) P(E_k) \tag{6.5}$$

This is the first example of an extremely important set of relationships, i.e., those relationships that allow us to 'break up' the probability of an *n*-ple intersection, $\left(P(E_i \cap E_j \cap E_k)\right)$, into conditionals and marginals of order $n - 1$ or lower. Once we have introduced joint probabilities (see the next section) the importance of this will be evident.

Exercise 13   Generalize the result to the case of *n* Boolean variables.

Clearly, this decomposition is not unique. For instance

$$P(E_i \cap E_j \cap E_k) = P(E_k \cap E_j \cap E_i) \tag{6.6}$$

and therefore

$$P(E_k \cap E_j \cap E_i) = P(E_k, |E_j \cap E_i) P(E_j, |E_i) P(E_i) \tag{6.7}$$

Equating the right-hand sides of Equations (6.5) and (6.7) we have

$$P(E_i, |E_j \cap E_k)P(E_j, |E_k)P(E_k) = P(E_k, |E_j \cap E_i)P(E_j, |E_i)P(E_i) \qquad (6.8)$$

Since, of course,

$$P(E_k, |E_j \cap E_i) = P(E_k, |E_j, E_i) \qquad (6.9)$$

and

$$P(E_i \cap E_j \cap E_k) = P(E_i, E_j, E_k)$$

we finally have

$$P(E_i, |E_j, E_k)P(E_j, |E_k)P(E_k) = P(E_k, |E_j, E_i)P(E_j, |E_i)P(E_i) \qquad (6.10)$$

and

$$\frac{P(E_i, |E_j, E_k)}{P(E_k, |E_j, E_i)} = \frac{P(E_j, |E_i)}{P(E_j, |E_k)} \frac{P(E_i)}{P(E_k)} \qquad (6.11)$$

or

$$P(E_i, |E_j, E_k) = \frac{P(E_j, |E_i)P(E_i)}{P(E_j, |E_k)P(E_k)} P(E_k, |E_j, E_i) \qquad (6.12)$$

This relationship gives us a link between one doubly-conditioned probability ($P(E_i, |E_j, E_k)$) in terms of another ($P(E_k, |E_j, E_i)$), and marginal and singly-conditioned probabilities ($P(E_i)$, $P(E_k)$, $P(E_j, |E_i)$ and $P(E_j, |E_k)$). This can be of help when we deal with Bayesian nets and we need to assign doubly-conditioned probabilities – always a difficult task. Sometimes it may be easier to have a good intuition for one such doubly-conditioned probability (in this case $P(E_k, |E_j, E_i)$) rather than the other. Then Equation (6.12) can provide help in determining the less 'intuitive' one.

6.2   Joint Probabilities

We are now ready to introduce the most powerful probabilistic piece of information at our disposal: the joint distribution. Unfortunately, we will have to get some of notation out of the way first.

First, we now allow for n events (to be a bit more precise, n two-valued Boolean random variables), $E_1, E_2, \ldots, E_n$. A joint event is any combination of T and F realizations for the n elementary events. I will denote the ith joint event by J_i. For two-valued Boolean random variables, there will be 2^n such joint events. We can therefore label them all with an index $i = 1, 2, \ldots, 2^n$. Let us suppose that we have done so. We can now associate a probability $p(i)$ to each joint event. If we normalize the size of the whole universe to 1, each joint probability is therefore given by the size of the intersection set:

$$J_i = \{E_1 = x, E_2 = y, \ldots, E_n = z\} \qquad (6.13)$$

where x, y and z assume the values T or F, as appropriate for event J_i.

It is essential to stress that no two joint events can happen at the same time. With unfortunate terminology, all joint events J_i are therefore disjointed. Therefore, the following requirements (which we can derive from the probability axioms presented above) must hold true:

$$p(i) \geq 0, \quad i = 1, 2, \ldots, 2^n \qquad (6.14)$$

$$\sum_{i=1}^{2^n} p(i) = 1 \qquad (6.15)$$

For $n = 3$ we can represent all of this very easily as follows:

$$
\begin{array}{c c c c c}
 & E_1 & E_2 & E_3 & \\
J_1 & 1 & 0 & 0 & p(1) \\
J_2 & 0 & 1 & 0 & p(2) \\
J_3 & 0 & 0 & 1 & p(3) \\
J_4 & 1 & 1 & 0 & p(4) \\
J_5 & 1 & 0 & 1 & p(5) \\
J_6 & 0 & 1 & 1 & p(6) \\
J_7 & 1 & 1 & 1 & p(7) \\
J_8 & 0 & 0 & 0 & p(8)
\end{array}
\qquad (6.16)
$$

The entries 1, 0, 0 in the first row (which is assigned to joint event J_1) indicate that for this joint event the first event happened, and the second and third did not. The same applies for the other rows.

Note the last two rows. The last one (J_8) is associated with the joint event 'none of the three elementary events occurred'. The second-to-last one is associated with the joint event 'all of the three elementary events happened'. If our elementary events are to be given the interpretation of rare stress events, $p(8)$ should be 'large' (close to 1), and $p(7)$ very, very small (smaller than or equal to the smallest stand-alone probability $P(E_i)$). These kinds of checks will become very important when we move on to the practical applications of the above to stress testing, but for the moment any set of values $p(i)$ compatible with Equations (6.14) and (6.15) will suffice.

The set of probabilities $[p(i)]$ is called the *joint distribution for the n Boolean random variables*.

We can now readily understand the links between the joint probabilities and the various possible intersections. Look again at the table that forms Equation (6.16). The size of the set $E_1 = T$ is given by

$$\{E_1 = T\} = P(E_1)$$
$$= p(1) + p(4) + p(5) + p(7) \qquad (6.17)$$

The size of the set $\{E_1 = T \cap E_2 = F\}$ is given by

$$\{E_1 = T \cap E_2 = F\} = P(E_1 \cap \tilde{E}_2)$$
$$= p(1) + p(5) \qquad (6.18)$$

The size of $\{E_1 = T \cap E_2 = F \cap E_3 = F\}$ is given by

$$\{E_1 = T \cap E_2 = F \cap E_3 = F\} = P(E_1 \cap \tilde{E}_2 \cap \tilde{E}_3)$$
$$= p(1) \qquad (6.19)$$

In general, therefore, each of the probabilities of the joint events J_i can be written as the probability of appropriate intersections of sets of the elementary events:

$$p(1) = P(E_1 \cap \tilde{E}_2 \cap \tilde{E}_3) \qquad (6.20)$$
$$p(2) = P(\tilde{E}_1 \cap E_2 \cap \tilde{E}_3) \qquad (6.21)$$
$$p(3) = P(\tilde{E}_1 \cap \tilde{E}_2 \cap E_3) \qquad (6.22)$$
$$p(4) = P(E_1 \cap E_2 \cap \tilde{E}_3) \qquad (6.23)$$

$$\cdots$$

$$p(8) = P(\tilde{E}_1 \cap \tilde{E}_2 \cap \tilde{E}_3) \qquad (6.24)$$

I said above that once we know the joint probabilities we can obtain any probabilistic information about the underlying Boolean variables. I therefore now have to show how to do this. But before doing so, however, it is high time to clean up the notation.

6.3   A Remark on Notation

Defining notation midway through my treatment may strike the reader as odd. However, I wanted to introduce all the concepts needed for our analysis first, rather than introducing at the start the notation for mysterious quantities that have not yet been defined.

So, let me begin with the joint probabilities I have just defined. As I have shown, the joint probabilities are just the probabilities of all the various possible intersections. Depending on the context, I will therefore denote joint probabilities in any of the following equivalent ways:

- $p(i)$: The probability of joint event J_i. Joint events are in turn given by the intersection of a particular combination of realizations for events $E_r, E_s, \ldots, E_t$, such as, for instance, $J_k = [E_1 = T \cap E_2 = F, \ldots, \cap E_n = T]$. This notation for the joint probability is compact, but not very transparent when we are interested in the occurrences of the underlying events.

- $P(E_1 = T, E_2 = F, \ldots, E_n = T)$: This more cumbersome notation has the advantage of being totally transparent, because it shows in full the particular set of joint realizations (T or F), for the n elementary events, $E_1 = T, E_2 = F, \ldots, E_n = T$.

- $P(E_1 = T \cap E_2 = F \cap \ldots \cap E_n = T)$: The same as above, emphasizing that the joint probability is the probability of the intersection of the realizations for the n elementary events, $E_1 = T$, $E_2 = F, \ldots, E_n = T$.

- $P\left(E_1 \cap \tilde{E}_2 \cap \ldots \cap E_n\right)$: The same as above, using the notation $\tilde{E}_2$ to denote $E_2 = F$ and E_1 to denote $E_1 = T$. This is the most delicate piece of notation, because now E_1 can mean either the Boolean random variable E_1 or its TRUE realization. So if I write $P(E_1 \cap E_2 \cap \ldots \cap E_n)$ I could be referring to a generic joint probability, or to the particular joint probability where all the events turned out to be TRUE. The context should make the meaning clear.

- $P(E_1, \tilde{E}_2, \ldots, E_n)$: The same as above, when there is no need to emphasize the intersections.

- $P(E_1 = x \cap E_2 = y \cap \ldots \cap E_n = z)$ or $P(E_1 = x, E_2 = y, \ldots, E_n = z)$ with x, y, $z = T, F$ to denote *all* the joint probabilities associated with the various possible realizations for the Boolean variables $E_1, E_2, \ldots, E_n$.

I will always denote marginal probabilities by $P(E_k)$, where $P(E_k)$ means the probability of event E_k being true. When I want to denote the marginal probability of event E_k being false, I will write $P(\tilde{E}_k)$ or $P(E_k = F)$.

As for conditional probabilities, the notation $P(E_j | E_k)$ suffers from the same ambiguity highlighted above in the case of joint probabilities: I could be referring to the generic conditional probability $P(E_j | E_k)$ or I could mean the specific conditional probability $P(E_j = T | E_k = T)$. Context, as usual, is everything.

When I mean, say, $P(E_j = T | E_k = F)$, to save ink I will often write $P(E_j | \tilde{E}_k)$.

And, finally, the notation $P(E_j = x | E_k = y)$ with x, $y = T, F$ will have the collective meaning of denoting *all* the possible conditional probabilities, exactly as in the case of joint probabilities.

Depending on the context, one notation can be more suggestive or transparent than the other, and I will therefore use them interchangeably.

6.4   From the Joint to the Marginal and the Conditional Probabilities

With the notation clearly defined, I return to the main thrust of the presentation. Our next task is to obtain the probabilities of the individual events, $P(E_k)$, $k = 1, 2, \ldots, n$ from the joint distribution – in practice we will often try to go in the opposite direction, but we worry about this later. To illustrate the concepts in the simplest case, let us consider the case of $n = 3$.

We start from $P(E_1)$. Since all the joint events J_i are disjoint, the probability of event E_1 occurring is simply given by the sum of the probabilities $p(i)$ associated with joint events J_i where E_1 occurs. A glance at Equation (6.16) shows that this is equal to

$$P(E_1) = p(1) + p(4) + p(5) + p(7) \tag{6.25}$$

We can, of course, proceed similarly for E_2 and E_3.

So much for marginal probabilities. What about the probability that both events E_2 and E_3 happen? Again, we can read it directly from Equation (6.16) above:

$$P(E_2 \cap E_3) = p(6) + p(7) \tag{6.26}$$

Of course, we also know that

$$P(E_2 \cap E_3) = \{E_2 \cap E_3\} \tag{6.27}$$

We can check this immediately from Equation (6.16), because event E_2 is true ($E_2 = T$) in joint events J_2, J_4, J_6 and J_7, and event event E_3 is true ($E_3 = T$) in joint events J_3, J_5, J_6 and J_7. So, the only two joint events that have events E_2 and E_3 in common are J_6 and J_7.

Exercise 14   Using the information in Equation (6.16) derive an expression for $P(E_2 \cup E_3)$.

Of course, if we know how to calculate from the joint probabilities the probability of the intersection between any two sets, we are only a small step away from calculating any conditional probability in terms of the joint probabilities. To see this, consider, say, $P(E_2|E_3)$. We know that

$$P(E_2|E_3) = \frac{\{E_2 \cap E_3\}}{\{E_3\}} = \frac{P(E_2 \cap E_3)}{P(E_3)} \tag{6.28}$$

The probability of event E_3 is immediately obtained as above:

$$P(E_3) = p(3) + p(5) + p(6) + p(7) \tag{6.29}$$

and therefore

$$P(E_2|E_3) = \frac{p(6) + p(7)}{p(3) + p(5) + p(6) + p(7)} \tag{6.30}$$

Exercise 15   Generalize the expression just derived to any j and k, and check that the expressions thus obtained satisfy the conditions for representing possible probabilities (i.e., they are all greater or equal to 0 and smaller or equal to 1, and they all add up to 1).

6.5   From the Joint Distribution to Event Correlation

As I said, from the knowledge of the joint distribution we can derive everything that we may statistically desire. And everything means everything, not just the marginal and conditional probabilities. Let me show, for instance, how to determine the event correlation between any two events. The result will be more than an exercise in manipulating joint probabilities, because it will have intrinsic interest when we deal with stress testing.

When we deal with stochastic processes (i.e., roughly speaking, random variables indexed by time) we have a simple intuitive understanding of what correlation 'means': after normalizing for the possibly different variance, the correlation coefficient gives an indication of the extent to which the two variables 'move together'. What interpretation should we give to the correlation coefficient in the case of Boolean variables? Let me give a formal definition first, and we will see the intuitive meaning after obtaining the result.

As a first step it is useful to associate with each event E_i a random variable, $\mathbf{1}_i$, i.e., the indicator function that assumes value 1 if E_i is true, and zero otherwise:

$$\mathbf{1}_i = 1 \text{ if } E_i = T$$

$$\mathbf{1}_i = 0 \text{ if } E_i = F \tag{6.31}$$

Then a natural definition of correlation ρ_{ij} is

$$\rho_{ij} = \frac{\mathbb{E}\left[(\mathbf{1}_i - \overline{\mathbf{1}}_i)(\mathbf{1}_j - \overline{\mathbf{1}}_j)\right]}{\sqrt{var\,(\mathbf{1}_i)\,var\,(\mathbf{1}_j)}} \tag{6.32}$$

where the symbols $\mathbb{E}[\cdot]$, $var\,(\cdot)$ and $\overline{\mathbf{1}}_i$ denote the expectation operator,[2] the variance operator and the expected value of the indicator function $\mathbf{1}_i$, respectively:

$$\overline{\mathbf{1}}_i = \mathbb{E}\,[\mathbf{1}_i] \tag{6.33}$$

Looking back at Equation (6.16) it is easy to calculate the expected value of $\mathbf{1}_i$. Take, for instance, $i = 1$. In this case the expectation will be equal to the sum of the products of the value of the indicator function $\mathbf{1}_1$ for each joint event J_k, times the probability of the joint event, $p(k)$. For $i = 1$ this gives

$$\overline{\mathbf{1}}_1$$

$$= 1 * p(1) + 0 * p(2) + 0 * p(3) + 1 * p(4) + 1 * p(5) + 1 * p(7) + 0 * p(8)$$

$$= 1 * p(1) + 1 * p(4) + 1 * p(5) + 1 * p(7)$$

$$= p(1) + p(4) + p(5) + p(7) = P(E_1) \tag{6.34}$$

Therefore

$$\overline{\mathbf{1}}_i = \mathbb{E}\,[(\mathbf{1}_i)] = P(E_i) \quad \text{for any } i \tag{6.35}$$

We can therefore rewrite Equation (6.32) as

$$\rho_{ij} = \frac{\mathbb{E}\left[(\mathbf{1}_i - P(E_i))(\mathbf{1}_j - P(E_j))\right]}{\sqrt{var\,(\mathbf{1}_i)\,var\,(\mathbf{1}_j)}} \tag{6.36}$$

---

[2] The expectation is taken, of course, over the joint probabilities $[p(i)]$.

To calculate the numerator, I can construct the following table:

$$
\begin{array}{lcccc}
 & E_1 & E_2 & E_3 & \\
J_1 & 1 - P(E_1) & 0 - P(E_2) & 0 - P(E_3) & p(1) \\
J_2 & 0 - P(E_1) & 1 - P(E_2) & 0 - P(E_3) & p(2) \\
J_3 & 0 - P(E_1) & 0 - P(E_2) & 1 - P(E_3) & p(3) \\
J_4 & 1 - P(E_1) & 1 - P(E_2) & 0 - P(E_3) & p(4) \\
J_5 & 1 - P(E_1) & 0 - P(E_2) & 1 - P(E_3) & p(5) \\
J_6 & 0 - P(E_1) & 1 - P(E_2) & 1 - P(E_3) & p(6) \\
J_7 & 1 - P(E_1) & 1 - P(E_2) & 1 - P(E_3) & p(7) \\
J_8 & 0 - P(E_1) & 0 - P(E_2) & 0 - P(E_3) & p(8)
\end{array}
\qquad (6.37)
$$

Now, each entry of the table has been expressed in a way that is suitable for direct use in Equation (6.36): suppose, for instance, that I want to calculate $\mathbb{E}\left[(\mathbf{1}_1 - P(E_1))(\mathbf{1}_2 - P(E_2))\right]$. All I have to do is to look at the first two columns of Equation (6.37) and obtain:

$$
\begin{aligned}
&[(1 - P(E_1))(0 - P(E_2))]\,p(1) + \\
&[(0 - P(E_1))(1 - P(E_2))]\,p(2) + \\
&[(0 - P(E_1))(0 - P(E_2))]\,p(3) + \\
&[(1 - P(E_1))(1 - P(E_2))]\,p(4) + \\
&[(1 - P(E_1))(0 - P(E_2))]\,p(5) + \\
&[(0 - P(E_1))(1 - P(E_2))]\,p(6) + \\
&[(1 - P(E_1))(1 - P(E_2))]\,p(7) + \\
&[(0 - P(E_1))(0 - P(E_2))]\,p(8)
\end{aligned}
\qquad (6.38)
$$

where, of course, $P(E_1)$ and $P(E_2)$ have been derived as above.

So much for the numerator. Let us move to the denominator. The variance of the indicator function $\mathbf{1}_i$ is given by

$$
var\,[\mathbf{1}_i] = \mathbb{E}\left[(\mathbf{1}_i)^2\right] - \mathbb{E}\left[(\mathbf{1}_i)\right]^2
\qquad (6.39)
$$

Now,

$$
\mathbb{E}\left[(\mathbf{1}_i)\right]^2 = P(E_i)^2
\qquad (6.40)
$$

But, because we have stipulated that the indicator function can only take values 1 or 0,

$$
(\mathbf{1}_i)^2 = (\mathbf{1}_i)
\qquad (6.41)
$$

It therefore follows that

$$
\mathbb{E}\left[(\mathbf{1}_i)^2\right] = \mathbb{E}\left[(\mathbf{1}_i)\right] = P(E_i)
\qquad (6.42)
$$

So, we obtain

$$var\left[\mathbf{1}_i\right] = P(E_i) - P(E_i)^2 \tag{6.43}$$

Reassuringly, as $P(E_i)$ is always smaller or equal to 1, the variance will always be positive.

Exercise 16   Comment on the variance in the case when $P(E_i) = 1$. Does the result make sense? What does it indicate?

As a final result I can rewrite Equation (6.36) as:

$$\rho_{ij} = \frac{\mathbb{E}\left[\left(\mathbf{1}_i - \overline{\mathbf{1}_i}\right)\left(\mathbf{1}_j - \overline{\mathbf{1}_j}\right)\right]}{\sqrt{\left[P(E_i) - P(E_i)^2\right]\left[P(E_j) - P(E_j)^2\right]}} \tag{6.44}$$

$$= \frac{\mathbb{E}\left[\left(\mathbf{1}_i - P(E_i)\right)\left(\mathbf{1}_j - P(E_j)\right)\right]}{\sqrt{\left[P(E_i) - P(E_i)^2\right]\left[P(E_j) - P(E_j)^2\right]}} \tag{6.45}$$

with the numerator given by Equation (6.39-1). Needless to say, the joint probabilities enter expression (6.44) via the expectation operator, $\mathbb{E}\left[\cdot\right]$.

So much for an algebraic expression for the correlation. What intuitive meaning can we ascribe to it? Consider a joint event, say, J_6. If in joint event J_6, elementary event E_i is true (occurs), the indicator function will have value 1 and the quantity $\mathbf{1}_i - P(E_i)$ will be greater than or equal to 0. Conversely, if the elementary event E_i does *not* occur, the same quantity $\mathbf{1}_i - P(E_i)$ will be smaller than or equal to 0. The same reasoning applies to the elementary event E_j. So, if both event E_i and event E_j occur in joint event J_6, the numerator will be positive (positive number times positive number). The numerator will also be positive if neither event occurs (negative number times negative number). The numerator will instead be negative when one event occurs and the other does not in joint event J_6. This positive or negative number will then be weighted by the probability of joint event J_6, $p(6)$.

So, the correlation coefficient tells us the following: when the indicator function for one event is greater than its expected value (i.e., than the marginal probability for that event, $P(E_i)$) and the indicator function for the other event is greater than its expected value (the probability for that event, $P(E_j)$), we have a positive contribution to the correlation coefficient (weighted by $p(6)$). The opposite occurs when the indicator function for one event is greater than its expected value but the indicator function for the other event is smaller than its expected value. The correlation coefficient therefore gives a measure of the concordance of occurrence of two events. It gives a quantitative answer to the question: 'Are the two events likely or unlikely to happen together, after taking into account their stand-alone probability of occurrence?'

Following Tzani and Polychronakos (2008), we can gain further insight by analysing in greater detail Equation (6.44):

$$\rho_{ij} = \frac{\mathbb{E}\left[\left(\mathbf{1}_i - P(E_i)\right)\left(\mathbf{1}_j - P(E_j)\right)\right]}{\sqrt{\left[P(E_i) - P(E_i)^2\right]\left[P(E_j) - P(E_j)^2\right]}} \tag{6.46}$$

Let us look at the term

$$\mathbb{E}\left[(\mathbf{1}_i - P(E_i))\left(\mathbf{1}_j - P(E_j)\right)\right]$$

This can be rewritten as

$$\mathbb{E}\left[(\mathbf{1}_i - P(E_i))\left(\mathbf{1}_j - P(E_j)\right)\right]$$
$$= \mathbb{E}\left[\mathbf{1}_i\mathbf{1}_j\right] - P(E_i)\mathbb{E}\left[\mathbf{1}_j\right] - P(E_j)\mathbb{E}\left[\mathbf{1}_i\right] + P(E_i)P(E_j)$$
$$= \mathbb{E}\left[\mathbf{1}_i\mathbf{1}_j\right] - P(E_i)P(E_j) \qquad (6.47)$$

where the last line follows because

$$E\left[\mathbf{1}_j\right] = P(E_j)$$

As for the denominator, note that

$$P(E_i) * (1 - P(E_i)) = P(E_i) - P(E_i)^2$$
$$= P(E_i)Q(E_i)$$

with

$$Q(E_i) \equiv 1 - P(E_i)$$

Therefore Equation (6.44) can be rewritten as:

$$\rho_{ij} = \frac{\mathbb{E}\left[(\mathbf{1}_i - P(E_i))\left(\mathbf{1}_j - P(E_j)\right)\right]}{\sqrt{\left[P(E_i) - P(E_i)^2\right]\left[P(E_j) - P(E_j)^2\right]}}$$

$$\rho_{ij} = \frac{\mathbb{E}\left[\mathbf{1}_i\mathbf{1}_j\right] - P(E_i)P(E_j)}{\sqrt{P(E_i)Q(E_i)P(E_j)Q(E_j)}} \qquad (6.48)$$

Note that

$$\mathbb{E}\left[\mathbf{1}_i\mathbf{1}_j\right] = P(E_i = T, E_j = T) \qquad (6.49)$$

Following again Tzani and Polychronakos (2008), from this result we can write for any two events E_i, E_j:

$$P(E_i, E_j) - P(E_i)P(E_j) = \rho_{ij}\sqrt{P(E_i)Q(E_i)P(E_j)Q(E_j)} \qquad (6.50)$$

where

$$P(E_i, E_j) = P(E_i = T, E_j = T) \qquad (6.51)$$

and

$$P(E_i, \tilde{E}_j) = P(E_i = T, E_j = F)$$

Also, it is always true that

$$P(E_i, \tilde{E}_j) + P(E_i, E_j) = P(E_i) \tag{6.52}$$

$$P(\tilde{E}_i, E_j) + P(E_i, E_j) = P(E_j) \tag{6.53}$$

$$P(\tilde{E}_i, \tilde{E}_j) + P(E_i, \tilde{E}_j) + P(\tilde{E}_i, E_j) + P(E_i, E_j) = 1 \tag{6.54}$$

From this we can readily obtain the following:

$$P(\tilde{E}_i, \tilde{E}_j) = Q(E_i)Q(E_j) + \rho_{ij}\sqrt{P(E_i)Q(E_i)P(E_j)Q(E_j)} \tag{6.55}$$

$$P(\tilde{E}_i, E_j) = Q(E_i)P(E_j) - \rho_{ij}\sqrt{P(E_i)Q(E_i)P(E_j)Q(E_j)} \tag{6.56}$$

$$P(E_i, \tilde{E}_j) = P(E_i)Q(E_j) - \rho_{ij}\sqrt{P(E_i)Q(E_i)P(E_j)Q(E_j)} \tag{6.57}$$

$$P(E_i, E_j) = P(E_i)P(E_j) + \rho_{ij}\sqrt{P(E_i)Q(E_i)P(E_j)Q(E_j)} \tag{6.58}$$

As these probabilities must all be non-negative, there are constraints on the correlations $\{\rho_{ij}\}$, such as

$$\rho_{ij} \leq \min\left[\sqrt{\frac{P(E_i)Q(E_j)}{P(E_j)Q(E_i)}}, \sqrt{\frac{P(E_j)Q(E_i)}{P(E_i)Q(E_j)}}\right] \tag{6.59}$$

$$\rho_{ij} \geq \max\left[-\sqrt{\frac{P(E_i)P(E_j)}{Q(E_j)Q(E_i)}}, -\sqrt{\frac{Q(E_j)Q(E_i)}{P(E_i)P(E_j)}}\right] \tag{6.60}$$

These conditions are distinct from the conditions of positivity of the eigenvalues of $\{\rho_{ij}\}$: there are correlation matrices (which, as such, have positive eigenvalues) for which the condition above is not satisfied; and there are quantities such that the same inequality is satisfied, but that do not constitute a correlation matrix. However, if Equation (6.59) holds as an equality,

$$\rho_{ij} = \min\left[\sqrt{\frac{P(E_i)Q(E_j)}{P(E_j)Q(E_i)}}, \sqrt{\frac{P(E_j)Q(E_i)}{P(E_i)Q(E_j)}}\right] \tag{6.61}$$

then an associated set of event probabilities exists and is unique. (See Tzani and Polychronakos (2008) for a simple proof.) This means that, for any given set of event probabilities, there is an absolute maximum in the associated event correlations.

Exercise 17   Derive the constraints on the correlations $\{\rho_{ij}\}$ coming from the condition that the probabilities must be smaller than or equal to 1.

6.6 From the Conditional and Marginal to the Joint Probabilities?

We have seen how to go from the joint probabilities, $p(i)$, to the conditional, $P(E_k|E_j)$, or marginal probabilities, $P(E_k)$. Can we go in the opposite direction? If, in other words, I gave you all the stand-alone probabilities, $P(E_k)$, and all the (singly-conditioned) conditional probabilities, $P(E_k|E_j)$, would you be able to reconstruct the joint probability distribution? Unfortunately, the answer is, in general, 'no'. Let us see why this is the case.

Suppose that we have somehow obtained all the singly-conditional probabilities, $P(E_k|E_j)$, and marginal probabilities, $P(E_k)$, for n Boolean variables: $j, k = 1, 2, \ldots, n$. Do we have enough information to deduce the joint probabilities, $p(i)$, $i = 1, 2, \ldots, 2^n$? Well, we have $n^2 - n$ conditional probabilities (n^2 because $P(E_k|E_j) \neq P(E_j|E_k)$ and $-n$ because the main diagonal is just filled with n 1s.) Knowledge of the marginal probabilities adds another n pieces of information. So, we seem to have in all n^2 quantities. However, once the marginal probabilities are given, the singly-conditioned probabilities are not independent, because they are linked by Bayes' theorem: given $P(E_j|E_k)$ (and the marginals $P(E_j)$ and $P(E_k)$) then $P(E_k|E_j)$ is fully specified. Therefore we only have $\frac{n^2-n}{2}$ pieces of independent information from the singly-conditioned probabilities, plus n from the marginals. Specification of the joint probabilities requires $2^n - 1$ numbers (where the -1 comes from the condition $\sum_{i=1}^{2^n} p(i) = 1$). The following table shows the number of unknowns against the number of known quantities for various values of n:

n	$\frac{n^2-n}{2} + n$	$2^n - 1$	
2	3	3	
3	6	7	
4	10	15	(6.62)
5	15	31	
6	21	63	
7	28	127	

As one can see, when there are more than two Boolean random variables, the information in the marginal and singly-conditional probabilities is in general not enough to determine uniquely the joint distribution.

Having said that, there are situations where we *can* derive the joint probabilities from the marginal and the singly-conditioned probabilities: this can happen when our knowledge of the problem suggests that there may be independence (absolute or conditional) between some of the variables. This is dealt with in the following two sections. Before moving to that task it is important to point out that there are other very interesting situations: we may not have enough information to specify fully the joint probabilities, but it is surprising how powerful even limited information about marginal and once-conditioned probabilities can be in producing very useful bounds for joint distributions or more highly-conditioned probabilities. This aspect is dealt with in Chapter 7.

6.7   Putting Independence to Work

I defined in Section 5.7 the concept of independence between two events. Let us see how, and when, we can make use of this extremely powerful tool in order to calculate joint probabilities. Suppose that we have decided that two events, E_1 and E_2, are independent, and that they have marginal probabilities of $P(E_1) = 0.6$ and $P(E_2) = 0.3$.[3] Recall that, in general,

$$P(E_1|E_2) + P\left(\tilde{E}_1|E_2\right) = 1 \tag{6.63}$$

and that

$$P(E_1 = x \cap E_2 = y \cap E_3 = z)$$
$$= P(E_1 = x|E_2 = y \cap E_3 = z) * P(E_2 = y \cap E_3 = z) \tag{6.64}$$

with $x, y, z = T, F$. Also, recall that in the case of independence

$$P(E_1 = x \cap E_2 = y) = P(E_1 = x)P(E_2 = y) \tag{6.65}$$

for $x, y = T, F$. If independence applies, the joint probabilities for E_1 and E_2 are then easily obtained:

$$P(E_1 \cap E_2) = P(E_1)P(E_2) = 0.6 * 0.3 = 0.18 \tag{6.66}$$

$$P\left(E_1 \cap \tilde{E}_2\right) = P(E_1)P(\tilde{E}_2) = 0.6 * (1 - 0.3) = 0.42 \tag{6.67}$$

$$P\left(\tilde{E}_1 \cap E_2\right) = P(\tilde{E}_1)P(E_2) = (1 - 0.6) * 0.3 = 0.12 \tag{6.68}$$

$$P\left(\tilde{E}_1 \cap \tilde{E}_2\right) = P(\tilde{E}_1)P(\tilde{E}_2) = (1 - 0.6) * (1 - 0.3) = 0.28 \tag{6.69}$$

Now assume that, on the basis of our knowledge of how the world works, we have decided that

$$P(E_3|E_1 \cap E_2) = 0.05 \tag{6.70}$$

$$P\left(E_3|E_1 \cap \tilde{E}_2\right) = 0.10 \tag{6.71}$$

$$P\left(E_3|\tilde{E}_1 \cap E_2\right) = 0.10 \tag{6.72}$$

$$P\left(E_3|\tilde{E}_1 \cap \tilde{E}_2\right) = 0.20 \tag{6.73}$$

How can we build the joint probabilities $P(E_1 = x \cap E_2 = y \cap E_3 = z)$ for $x, y, z = T$, F from this information?

---

[3] The following example has been adapted from Moore (2001).

To begin with let us make use of Equation (6.63) to obtain the following:

$$P\left(\tilde{E}_3|E_1 \cap E_2\right) = 1 - P\left(E_3|E_1 \cap E_2\right) = 0.95 \tag{6.74}$$

$$P\left(\tilde{E}_3|E_1 \cap \tilde{E}_2\right) = 1 - P\left(E_3|E_1 \cap \tilde{E}_2\right) = 0.90 \tag{6.75}$$

$$P\left(\tilde{E}_3|\tilde{E}_1 \cap E_2\right) = 1 - P\left(E_3|\tilde{E}_1 \cap E_2\right) = 0.90 \tag{6.76}$$

$$P\left(\tilde{E}_3|\tilde{E}_1 \cap \tilde{E}_2\right) = 1 - P\left(E_3|\tilde{E}_1 \cap \tilde{E}_2\right) = 0.80 \tag{6.77}$$

Next, we write in full the expression $P(E_1 = x \cap E_2 = y \cap E_3 = z)$ for all the cases of interest making use of Equation (6.64) (and remembering, of course, that, e.g., $P(E_i \cap E_j \cap E_k) = P(E_k \cap E_i \cap E_j)$, for any permutation of i, j, k):

$$P\left(E_3 \cap E_1 \cap E_2\right) = P\left(E_3|E_1 \cap E_2\right) * P\left(E_1 \cap E_2\right) = 0.05 * 0.18 = \mathbf{0.009} \tag{6.78}$$

$$P\left(\tilde{E}_3 \cap E_1 \cap E_2\right) = P\left(\tilde{E}_3|E_1 \cap E_2\right) * P\left(E_1 \cap E_2\right) = 0.95 * 0.18 = \mathbf{0.171} \tag{6.79}$$

$$P\left(E_3 \cap \tilde{E}_1 \cap E_2\right) = P\left(E_3|\tilde{E}_1 \cap E_2\right) * P\left(\tilde{E}_1 \cap E_2\right) = 0.10 * 0.12 = \mathbf{0.012} \tag{6.80}$$

$$P\left(\tilde{E}_3 \cap \tilde{E}_1 \cap E_2\right) = P\left(\tilde{E}_3|\tilde{E}_1 \cap E_2\right) * P\left(\tilde{E}_1 \cap E_2\right) = 0.90 * 0.12 = \mathbf{0.108} \tag{6.81}$$

$$P\left(E_3 \cap E_1 \cap \tilde{E}_2\right) = P\left(E_3|E_1 \cap \tilde{E}_2\right) * P\left(E_1 \cap \tilde{E}_2\right) = 0.10 * 0.42 = \mathbf{0.042} \tag{6.82}$$

$$P\left(\tilde{E}_3 \cap E_1 \cap \tilde{E}_2\right) = P\left(\tilde{E}_3|E_1 \cap \tilde{E}_2\right) * P\left(E_1 \cap \tilde{E}_2\right) = 0.90 * 0.42 = \mathbf{0.378} \tag{6.83}$$

$$P\left(E_3 \cap \tilde{E}_1 \cap \tilde{E}_2\right) = P\left(E_3|\tilde{E}_1 \cap \tilde{E}_2\right) * P\left(\tilde{E}_1 \cap \tilde{E}_2\right) = 0.20 * 0.28 = \mathbf{0.056} \tag{6.84}$$

$$P\left(\tilde{E}_3 \cap \tilde{E}_1 \cap \tilde{E}_2\right) = P\left(\tilde{E}_3|\tilde{E}_1 \cap \tilde{E}_2\right) * P\left(\tilde{E}_1 \cap \tilde{E}_2\right) = 0.80 * 0.28 = \mathbf{0.224} \tag{6.85}$$

If we redefine as follows:

	E_3	E_1	E_2	
J_1	1	1	1	$p(1)$
J_2	0	1	1	$p(2)$
J_3	1	0	1	$p(3)$
J_4	0	0	1	$p(4)$
J_5	1	1	0	$p(5)$
J_6	0	1	0	$p(6)$
J_7	1	0	0	$p(7)$
J_8	0	0	0	$p(8)$

(6.86)

we then have

$$p(1) = \mathbf{0.009} \tag{6.87}$$

$$p(2) = \mathbf{0.171} \tag{6.88}$$

$$p(3) = \mathbf{0.012} \tag{6.89}$$

$$p(4) = \mathbf{0.108} \tag{6.90}$$

$$p(5) = \mathbf{0.042} \tag{6.91}$$

$$p(6) = \mathbf{0.378} \tag{6.92}$$

$$p(7) = \mathbf{0.056} \tag{6.93}$$

$$p(8) = \mathbf{0.224} \tag{6.94}$$

that is, thanks to the assumption of independence, we have determined the $8 - 1$ joint probabilities from two marginal probabilities and four conditional probabilities. (The -1 of course comes from the normalization condition $\sum_{i=1}^{2^n} p(i) = 1$.) Reassuringly, all these probabilities nicely add up to 1. And we did it by assigning six numbers instead of seven! You may not be overwhelmed, but the savings become substantial as soon as we begin to deal with a larger number of variables.

Clearly, there is no 'universal trick' that can conjure information out of thin air. The success of a strategy like the one above is predicated on the nature of the problem; that is, on whether it is indeed possible to identify independence between some of the variables. As we shall see in the following, even when full independence is not there we can still be helped by invoking the related property of *conditional* independence. The general point does not change, however: whether conditional independence can or cannot be invoked depends on the nature of the problem, not on our desire to make the task at hand more manageable.

6.8 Conditional Independence

As we saw above, when we can safely assume that two variables are independent the probabilistic problem simplifies considerably. Full independence, however, is a very strong condition, rarely met when one deals with financial variables. Conditional independence gives us a slightly less powerful, but more easily justifiable, tool to simplify the problem at hand. Let us see what conditional independence means. In order to help intuition we abandon for a moment the world of two-valued Boolean variables, and deal instead with Brownian processes, with which most readers are likely to be familiar.

So, consider for a moment the processes for two asset prices:

$$\frac{dS_1}{S_1} = \mu_1 dt + \sigma_1^1 dw + \sigma_1^2 dz_1 \tag{6.95}$$

$$\frac{dS_2}{S_2} = \mu_2 dt + \sigma_2^1 dw + \sigma_2^2 dz_2 \tag{6.96}$$

Suppose that the Brownian shock dw represents a shock to a common factor (if S_1 and S_2 are equity prices, dw could be a shock to the same equity index of which they are components; if they represent the assets of two firms in a Merton-like model, dw could be a shock to the economy; etc.). Clearly, the processes for S_1 and S_2 are not independent – and the greater σ_i^1 is with respect to σ_i^2, the more the two processes will be correlated. However, let us assume that

$$\mathbb{E}\,[dz_1 dz_2] = 0 \qquad\qquad (6.97)$$

that is, the *idiosyncratic* shocks dz_1 and dz_2 are uncorrelated.[4] But, if this is the case, *conditional on a particular shock, $d\tilde{w}$, having been realized*, the variables S_1 and S_2 become independent: once we know the sign and magnitude of the common shock, $d\tilde{w}$, knowledge of what 'else' happened to S_1 because of the shock dz_1 will not help us at all in predicting what S_2 does. Even if the unconditional correlation between S_1 and S_2 were 99.9%, they would still remain conditionally independent.

In this book I do not deal with Brownian processes, but since many readers are likely to come from a derivatives or stochastic calculus background, the simple example above can give an intuitive understanding of the concept of conditional independence, which I now introduce for the case of Boolean variables.

Given three events, E_1, E_2 and E_3, E_1 and E_2 are said to be conditionally independent given E_3 if[5]

$$P\,(E_1|E_2, E_3) = P\,(E_1|E_3) \qquad\qquad (6.98)$$

and

$$P\left(E_1|E_2, \tilde{E}_3\right) = P\left(E_1|\tilde{E}_3\right) \qquad\qquad (6.99)$$

As Moore (2001) points out, the simplest way to think about conditional independence is the following:

> Given knowledge of whether E_3 has occurred or not, knowledge of whether E_2 has happened or not would not help in predicting whether E_1 has happened or not.

With more general notation, if E_1 and E_2 are conditionally independent given E_3, then

$$P\,(E_1 = x|E_2 = y \cap E_3 = z) = P\,(E_1 = x|E_3 = z) \qquad\qquad (6.100)$$

where x, y and z, as usual, take on the values x, y, $z = T, F$.

---

[4]Since we are dealing in this example with a Brownian process, we can interchangeably speak of lack of correlation and independence. This is not correct in general (i.e., for non-elliptic distributions).

[5]For the definition of conditional independence to make sense, we must, of course, also require that $P(E_2, E_3) \neq 0$. In principle this requires knowledge of the joint probabilities, $P(E_2, E_3)$, which in general we do not have – remember that our plan is to *build* the joint probabilities from the marginals and conditionals. However, the only thing we need to know about $P(E_2, E_3)$ is that this probability should be non-zero, i.e., that the two elementary events, E_2, E_3, can happen at the same time.

Let us see what conditional independence implies.

We can start from an expression for the joint probability $P(E_1, E_2, E_3)$ in the case when E_1 and E_2 are conditionally independent given E_3, that is, when $P(E_1|E_2, E_3) = P(E_1|E_3)$:

$$P(E_1, E_2, E_3) = P(E_1|E_2, E_3)P(E_2, E_3)$$

$$= P(E_1|E_2, E_3)P(E_2|E_3)P(E_3)$$

$$= P(E_1|E_3)P(E_2|E_3)P(E_3) \qquad (6.101)$$

where the last line follows from the assumed conditional independence.

However, since $P(E_1, E_2, E_3) = P(E_2, E_1, E_3)$, I can also write

$$P(E_1, E_2, E_3) = P(E_2, E_1, E_3) = P(E_2|E_1, E_3)P(E_1, E_3)$$

$$= P(E_2|E_1, E_3)P(E_1|E_3)P(E_3) \qquad (6.102)$$

Equating Equations (6.101) and (6.102) therefore gives

$$P(E_1|E_2, E_3) = P(E_1|E_3) \Longleftrightarrow P(E_2|E_1, E_3) = P(E_2|E_3) \qquad (6.103)$$

In words: if conditioning the probability of E_1 on E_2 and E_3 is the same as conditioning the probability of E_1 just on E_3, then conditioning the probability of E_2 on E_1 and E_3 is equivalent to conditioning the probability of E_2 just on E_3.

The reader can profitably compare Equation (6.103) with Equations (5.23) and (5.24).

6.9   Obtaining Joint Probabilities with Conditional Independence

Let us use an example to see how the above can help us in obtaining joint probabilities. Consider again three events, E_1, E_2 and E_3, and assume that E_1 and E_2 are conditionally independent given E_3. Suppose that we have exogenously established the following:[6]

$$P(E_3) = 0.6 \qquad (6.104)$$

$$P(E_2|E_3) = 0.085 \qquad (6.105)$$

$$P\left(E_2|\tilde{E}_3\right) = 0.17 \qquad (6.106)$$

$$P(E_1|E_3) = 0.3 \qquad (6.107)$$

$$P\left(E_1|\tilde{E}_3\right) = 0.6 \qquad (6.108)$$

This information and the assumption that E_1 and E_2 are conditionally independent given E_3 comes from our knowledge of 'how the world works'. The task, as usual, is to determine

---

[6]This example is also adapted from Moore (2001).

the joint probabilities, $P(E_1 = x \cap E_2 = y \cap E_3 = z)$, with x, y, $z = T, F$. The tools we are going to use are given by Equations (6.98) to (6.100).

We start from $P(E_1, E_2, E_3)$:

$$P(E_1, E_2, E_3) = P(E_1|E_2, E_3)P(E_2, E_3)$$
$$= P(E_1|E_3)P(E_2, E_3)$$
$$= P(E_1|E_3)P(E_2|E_3)P(E_3)$$
$$= 0.3 * 0.085 * 0.6 = 0.0153 \tag{6.109}$$

where the left-hand side on the second line follows from the assumption of conditional independence. We build another joint probability, say, $P(\tilde{E}_1, E_2, \tilde{E}_3)$:

$$P(\tilde{E}_1, E_2, \tilde{E}_3) = P(\tilde{E}_1|E_2, \tilde{E}_3)P(E_2, \tilde{E}_3)$$
$$= P(\tilde{E}_1|\tilde{E}_3)P(E_2, \tilde{E}_3)$$
$$= P(\tilde{E}_1|\tilde{E}_3)P(E_2|\tilde{E}_3)P(\tilde{E}_3) \tag{6.110}$$
$$= 0.4 * 0.17 * 0.4 = 0.0272 \tag{6.111}$$

where we have used the fact that

$$P\left(E_1|\tilde{E}_3\right) + P\left(\tilde{E}_1|\tilde{E}_3\right) = 1 \tag{6.112}$$

and, again, the conditional independence.

Exercise 18   Complete the derivation of the remaining joint probabilities.

Exercise 19   Draw a Venn diagram for three events A, B and C when $P(A|B, C) = P(A|B)$.

Conditional independence will be one of the most powerful tools at our disposal when we deal with Bayesian networks.

6.10   At a Glance

Here are the relationships we are going to use in the next chapter, neatly collected in one place:

$$P(B) = P(B|A)P(A) + P(B|\tilde{A})P(\tilde{A}) \tag{6.113}$$
$$P(A|B) = \frac{P(A \cap B)}{P(B)} \tag{6.114}$$
$$P(A \cap B) = P(A|B)P(B) \tag{6.115}$$
$$P(A \cap B \cap C) = P(A|B \cap C)P(B|C)P(C) = P(C|B \cap A)P(B|A)P(A) \tag{6.116}$$
$$P(A) + P(\tilde{A}) = 1 \tag{6.117}$$
$$P(A|B) + P(\tilde{A}|B) = 1 \tag{6.118}$$

6.11   Summary

In this chapter I first cleaned up the notation. I then gave the definition of stand-alone (marginal) probabilities for the two-valued Boolean-valued variables (true-or-false events) that we are going to use to model stress events. Finally, for the same variables I introduced the concepts of conditional and joint probabilities, and of absolute and conditional independence. All the rest has been a manipulation of these fundamental concepts.

The most important message from this chapter is that, once we have the joint probabilities, we have everything else. The converse, however, is in general not true. The joint probabilities are king: they contain all the (probabilistic) information we can possibly want.

Unfortunately it is very difficult to assign or estimate these joint probabilities: there are very many of them, and it is difficult even for an expert risk manager to make an informed guess. (Would you like to venture a guess, or to estimate from your data, the joint probability of the S&P falling by 20% and of the US yield Treasury curve not steepening by at least 60 bp, and of the winter/summer gas spread falling by more than 40%?)

Therefore, a lot of non-data information (which we often translate in absolute and conditional independence) must go into the construction of the joint probabilities if we want to derive them from quantities for which we have a better intuitive feel, and which are easier to estimate from our data. These easier-to-estimate quantities are the marginal and conditional probabilities. As I have shown above, unfortunately these quantities rarely define the whole joint distribution – unless, that is, we are prepared to provide very-highly-conditioned probabilities, or to make strong assumptions about the nature of the dependencies among the variables at play. Bayesian nets provide a useful tool to organize and visualize the information contained in the marginal and conditional probabilities, and to help us in thinking correctly. (I discuss this topic in Chapters 8 and 9.) The power of Bayesian nets is remarkable, and their strengths come via the exploitation of conditional independence and the simplification of the causal structure among the underlying variables. This simplification, as I will show, reduces the degree of conditioning of the probabilities required to obtain exactly the joint distribution.

Sometimes, however, the risk manager may feel too daunted by the prospect of supplying even these relatively-lowly-conditioned probabilities. However, I show in the next chapter that even limited knowledge of the marginal probabilities and a few singly-conditioned probabilities can create very tight bounds for the joint probabilities we want to determine. It is to this task that I therefore turn.

6.12   Suggestions for Further Reading

The approach I have followed in this chapter mirrors closely that chosen by Moore (2001). The conceptual framework of probability is very well presented in Williams (2001). His book is as demanding as it is rewarding, and is particularly useful for the reader who wants to understand conditional probabilities well, because it takes conditional probabilities as one of its central themes.

A book at a mathematically much simpler level, but with proper care paid to the logical aspects of the problems at hand, and of conditional probability in particular, is

Hacking (2001). For a gentle introduction to Williams' book, I recommend Stirzacker (1999). Stirzacker's emphasis on Venn diagrams is particularly consonant with the approach taken in this book. He also provides a brief introduction to networks (trees and graphs), which, however, only touches on some of the aspects needed for the Bayesian network approach presented in the following chapters.

Chapter 7

Creating Probability Bounds

7.1 The Lay of the Land

As far as probabilities are concerned, our final goal is obtaining *joint* probabilities.[1] For n variables, we have seen that to do so we have to specify $(n - 1)$-conditioned and marginal probabilities: see, for instance, Equation (6.12) in Chapter 6. I will derive more, and more handy, expressions in the following pages (i.e., expressions in terms of different conditioned and marginal probabilities), but the general result does not change. For n greater than about 3, the task would therefore seem hopeless.

Our strategy to escape this curse of dimensionality will be two-fold: first we will so restrict the type of causal links among our variables as to require at-most-doubly-conditioned probabilities. Conditional independence will then be the indispensable tool to obtain the joint probabilities from these at-most-doubly-conditioned ones.

Even assigning doubly-conditioned probabilities on the basis of expert judgement may be too much for the cognitive abilities of human beings, let alone risk managers. Fortunately, I show in this chapter how, from the knowledge of marginal and singly-conditioned probabilities, it is possible to obtain usefully tight bounds on the joint probabilities that we are after. And if the risk manager feels bold enough to provide just one or two doubly-conditioned probabilities, the bounds on the joint probabilities become very tight indeed.

Having bounds rather than point estimates is not necessarily a bad thing, because they can give us an idea of the uncertainty around our stress estimates. I deal with this topic in Part III. My current task is to derive these bounds.

7.2 Bounds on Joint Probabilities

So, if I have n Boolean variables, in order to determine uniquely the associated joint probabilities, I need to specify all the independent $(n - 1)$-conditioned probabilities. Consider,

---

[1]This 'final' goal should be considered final only from a probabilistic point of view. As I discussed at the end of Chapter 4, there is more to life, and to quantitative risk management, than determining joint probabilities (which underpin an associative view of events). Causal links are richer and more powerful.

for instance, $n = 3$:

$$P(A, B, C) = P(A|B, C)P(B, C) =$$

$$P(A|B, C)P(B|C)P(C) \tag{7.1}$$

In general

$$P(A, B, C, \ldots, Z) = P(A|B, C, \ldots, Z)P(B, C, \ldots, Z) \tag{7.2}$$

and so on. When Bayesian nets are introduced I will show that, by restricting our analysis to a subset of the most general nets, we can reduce the problem to, say, providing at most doubly-conditioned probabilities. But I have also pointed out that, in practice, even this can become a daunting task. (See also Chapter 12.) Therefore, In this section I draw directly from work by Moskowitz and Sarin (1983) to show that very useful bounds can be set on the joint probabilities even if only the marginal and the singly-conditioned probabilities are provided – and, sometimes, even if only the marginals are available. Following their treatment the reasoning goes as follows.

Consider again the following table:

	E_1	E_2	E_3	
J_1	1	1	1	$p(1)$
J_2	0	1	1	$p(2)$
J_3	1	0	1	$p(3)$
J_4	0	0	1	$p(4)$
J_5	1	1	0	$p(5)$
J_6	0	1	0	$p(6)$
J_7	1	0	0	$p(7)$
J_8	0	0	0	$p(8)$

$$(7.3)$$

Define by a_i the column vector containing 1s or 0s for event i. Its jth element will be denoted by a_i^j. So, for instance,

$$a_1 = \begin{bmatrix} 1 \\ 0 \\ 1 \\ 0 \\ 1 \\ 0 \\ 1 \\ 0 \end{bmatrix} \tag{7.4}$$

and $a_1^3 = 1$ and $a_i^8 = 0$ for any i.

Now, denote by p the column vector of components $p(k) = p_k$, containing the n joint probabilities, and p^T its transpose. Let, as usual, $P(E_i)$ be the marginal probability and

$P(E_i, Ej)$ and $P(E_i.E_j, E_k)$ be the joint probabilities. Then, given these definitions it is straightforward to prove that, for $n = 3$,

$$P(E_i) = \boldsymbol{p}^T \cdot \boldsymbol{a}_i \text{ for } i = 1, 2, 3 \tag{7.5}$$

$$P(E_i, E_j) = \boldsymbol{p}^T \cdot (\boldsymbol{a}_i * \boldsymbol{a}_j) \text{ for } i = 1, 2 \tag{7.6}$$

$$P(E_i, E_j, E_k) = \boldsymbol{p}^T \cdot (\boldsymbol{a}_i * \boldsymbol{a}_j * \boldsymbol{a}_k) \text{ for } i = 1 \tag{7.7}$$

where the symbol '·' denotes the row-by-line product between two vectors, and $\boldsymbol{a}_i * \boldsymbol{a}_j$ indicates the column vector whose elements are given by the element-by-element multiplication of the vectors $\boldsymbol{a}_i$ and $\boldsymbol{a}_j$.

Exercise 20 Prove the three relationships above.

The generalization of the results to the case of n variables above is obvious:

$$P(E_i) = \boldsymbol{p}^T \cdot \boldsymbol{a}_i \text{ for } i = 1, \ldots, n \tag{7.8}$$

$$P(E_i, E_j) = \boldsymbol{p}^T \cdot (\boldsymbol{a}_i * \boldsymbol{a}_j) \text{ for } i = 1, \ldots, n - 1, \ j > i \tag{7.9}$$

$$P(E_i, E_j, E_k) = \boldsymbol{p}^T \cdot (\boldsymbol{a}_i * \boldsymbol{a}_j * \boldsymbol{a}_k) \text{ for } i = 1, \ldots, n - 2, k > j > i \tag{7.10}$$

$$\ldots$$

$$P(E_1, E_2, E_3, \ldots, E_n) = \boldsymbol{p}^T \cdot (\boldsymbol{a}_1 * \boldsymbol{a}_2 * \boldsymbol{a}_3 * \ldots * \boldsymbol{a}_n) \tag{7.11}$$

In addition we have the usual normalization condition:

$$\sum_{i=1}^{2^n} p_i = 1 \tag{7.12}$$

As we have seen, the fullest specification of the joint probabilities can be given in terms of $(n - 1)$-conditional and marginal probabilities. Suppose, however, that the risk manager only felt able to supply a subset of the conditions above, say, the normalization condition, the marginals and the singly-conditioned probabilities, $P(E_i|E_j)$. (Of course, providing the marginals and the singly-conditioned probabilities is equivalent to supplying the two-event joint probabilities, as, for any j and k, $P(j, k) = P(j|k)P(k)$.) Call this subset X:

$$X = \left[\sum_{i=1}^{2^n} p_i = 1 \cup \right.$$

$$P(E_i) = \boldsymbol{p}^T \cdot \boldsymbol{a}_i \text{ for } i = 1, \ldots, n \ \cup$$

$$\left. P(E_i|E_j)P(E_j) = \boldsymbol{p}^T \cdot (\boldsymbol{a}_i * \boldsymbol{a}_j) \text{ for } i = 1, \ldots, n - 1, \ j > i \right]$$

Consider now the jth joint probability, p_j. We can determine an upper or a lower bound for this probability by solving the simple Linear Programming[2] problems

$$\text{Minimize } p_j \text{ subject to } \boldsymbol{p} \in X \qquad (7.13)$$

and

$$\text{Maximize } p_j \text{ subject to } \boldsymbol{p} \in X \qquad (7.14)$$

where the expression $\boldsymbol{p} \in X$ means that the joint probabilities $\boldsymbol{p}$ must belong to the constraint set X. Of course, the more elements in the set X, the tighter the bounds we will obtain. The good news, however, is that even if the set X is rather small (i.e., even if the risk manager only feels confident to provide relatively few probabilities), the bounds can still be usefully tight. (See the examples below.)

Following the same approach, we can ask a lot of related and useful questions. For instance, as Moskowitz and Sarin (1983) point out, we can ask whether one joint scenario, say, J_r, has a higher probability than another joint scenario, say, J_s. We can answer the question by defining the variable $p_r - p_s$, and checking whether the solution to

$$\text{Minimize } p_r - p_s \text{ subject to } \boldsymbol{p} \in X \qquad (7.15)$$

gives an answer greater than 0.

7.3   How Tight are these Bounds in Practice?

Bounds are all well and good, but to be useful they have to be reasonably tight. The good news is that even very sparse information can produce highly useful bounds. I first present the results obtained by Moskowitz and Sarin (1983), and then the results obtained for an example that is of greater relevance to the low probabilities found in stress testing.

Moskowitz and Sarin looked at a 3-event and a 4-event case. For each one, first they randomly sampled from the uniform, $\mathcal{U}[0, 1]$, distribution, but the assignments of the numbers thus drawn to the marginal or conditional probabilities were made by ensuring internal consistency (i.e., by ensuring that the numbers chosen *could* be marginal and conditional probabilities – see Chapter 11). As a next step, Moskowitz and Sarin considered two cases: either they availed themselves of the knowledge just of marginals or they assumed that they had at their disposal both the marginal and the singly-conditioned probabilities. Using the Linear Programming approach described above they then determined the bounds to the joint probabilities. Finally, they repeated this procedure 100 times for each of the four cases (3- or 4-event, marginals only or marginals plus conditionals). Their results were as follows:

- 3-event case, only marginal probabilities provided: in 95% of the cases the difference between upper and lower bound for the joint probabilities was ≤ 0.1641.

---

[2]I provide a simple introduction to Linear Programming in the Appendix in Chapter 15.

- 3-event case, marginals and conditionals provided: in 95% of the cases the difference between upper and lower bound for the joint probabilities was ≤ 0.0567.

- 4-event case, only marginal probabilities provided: in 95% of the cases the difference between upper and lower bound for the joint probabilities was ≤ 0.058.

- 4-event case, marginals and conditionals provided: in 95% of the cases the difference between upper and lower bound for the joint probabilities was ≤ 0.0073.

Two observations. The first is obvious: supplying also the conditional probabilities makes the bounds tighter. The second observation is not so obvious: increasing the number of variables tightens the bounds. The intuition behind this second result is that new variables bring in more and more hyperplanes of acceptability, which progressively limit the solution space.

So much for tests with the probabilities drawn from the uniform, $\mathcal{U}[0, 1]$, distribution. What about the situation when the probabilities are of magnitudes more likely to be met in stress-testing situations? To answer this question, look at the case of four variables with joint probabilities given by

$$
\begin{bmatrix}
 & E_1 & E_2 & E_3 & E_4 & p(i) \\
J_1 & 1 & 0 & 1 & 1 & 0.001369 \\
J_2 & 0 & 1 & 1 & 1 & 0.000006 \\
J_3 & 1 & 1 & 1 & 1 & 0.000028 \\
J_4 & 0 & 0 & 1 & 1 & 0.000016 \\
J_5 & 1 & 0 & 0 & 1 & 0.000013 \\
J_6 & 0 & 1 & 0 & 1 & 0.000034 \\
J_7 & 1 & 1 & 0 & 1 & 0.000010 \\
J_8 & 0 & 0 & 0 & 1 & 0.000123 \\
J_9 & 1 & 0 & 1 & 0 & 0.000529 \\
J_{10} & 0 & 1 & 1 & 0 & 0.000248 \\
J_{11} & 1 & 1 & 1 & 0 & 0.000980 \\
J_{12} & 0 & 0 & 1 & 0 & 0.000023 \\
J_{13} & 1 & 0 & 0 & 0 & 0.000081 \\
J_{14} & 0 & 1 & 0 & 0 & 0.000104 \\
J_{15} & 1 & 1 & 0 & 0 & 0.000090 \\
J_{16} & 0 & 0 & 0 & 0 & 0.996345
\end{bmatrix}
\tag{7.16}
$$

and marginal probabilities given by

$$P(E_1) = 0.00310 \tag{7.17}$$

$$P(E_2) = 0.00150 \tag{7.18}$$

$$P(E_3) = 0.00320 \tag{7.19}$$

$$P(E_4) = 0.00160 \tag{7.20}$$

We assume that the risk manager only feels confident enough to provide the marginal probabilities. Normally we should be able to do better than this, but we want to see to what extent even very limited information can impose useful bounds on the joint probabilities. Of course, the table of joint probabilities in Equation (7.16) is not assumed to be known by the risk manager – it is only presented to allow the reader to 'peek behind the curtains'.

Now, Linear Programming is a beautiful tool, but rather opaque. For this super-simple example I am therefore going to take a more transparent approach. Here is one intuitive way to look at the problem: the four marginal probabilities pin down any four joint probabilities. To make my algebra easy I have chosen these four joint probabilities to be associated with events J_1, J_9, J_{10} and J_{12}.

Exercise 21   For the net depicted in Figure 11.1 (page 157), derive the expression for $p(1)$, $p(9)$, $p(10)$ and $p(12)$ in terms of the pre-assigned marginal probabilities $P(E_i)$, $i = 1, \ldots, n$, and other joint probabilities.

The constraint from the normalization condition then pins down another joint probability, which I have chosen to be the one associated with J_{16}. I can then move the remaining joint probabilities – $p(2)$, $p(3)$, $p(4)$, $p(5)$, $p(6)$, $p(7)$, $p(8)$, $p(11)$, $p(13)$, $p(14)$ and $p(15)$ – from their true value (in correspondence of which there obviously exists a solution) until any of the other joint probabilities becomes either negative or greater than 1.

It is then not difficult, following the approach described above, to show the following:

- $0 \leq p(2) \leq 0.00024$
- $0.000005 \leq p(3) \leq 0.00026$
- $0 \leq p(4) \leq 0.00003$
- $0 \leq p(5) \leq 0.0013$
- $0.000014 \leq p(6) \leq 0.00024$
- $0 \leq p(7) \leq 0.00024$
- $0 \leq p(8) \leq 0.0013$
- $0.000960 \leq p(11) \leq 0.00118$
- $0.000060 \leq p(13) \leq 0.00060$
- $0.000081 \leq p(14) \leq 0.00034$
- $0.000079 \leq p(15) \leq 0.00033$

For our applications, of course, these bounds must be looked at in the context of stress events. From this point of view a bound like the one for $p(4)$ is indeed tight and useful; the one for, say, $p(8)$, less so. Recall, however, that no conditional probabilities were provided for this analysis.

These results are very encouraging, and should be used in conjunction with the Bayesian-net treatment presented in the following chapters.

Chapter 8

Bayesian Nets I: An Introduction

8.1 Bayesian Nets: An Informal Definition

Before we get started, let me make my game plan as clear as possible. What we want to get are joint probabilities. We have seen that assigning marginal and conditional probabilities of low order is in general not enough to pin down the joint probabilities we want (see Section 6.6). But we do not think that complex, highly-conditioned probabilities can be reliably assigned by a risk manager. At most we are ready to trust order-of-magnitude estimates of marginal and simple, lowly-conditioned probabilities. What can we do?

To get out of this impasse we need extra information, which is provided by the causal links among the variables in our problems. Bayesian nets are the tools that will assist us with the necessary book-keeping, and more importantly, will help us to think constructively about the problem. The rest of the chapters will clarify what 'thinking constructively' means.

For our purposes, Bayesian nets (or networks) can be defined as directed, acyclical graphs where each node (or vertex) is associated with a two-valued (Boolean) random variable and with a list of numbers called a conditional probability table. Let us see what this means in detail.

I will discuss conditional probability tables later on in Section 8.4. Let me therefore start to explain what directed, acyclical graphs are. A *graph* is a set of points (the *nodes* that represent random variables) connected by lines (*arcs* or *edges*). For the applications of interest to us, the edges are *directed* – they have an arrow that goes from one node to another. And for our applications the directed graphs we work with are acyclical. This means that, starting from any node, we cannot go back to the same node following the arrows that connect the other nodes.

A few more pieces of terminology: first, if an arrow points from node A to node B, node A is said to be the *parent* of node B (the *child*) (see Figure 8.1). Then, the parents, the parents of the parents of a node, their parents, the parents of these and so on, are collectively called the *ancestors*. Similarly, the children, the children of children, their children, the children of these, and so on are called the *descendants*.

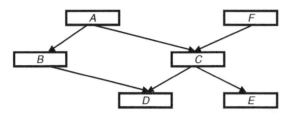

Figure 8.1   In this net, A causes B and C, F causes C, B and C causes D and C causes E.

The power of Bayesian nets comes from the fact that we can interpret the existence of an arrow between two nodes as representing a causal link between the associated random variables. This is where we begin to enrich the associative approach to uncertain events afforded by a purely probabilistic treatment. We do so by injecting information about how the world works. I have discussed in Chapter 3 and at the end of Chapter 4 how important and powerful this approach can be.

What do we mean by 'causal link'? As a bare minimum, when we say that there is a causal link between A and B we are saying that knowledge of A (the parent) will help us in our assessment of the probability of B (the child) happening.[1] This is always true. However, there is more to a causal link than an alteration of their marginal probabilities. For instance, knowing that on a given day it was raining changes my probability assessment that that day was in autumn. Conversely, knowing that it is autumn changes my assessment of the marginal probability that it will rain tomorrow. Both marginal (prior) probabilities are modified by knowledge of occurrence of the other event. However, we do not think that a rainy day 'causes' the season to become autumn. A causal relationship is linked to a model of how the world works. Availability of such a model helps our understanding, tells us what is essential and what is accidental, and alerts us to when the world has changed – and when, therefore, we should abandon the model.[2] It is no surprise, then, that when we can establish a causal link, our minds find assigning conditional probabilities much easier and 'natural'.[3]

This last feature of causal links is particularly useful because, as we shall see, in order to use Bayesian nets we have to associate to each node either a marginal probability or a conditional probability table. Once this information is given, Bayesian nets provide a full graphical (and, via the tables, numerical) representation of the joint distribution. But the construction of these conditional probability tables can be carried out much more efficiently if we are aware, and fully exploit, the causal structure of the underlying phenomenon. If you need convincing about this, you may want to revisit the wet pavement example (see also Pearl (2009)) presented in Chapter 4, Section 4.4.

This point is important, so let me clarify it a bit. What do I mean when I say that understanding of the causal structure of the problem can make the construction of the Bayesian nets more efficient? Bayesian nets are made up of nodes, lines, arrows *and conditional probability tables*. Not surprisingly, these are populated by conditional probabilities. Now, different conditional probabilities (say, $P(A|B)$ rather than $P(B|A)$) may well be equivalent from the mathematical point of view (and are linked, once the marginals are given, by

---

[1] This is just a necessary condition for causation. See the discussion below.

[2] It is for this reason that the availability of alternative models of reality discussed in Chapter 3 is so important.

[3] Truth be told, sometimes causal links can make us *over*estimate the revision of the stand-alone probability. See the discussion in Chapter 12.

Bayes' theorem). However, very often they are not at all as easy to assign (cognitively resonant) during the process of expert elicitation. Choosing the causal rather than diagnostic 'direction' (see Section 12.4) can make an enormous difference in producing a good-quality conditional–probability table. We shall see many examples of this in the following.

Keeping these considerations in mind, in order to make use of Bayesian nets we have to be able to answer a few questions:

1. How do we 'map' the causal relationships among the variables into the structure (arcs and arrows) or the net? I'll answer these questions in the next section.

2. What goes in the conditional probability tables? This is dealt with in Section 8.4

3. Assuming that the conditional probability tables have been given, how do we go from these to the joint probabilities? I'll also deal with this topic in this chapter (Section 8.7).

4. Now that we know what we should put in the conditional probability tables, how do we actually populate their entries? How do we assign the conditional probabilities that are required? I deal with this question in Chapters 9 and 10.

Once all these questions have been answered the structure of the Bayesian net and the inputs required to use it will be in place, and I will show in Chapter 11 how to put all the pieces together and obtain a solution (a set of joint probabilities) in the general case.

8.2 Defining the Structure of Bayesian Nets

How do we build Bayesian nets? More precisely, how do we translate the causal links among the variables into the topology of a Bayesian net?

First, we must identify the variables relevant to our application (in our context, to our joint scenario). Each variable will typically be a stand-alone stress event. Each event can either happen (in which case the variable has value T) or not (in which case it has value F).

Next, we associate each variable to a node.

As a next step we draw arcs between the nodes. We do so keeping in mind that whenever we draw an arc (a line) between two nodes we mean that there is a causal link between the two variables.

Now, wherever we find a line we put an arrow at one end or the other. The causal link goes in the direction of the arrow: from the *parent* to the *child*.

Causality is a very complex topic. Philosophers have been discussing it for about 2500 years, and they are not quite done yet. I am therefore understandably reluctant to enter the fray. Still, it is important to make a few, uncontroversial, points.

First of all, a *necessary* condition for the existence of a causal link is that knowledge of whether the parent Boolean random variable is true or false should help us in telling whether the child Boolean random variable is true or false. It may help us a lot (perhaps completely, in the case of deterministic causation), or very little, but this is a different matter.[4] I stress that also knowledge of whether a child is true or false can help in deciding

---

[4]For pragmatic reasons, very often we will set very low degrees of causation (very low degrees of influence) to zero in order to simplify our life, but this is (yet) another matter.

whether the parent was true or false. Therefore the criterion I gave above (help in prediction) is a necessary but not sufficient condition for causation. To be clear: if knowledge of A does not help us at all in predicting whether B is true or false, then A cannot possibly be a cause for B, but the reverse is not true: A (a sudden large increase in equity implied volatilities) may help us in determining whether B (an equity market crash) occurred, but may be the consequence not the cause of B.

Having settled this point about causation, we can begin to look in turn at our variables (our elementary stress events). Given our knowledge of the world, there will be a set of variables that have no parents (those we believe are caused by no other variables in our set). We will draw these primary parents in such a way that no arrows point into them. They will only have arrows originating away from them. In Figure 8.1, variables A and F are the only primary parents: either one or the other directly or indirectly influences all the other variables, but they are not influenced by any of them (and they do not influence each other). Note already how the graphical depiction naturally reflects this concept, and therefore aids our intuition.

One more comment about these Ur-parents in Figure 8.1, nodes A and F. We have decided to draw no connecting lines between them, and they have no common parents. This means that we believe that they are *statistically independent*: $P(A|F) = P(A)$ and $P(F|A) = P(F)$.

We have seen that the existence of an arrow indicates causal relationship from parent to child. If the causal relationship is deterministic this is signified by putting 0s or 1s, as appropriate, in the conditional probability table – this is what we called above incompatibility and deterministic causation. This is a rather trivial result. What is far more interesting is that the conditional probability tables we associate with nodes can allow us to express far more nuanced relationships between variables than incompatibility or deterministic causation. In particular, our understanding of the nature of the causal relationships among the variables will enable us to embed in the structure of the net not only absolute, but also conditional, independence. How can this be done?

Simply by exploiting the fact that, once we have drawn all the nodes and arrows in a Bayesian net, given the parents of node X, *node X is conditionally independent of all the nodes that are not its own descendants*. So, in Figure 8.1, conditional on C and B, node D is conditionally independent of A and E. It is this condition that dramatically reduces the entries in the conditional probability table required to compute the joint probabilities. At this stage I will say only that this is the case because providing probabilities of D conditioned on events other than B or C would be informationally redundant once the quantities $P(D = x | B = y, C = z)$ have been provided. This may not be totally clear at this stage, and I will discuss this important point at length in this chapter.

These ideas can be made more precise by introducing the concept of d-separation.[5] Here is how it works. Let Y, Z and X be sets of nodes. Then the set of nodes X is said to d-separate sets Y and Z if every undirected path from a node in set Y to a node in set Z is blocked by X. It is then easy to show that, if X d-separates Y and Z, then Y and Z are conditionally independent given X.

---

[5]The d in d-separation stands for 'direction-dependent'.

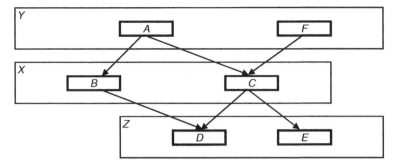

Figure 8.2   In this net, the block X d-separates blocks Z and Y.

Let us look at what this means in practice with reference to Figure 8.2. Let $Y = \{A\&F\}$, $Z = \{D\&E\}$ and $X = \{B\&C\}$. Then, by the definition above X d-separates Y and Z. This means that any node in Z is conditionally independent of any node in Y given X.[6]

Therefore, when we build Bayesian nets we make the fundamental assumption that, *conditional on its parents*, any variable is independent of all other variables apart from its descendants. Looking back at Figure 8.1, this means that, say, D clearly depends on A, F, B and C, but, once we know B and C, there is no residual A- and F-dependence on D: knowledge of A and F does not help us in predicting D any more than just knowledge of B and C does. *This also means that there is no path-dependence in our net*: the probability of D happening does not depend on whether C was caused by A or F.

This condition of path independence is very closely linked to the Markov condition, and plays an essential role in the developments below. Why Markov? For a time-ordered process, X_i, we commonly call it a Markov process if

$$P(X_k|X_{k-1}, X_{k-2}, \ldots, X_{k-n}) = P(X_k|X_{k-1}) \qquad (8.1)$$

that is, if knowledge of the realization of the process at times earlier than $k - 1$ does not help the time-$k - 1$ prediction of its realization at time k. It is easy to see the analogy in the case of Bayesian nets: ancestors other than parents are equivalent to 'earlier events' that do not affect the probability of the current realization.[7]

Conditional independence is so central to Bayesian nets that I discuss this point in more detail in the next section.

Exercise 22   We know from Section 6.8 (Equation (6.103) in particular) that, if $P(E|D, C) = P(E|C)$ then $P(D|E, C) = P(D|C)$. Convince yourself that this is borne out by the topology of our Bayesian net.

---

[6]In providing the criterion for conditional independence based on d-separation I have cheated a bit, because I have not really defined what I mean when I say that the set Z 'blocks off' the sets X and Y.

Explaining 'blocking' in a precise manner is actually very easy, but rather tedious, and I trust that the reader can go with the flow. If desired, a precise definition can be found in Pearl (2009).

[7]In the Bayesian nets we work with in this book there is no time dimension. It is possible to interpret the arrows as conveying time ordering, but this route is not taken in the present treatment.

Exercise 23   Looking at Figure 8.1, are variables A and E correlated? What about B and C? A and F?

8.3   More About Conditional Independence

When I introduced d-separation I stated that, conditional on its parents, any variable is independent of all other variables *apart from its descendents*. What does this last qualification mean? In general a node is *not* conditionally independent of its descendents given its parents. Looking at Figure 8.3, this means that D is conditionally independent of A and F given B and C (which together d-separate $\{A\&F\}$ from $\{D\&E\}$):

$$P(D|A, F, B, C) = P(D|B, C) \tag{8.2}$$

but it is not conditionally independent of G:

$$P(D|A, F, B, C, G) \neq P(D|B, C) \tag{8.3}$$

This is because knowledge of whether G is true or false does help in deciding whether its parent occurred or not: if D is an equity market crash, and G a sharp increase in equity implied volatilities ('caused' by the equity market crash), observing that the sharp rise in volatility has not occurred can help us (a lot) in deciding whether the equity crash occurred – probably not.

Therefore, even if a node only has, say, two parents, we cannot say that, in general, there can be at-most-doubly-conditioned probabilities associated with it. Since what we want to obtain are joint probabilities this seems to create a big problem: was the strategy advertised in the first paragraph of this chapter not predicated on the need to provide only simple, low-conditioned probabilities? Fortunately, when we consider joint probabilities we can always order the variables in such a way that the conditional probability tables required to build them only contain at-most-m-conditioned probabilities, where m is the maximum number of parents a node can have. As a consequence, we can still always build the joint distribution by supplying at-most-m-conditioned probabilities.

Let us see how this can be done. To begin, note that any Bayesian net (which is made up, remember, of a directed, *acyclical* graph) induces a partial ordering among its variables.

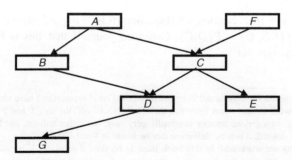

Figure 8.3   In this net, D is conditionally independent of A and F given B and C, but is not conditionally independent of G.

Inducing an ordering means establishing a rule by means of which, given A and B, we can always say whether $A \geq B$ or $B \geq A$. For acyclical graphs this ordering can be achieved by defining

$$X \leq Y \text{ if and only if } X \text{ is a descendant of } Y \tag{8.4}$$

So, for the net in Figure 8.3, $G \leq D \leq B \leq A$.

Now, we can always break down a joint probability in such a way that the conditional probability for a node has only non-descendants in the condition. It is thanks to this property that in a Bayesian net with at most m parents per node the conditional probability tables necessary to build the joint probabilities only contain at-most-m-conditioned probabilities.

Let us see how this works. Looking at Figure 8.3 again, consider the joint probability $P(A, B, C, D, E, F, G)$. Thanks to the ordering defined above, I can rearrange the variables from 'smallest' to 'largest' as

$$P(A, B, C, D, E, F, G) = P(G, D, E, B, C, F, A) \tag{8.5}$$

Therefore

$$
\begin{aligned}
P(G, D, E, B, C, F, A) &= P(G|D, E, B, C, F, A)P(D, E, B, C, F, A) \\
&= P(G|D)P(D, E, B, C, F, A) = P(G|D)P(D|E, B, C, F, A)P(E, B, C, F, A) \\
&= P(G|D)P(D|B, C)P(E|B, C, F, A)P(B, C, F, A) \\
&= P(G|D)P(D|B, C)P(E|C)P(B, C, F, A) \\
&= P(G|D)P(D|B, C)P(E|C)P(B|C, F, A)P(C, F, A) \\
&= P(G|D)P(D|B, C)P(E|C)P(B|A)P(C, F, A) \\
&= P(G|D)P(D|B, C)P(E|C)P(B|A)P(C|F, A)P(F, A) \\
&= P(G|D)P(D|B, C)P(E|C)P(B|A)P(C|F, A)P(A)P(F) \tag{8.6}
\end{aligned}
$$

This example shows that, in order to calculate the joint probability $P(A, B, C, D, E, F, G)$, we have used at-most-doubly-conditioned probabilities despite the fact that D is not conditionally independent of its descendant G, given B and C.

The reader can easily prove to herself that this property holds true in general, and that there was nothing special about the topology of the net in Figure 8.3 that allowed us to derive this result.

For short I will therefore often say in the following that, for a Bayesian net with at most m parents we will need at-most-m-conditioned probabilities to build all the joint probabilities, without specifying that this holds after a suitable rearrangement of the variables in ascending order.

A last observation is worth repeating: in the chain of equalities above I have set $P(B|C, A) = P(B|A)$. This is not because C does not help us in predicting whether B happened – in general it does! For instance, now let A be an equity market crash, B a sharp increase in implied volatilities and C a widening of credit spreads. Knowing that credit spreads have widened ($C = T$) *does* help us in adjusting our unconditional probability,

$P(B)$, of a sharp increase in implied volatilities:

$$P(B) \neq P(B|C) \tag{8.7}$$

However, *once we are told whether the equity market crash (the common parent) happened or not*, there is no extra information left in C! The additional information about B (the increase in implied volatilities) that we could extract from knowledge of the occurrence or otherwise of the credit spread widening, C, was only 'coming from' our knowledge of whether the equity market crash, A, had occurred or not. Therefore, indeed,

$$P(B|A, C) = P(B|A) \tag{8.8}$$

This is all we need to know to translate our understanding of the causal links among the variables at play into a topological structure for the net. The topology is not just made up of the nodes, lines and arrows. It also establishes an ordering among the variables and tells us which entries of the conditional probability tables are required (or, rather, which entries convey non-redundant information to build the joint probabilities). We have not been able to say anything yet about the strength of the causal links. To do this we have to provide conditional probability tables. There is one class of probability table per structure of Bayesian net – where by structure I mean order of conditioning and number of entries in the table. It is the actual numerical numbers we put in the tables that quantify the strength of the links.

8.4   What Goes in the Conditional Probability Tables?

In general, given n variables with an unspecified causal structure among them, *a priori* there is information in all the conditional probabilities, that is, in very complex quantities such as, say, $P(E_1, E_2, \ldots, E_j | E_k, E_l, \ldots, E_n)$. However, once the topology of the net has been assigned (i.e., once we have specified the causal structure among the variables) only a very small subset of the whole universe of conditional probabilities will be needed. We now examine in detail and systematically what goes in the tables.

We can start from the earliest ancestors.[8] If a node has no parents (such as node A in Figure 8.1), we assign a marginal probability to the event associated with the random variable of that node. For the earliest ancestors, this is all we need.

We next consider any of the descendants of A, not necessarily a child of A. Let us consider, for instance, node D. A conditional probability table for D lists all the conditional probabilities of D being true or false given its parent(s) being true or false. So, for instance, the conditional probability table for node D in Figure 8.1 is given by

$$\begin{bmatrix} P(D|C \cap B) & P(D|\tilde{C} \cap B) \\ P(D|C \cap \tilde{B}) & P(D|\tilde{C} \cap \tilde{B}) \end{bmatrix} \tag{8.9}$$

---

[8]In the actual computational we start from the opposite end, i.e., from the children. However, in order to see what the conditional probability tables should contain it is better to start from the opposite end of the net.

plus its 'mirror image'

$$\begin{bmatrix} P(\widetilde{D}|C \cap B) & P(\widetilde{D}|\widetilde{C} \cap B) \\ P(\widetilde{D}|C \cap \widetilde{B}) & P(\widetilde{D}|\widetilde{C} \cap \widetilde{B}) \end{bmatrix} \qquad (8.10)$$

This entails a very substantial reduction of the non-zero conditional probabilities connected with node D: for instance, $P(D|A, F)$ is certainly not zero, and in itself, carries information. But, given the topology of a particular net, we know which conditional probabilities carry the minimal information required to build the joint probabilities. Therefore we do not have to assign the conditional probability $P(D|A, F)$ in order to build the joint probabilities. The point is that the entry $P(D|A, F)$ will carry no extra information that we cannot recover once the conditional probabilities in the tables in Equations (8.9) and (8.10) have been given (and, of course, the marginal probability for A).[9]

We proceed in the same manner for all the descendants of the ancestors. In general each node will contain the marginal probability for that node, and conditioned probabilities of order as high as the number of direct parents into that node. And, of course, the conditioning will then only be on the parents of each node.

8.5   Useful Relationships

We saw in Section 8.3 that the ability to rearrange the variables of a joint probability according to their ordering was crucial in reducing the highest order of conditionality required to obtain any joint probability. This is but one of the relationships that we will use in order to fill efficiently the conditional probability matrices.

Here is a useful list of simple relationships that we will use over and over again when we tackle real applications.

1. Breaking down the joint

$$P(E_1 = x \cap E_2 = y \cap \ldots E_n = z)$$
$$= P(E_1 = x|E_2 = y \cap \ldots E_n = z)P(E_2 = y \cap \ldots E_n = z) \qquad (8.11)$$

with, as usual, $x, y, \ldots, z = T, F$.

Lightening the notation, we can present the breaking-down-the-joint rule as follows:

$$P(E_1, E_2, \ldots, E_n) = P(E_1|E_2, \ldots, E_n)P(E_2, \ldots, E_n)$$
$$= P(E_1|E_2, \ldots, E_n)P(E_2|\ldots, E_n)P(E_3, \ldots, E_n) = \ldots$$
$$= P(E_1|E_2, \ldots, E_n)P(E_2|\ldots, E_n)P(E_3|\ldots, E_n)\ldots, P(E_{n-1}|E_n)P(E_n) \quad (8.12)$$

---

[9]In case the reader is daunted by the number of entries required to populate the table, let me make clear straightaway that most of these entries can be derived from the applications of Bayes' theorem, and from the closure relationships.

So, given an n-dimensional joint distribution we can always break it down into the product of an $n - 1$-conditioned probability, an $n - 2$-conditioned probability, ..., a singly-conditioned probability and a marginal probability.

2. Order of conditioning

As discussed above, if we have n two-valued Boolean variables, and each can have at most m parents, then the specification of all the n-dimensional joint probabilities never requires anything more complex than m-conditioned probabilities.

3. Commutativity

We can reorder variables without crossing a conditionality sign ($|\cdot|$) any way we like:

$$P(E_1 = x | E_n = y, \ldots, E_2 = z) = P(E_1 = x | E_2 = y, \ldots, E_n = z) \tag{8.13}$$

$$P(E_1 = x, E_2 = y, \ldots, E_n = z) = P(E_n = x, E_{n-1} = y, \ldots, E_1 = z) \tag{8.14}$$

$$P(E_1 = x, E_2 = y, \ldots, E_k = w | E_n = z) = P(E_k = x, E_{k-1} = y, \ldots, E_1 = w | E_n = z) \tag{8.15}$$

Trivial at it may seem this condition is extremely useful, because it allows us to rearrange variables in a way that the conditional probability for a given node only has non-descendants in the breakdown of the joint above. Putting the breakdown rule and the commutativity property together we can always write the joint probabilities in terms of the entries in the conditional probability tables.

4. Closure

$$P(E_1 = x | E_2 = y \cap \ldots E_n = z) + P(\tilde{E}_1 = x | E_2 = y \cap \ldots E_n = z) = 1 \tag{8.16}$$

5. Conditional independence

If the probability of E_1 given E_2 is equal to the probability of E_1, then the probability of E_2 given E_1 is equal to the probability of E_2:

$$P(E_1 | E_2) = P(E_1) \Longleftrightarrow P(E_2 | E_1) = P(E_2) \tag{8.17}$$

Similarly for double conditioning:

$$P(E_1 | E_2, E_3) = P(E_1 | E_3) \Longleftrightarrow P(E_2 | E_1, E_3) = P(E_2 | E_3) \tag{8.18}$$

In words: if conditioning the probability of E_1 on E_2 and E_3 is the same as conditioning the probability of E_1 just on E_3, then conditioning the probability of E_2 on E_1 and E_3 is equivalent to conditioning the probability of E_2 just on E_3.

6. Splitting of the marginal

For any E_1 and E_2

$$P(E_1|E_2)P(E_2) + P(E_1|\tilde{E}_2)P(\tilde{E}_2) = P(E_1) \qquad (8.19)$$

Exercise 24 Prove the equality above using a Venn diagram.

8.6 A Worked-Out Example

All of this may seem a bit abstract, and so I now show how it works in practice with a very stylized example.[10] We will look at more interesting cases in Chapter 11.

Consider the net in Figure 8.4. What information has been embedded in the net? We believe that A and B are 'primary variables', in the sense that knowledge of no other variable would help us making a prediction about either A or B. We believe that D depends on B but not on A. We also think that C depends both on A and B, and that, once we know C, we do not need to know anything else in order to predict E.

The probability tables must therefore contain the following information:

- for node A, the marginal probability, $P(A)$;

- for node B, the marginal probability, $P(B)$;

- for node C, the marginal probability, $P(C)$, and the conditional probability table

$$P(C = x|A = y \cap B = z) \quad \text{for } x, y, z = T, F \qquad (8.20)$$

- for node D, the marginal probability, $P(D)$, and the conditional probability table

$$P(D = x|B = y) \quad \text{for } x, y = T, F \qquad (8.21)$$

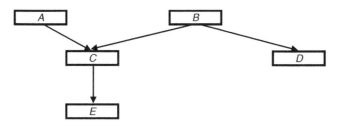

Figure 8.4 Which variables display zero correlation?

---

[10]This example has been adapted from Moore (2001).

- for node E, the marginal probability, $P(E)$, and the conditional probability table

$$P(E = x|C = y) \quad \text{for } x, y = \boldsymbol{T}, \boldsymbol{F} \tag{8.22}$$

Remembering the closure property above ($P(E_1 = x|E_2 = y \cap \ldots E_n = z) + P(\tilde{E}_1 = x| E_2 = y \cap \ldots E_n = z) = 1$), one can easily see that all of the above amounts to just 13 numbers (5 marginal probabilities; 4 entries for the conditional probability table for node C; 2 entries for the conditional probability table for node D; and 2 entries for the conditional probability table for node E). This will allow us to determine the $2^5 - 1 = 31$ joint probabilities (where the -1 comes, as usual, from the normalization condition).

How exactly can we do this? Let us start from one particular entry, say, $P(E \cap \tilde{D} \cap C \cap \tilde{B} \cap A)$, that is, the joint probability that events E, C and A happened and events D and B did not happen. Note, to begin with, that I have made use of the commutativity condition (8.13) to rearrange the order of the variables in (what will turn out to be) the most convenient order. Then, by Equation (8.11) we can write:

$$P(E \cap \tilde{D} \cap C \cap \tilde{B} \cap A) = P(E|\tilde{D} \cap C \cap \tilde{B} \cap A)P(\tilde{D} \cap C \cap \tilde{B} \cap A) \tag{8.23}$$

We look at the first term on the right-hand side. The way we have drawn our Bayesian net means that once I know C I know everything I need to know to predict E. (Of course, A and B indirectly influence E, but once A and B have influenced C, there is no residual dependence left – this is the Markov condition at play.) Therefore

$$P(E|\tilde{D} \cap C \cap \tilde{B} \cap A) = P(E|C) \tag{8.24}$$

and Equation (8.23) simplifies to:

$$P(E \cap \tilde{D} \cap C \cap \tilde{B} \cap A) = P(E|\tilde{D} \cap C \cap \tilde{B} \cap A)P(\tilde{D} \cap C \cap \tilde{B} \cap A)$$
$$P(E|C)P(\tilde{D} \cap C \cap \tilde{B} \cap A) \tag{8.25}$$

The quantity $P(E|C)$ is known from our conditional probability table for E. So, we are left with the task of decomposing $P(\tilde{D} \cap C \cap \tilde{B} \cap A)$. We can play the same trick again:

$$P(\tilde{D} \cap C \cap \tilde{B} \cap A) = P(\tilde{D}|C \cap \tilde{B} \cap A)P(C \cap \tilde{B} \cap A) \tag{8.26}$$

Let us focus on $P(\tilde{D}|C \cap \tilde{B} \cap A)$. Looking at our Bayesian net it is clear that D only depends on B. Therefore

$$P(\tilde{D}|C \cap \tilde{B} \cap A) = P(\tilde{D}|\tilde{B}) \tag{8.27}$$

From the conditional probability table for D we have $P(D|\tilde{B})$. But we know that

$$P(D|\tilde{B}) + P(\tilde{D}|\tilde{B}) = 1 \Longrightarrow P(\tilde{D}|\tilde{B}) = 1 - P(D|\tilde{B}) \tag{8.28}$$

and therefore

$$P(\tilde{D} \cap C \cap \tilde{B} \cap A) = P(\tilde{D}|C \cap \tilde{B} \cap A)P(C \cap \tilde{B} \cap A) = P(\tilde{D}|\tilde{B})P(C \cap \tilde{B} \cap A) \quad (8.29)$$

Exercise 25 Complete the example above to show that

$$P(E \cap \tilde{D} \cap C \cap \tilde{B} \cap A)$$
$$= P(E|C)\, P(\tilde{D}|\tilde{B})P\left(C|\tilde{B} \cap A\right) P\left(\tilde{B}\right) P(A) \quad (8.30)$$

Exercise 26 Looking at Figure 8.4 state which variables have zero correlation.

8.7 A Systematic Approach

For the size of Bayesian nets that I propose to use for stress-testing purposes (i.e., five-to-ten well chosen variables) a 'manual' approach such as the one highlighted in the previous section may sometimes be sufficient. The procedure, however, soon becomes too tedious and time-consuming. This section provides an algorithm for a systematic derivation of the joint probabilities from the (marginal or conditional) probability tables.

By extending the line of reasoning we followed in the worked-out example presented in the previous section, we can write a general prescription for going from a Bayesian net and its associated conditional probability tables to the joint probabilities as follows. To do so I will make a minor modification to the notation used so far: instead of writing, say, $P(E_1 = w \cap E_2 = x \cap \ldots \cap E_{n-1} = y \cap E_n = z)$ with $w, x, y, z = T, F$, I will write $P(E_1 = e_1 \cap E_2 = e_2 \cap \ldots \cap E_{n-1} = e_{n-1} \cap E_n = e_n)$, $e_i = T, F$. This is simply because I may otherwise run out of letters of the alphabet, or lack a simple way to indicate the previous or following letter.

For n variables (and n nodes) a generic joint probability entry will therefore have the following form:

$$P(E_1 = e_1 \cap E_2 = e_2 \cap \ldots \cap E_{n-1} = e_{n-1} \cap E_n = e_n) \quad (8.31)$$

where the values, $e_1, e_2, \ldots, e_{n-1}, e_n$, which the variables $E_1, E_2, \ldots, E_{n-1}, E_n$ can assume, are T and F. If we have labelled ancestors and descendants in ascending order, the first step is to reorder the joint probability entry that we want to evaluate from descendants to ancestors:

$$P(E_1 = e_1 \cap E_2 = e_2 \cap \ldots \cap E_{n-1} = e_{n-1} \cap E_n = e_n)$$
$$= P(E_n = e_n \cap E_{n-1} = e_{n-1} \cap \ldots \cap E_2 = e_2 \cap E_1 = e_1) \quad (8.32)$$

Next we decompose as follows:

$$P(E_n = e_n \cap E_{n-1} = e_{n-1} \cap \ldots \cap E_2 = e_2 \cap E_1 = e_1)$$
$$= P(E_n = e_n|E_{n-1} = e_{n-1} \cap \ldots \cap E_2 = e_2 \cap E_1 = e_1)^*$$
$$P(E_{n-1} = e_{n-1} \cap \ldots \cap E_2 = e_2 \cap E_1 = e_1)$$

Let us consider the term in the third line:

$$P(E_{n-1} = e_{n-1} \cap \ldots \cap E_2 = e_2 \cap E_1 = e_1) \tag{8.33}$$

It is easy to see that the same strategy can be employed, progressively reducing the joint entry to a product of conditional and marginal probabilities:

$$P(E_{n-1} = e_{n-1} \cap \ldots \cap E_2 = e_2 \cap E_1 = e_1)$$
$$= P(E_{n-1} = e_{n-1} | E_{n-2} = e_{n-2} \cap \ldots \cap E_2 = e_2 \cap E_1 = e_1) *$$
$$P(E_{n-2} = e_{n-2} \cap \ldots \cap E_2 = e_2 \cap E_1 = e_1)$$

This is just the break-down-the-joint property in action. Continuing with the same approach, one can generalize to

$$P(E_1 = e_1 \cap E_2 = e_2 \cap \ldots \cap E_{n-1} = e_{n-1} \cap E_n = e_n)$$
$$= \prod_{i=1}^{n} P(E_i = e_i | E_{i-1} = e_{i-1} \cap \ldots \cap E_1 = e_1) \tag{8.34}$$

or, more synthetically,

$$P(E_1 = e_1 \cap E_2 = e_2 \cap \ldots \cap E_{n-1} = e_{n-1} \cap E_n = e_n)$$
$$= \prod_{i=1}^{n} P(E_i = e_i | \text{Parents of } E_i) \tag{8.35}$$

where the last line follows from the Markov assumption (and what this implies about conditional independence).

   One important observation: the joint probabilities can be 'solved' by the formula above once the marginal and conditional probability tables are provided. But where can the risk manager get *these* from? In particular, from where can the risk manager get a beast such as:

$$P(E_{n-1} = e_{n-1} | E_{n-2} = e_{n-2} \cap \ldots \cap E_2 = e_2 \cap E_1 = e_1) \tag{8.36}$$

even for a relatively tame case of, say, five or six variables? I will discuss in detail how to assign conditional probabilities in Chapter 11, but we can already see that it is a super-human feat to expect the risk manager to prescribe the conditional probability of event E_6, given that, say, event E_5 has happened, events E_4 and E_3 have not happened, event E_2 has happened and event E_1 has not happened. As I mentioned above, the answer to this question comes at the stage of the specification of the causal links among the variables. Much as the world might be a subtly complex place, we may want to restrict the universe of possible Bayesian (directed, acyclical) nets associated with n variables to a simpler 'approximating' subspace – see the discussion in the next section, which looks at the approximation problem from a different, and complementary, angle. For, instance, we may want to restrict our attention to children who can have at most two parents.

This simplifies the problem enormously, and brings it (close) to the cognitive abilities of someone as smart as a risk manager. As promised, more about this aspect in Chapter 11.

Exercise 27 Prove that, if a child can have at most two parents, then the conditional probabilities terms of the form $P(E_{n-1} = e_{n-1}|E_{n-2} = e_{n-2} \cap \ldots \cap E_2 = e_2 \cap E_1 = e_1)$ contain at most two events after the conditioning sign ($|$).

8.8 What Can We Do with Bayesian Nets?

Bayesian nets have a variety of applications. From the point of view of stress testing, they can be looked at from two different angles.

8.8.1 Unravelling the Causal Structure

If we had the joint probabilities, Bayesian nets could help us in clarifying which causal structure the underlying variables are likely to display. The idea is conceptually simple – if, at times, computationally complex. See Williamson (2005) for an excellent discussion. Let us denote the set of the true joint probabilities by $[p(i)]$.[11] As I said, when we look at Bayesian nets from this angle, we assume that we already have the joint probabilities. For computational tractability we then restrict our attention to a subset of Bayesian nets simpler than the most general possible one. For instance, we may restrict our search to Bayesian nets with nodes with at most two parents. The set of these nets, call it $\mathbb{S}_2$, is clearly a subset of the full set of possible Bayesian nets, $\mathbb{B}$. Any possible net in $\mathbb{S}_2$ (equipped with its conditional probability tables) will produce joint probabilities, $[p_{\mathbb{S}_2}(i)]$. When we try to unravel the causal structure, we want to establish the links between the nodes in our subset $\mathbb{S}_2$ in such a way that, in some sense, the probabilities $[p_{\mathbb{S}_2}(i)]$ are as close as possible to the probabilities $[p(i)]$. The terms 'links' refers to the topology of the Bayesian nets (which nodes are connected and in which direction the arrows point) and to the associated probability tables. In a way the topology of the net and the entries in the associated conditional probability tables are the degrees of freedom that we use to make our approximate joint probabilities, $[p_{\mathbb{S}_2}(i)]$, as close as possible to the true joint probabilities, $[p(i)]$. To give a precise meaning to the expression 'as close as possible' we have to define the distance between the two distributions, $\mathcal{D}[p_{\mathbb{S}}, p]$. This is often taken to be given by the cross-entropy measure between the two sets of probabilities (see Williamson (2005)):[12]

$$\mathcal{D}[p_{\mathbb{S}_2}, p] = \sum -p(i) \ln \frac{p(i)}{p_{\mathbb{S}_2}(i)} \tag{8.37}$$

What we want to achieve is the minimization of this distance. Doing this 'properly' is computationally very hard. There are, however, computational techniques, such as greedy algorithms, that provide good approximating joint probabilities, $[p_{\mathbb{S}_2}(i)]$, constructed using

---

[11]For simplicity, I neglect the possible difference between the true probabilities, and the probabilities that have been statistically estimated.

[12]As is well known, the cross-entropy distance is not a true distance because of its lack of symmetry: $\mathcal{D}[f, g] \neq \mathcal{D}[g, f]$. However, this measure shares the other two important properties of a distance, i.e., it is non-negative and is equal to zero if and only if $f = g$.

Bayesian nets in $\mathbb{S}_2$ to the target $[p(i)]$. Again, Williamson (2005) has a very good discussion.

Could we use this approach for stress testing? Probably not. My starting point in this book has been that establishing the tail co-dependence for rare and extremely rare events using frequentist methods is just too hard. This being the case, we do not have direct access to the joint distribution. A brave risk manager could perhaps proceed as follows. She could estimate the joint probabilities from the data at her disposal, hoping that the correlation (not co-dependence!) structure she estimates will be valid in the tails as well. She would then have access to $[p(i)]$. She could then use the techniques alluded to above to understand the causal structure among the variables in her problem. This means that she would be able to construct the Bayesian net in the chosen subset $\mathbb{S}_n$ that best accounts for the estimated probabilities $[p(i)]$. In itself this is extremely valuable. Doing so would also allow the risk manager to 'stress' the Bayesian net, say, by altering the conditional probability tables in such a way to reflect her understanding of the weaknesses of the estimated co-dependencies. This has a certain appeal, but as soon as the risk manager begins to tinker with the conditional probability tables, whatever optimality the net so painfully constructed might have enjoyed is lost.

Tempting as it is, I will not pursue this route in this book. The determined reader is strongly encouraged to read Williamson (2005), especially Chapter 4.

8.8.2   Estimating the Joint Probabilities

The line I take in this book is different, in that I attempt to estimate the joint probabilities given the Bayesian net. The treatment above is tailored to this task. The approach is, in a way, complementary to the one above, which assumed that we know everything about the joint probabilities, and nothing about the causal structure that generated them. For our problem, which leads from the marginal and conditional to the joint probabilities, we must throw at the problem everything we have: our understanding of which data are relevant to the problem at hand; our data-based (frequentist) information; our subjective estimates for the conditional probabilities; and our understanding of how the world might work. Or, more realistically and more in line with the thoughts expressed in Chapter 3, our awareness about how little we know about how the world works, and our understanding that different models of reality may be similarly plausible. Perhaps we may end up with two or three plausible Bayesian nets (and joint probabilities). Not a bad thing in itself.

In the following chapters I will explain more precisely how all these various components can be gathered. In particular, I assumed in this chapter that somehow we have at our disposal the conditional probabilities needed to fill the node-specific tables. But where do these come from? I discuss this in the next chapter.

One more important point: human intuition can be faulty when we deal with probabilistic matters in general, and with conditional probabilities in particular. Even when we have put in our best efforts it is therefore likely that the conditional probability matrix we have built will not be a 'feasible' one. In general we have to clean it, that is, create the feasible conditional matrix closest to the one we devised. This is dealt with in Chapters 9 and 10. Some of the tools we require are narrowly technical ones – for example, some rudiments of Linear Programming. However, I will show that a less systematic set of 'pre-cleansing' checks can both simplify the task and enhance our understanding of the problem. The reader who is familiar with Linear Programming can safely skip the pedestrian review in the Appendix in

Chapter 15, which is simply included to make the book self-contained. All readers should read carefully, however, Chapter 9.

8.9 Suggestions for Further Reading

The literature on Bayesian nets is very large, but only touches risk management in passing. In my treatment I have presented the simplest introduction for the task at hand. By doing so, I have left by the wayside many important definitions and concepts. My most glaring omission has been a proper discussion of *d*-separation. I have trusted that the reader can find the link between *d*-separation and conditional independence plausible, just by looking at which paths are blocked by certain nodes. One of the great advantages of Bayesian nets, after all, is their intuitional appeal, and I have decided to exploit this feature to the fullest. I have also avoided the very interesting and deep conceptual issues about causation and probability. For those readers who may want a more satisfactory treatment of these aspects, here are some suggestions.

A very good conceptual treatment of Bayesian nets in general can be found in Williamson (2005). Much of the emphasis of the book is unfortunately *from* the probabilities (which the author assumes exogenously available) *to* the discovery of the underlying net (and hence causal structure). This is the opposite direction to the one taken in this book. As a consequence, much of the numerical work (e.g., greedy algorithms, simulated annealing, etc.) has little relevance to our applications.

Pearl (2009) provides an excellent discussion of causality. His introductory chapter about probability, graphs and causal models uses a similar framework to the one employed in this book, and provides additional material (e.g., a deeper treatment of the *d*-separation criterion) that can be useful for more advanced applications. In keeping with the treatment I have followed, it focuses on the much simpler setting of a finite number of discrete variables. The book makes clear the link between probability and causation. Pearl's approach, which is deeply Bayesian in nature, also establishes a profound link between mathematical expressions (such as Bayes' theorem) and cognitive structures (see, e.g., his remarks on page 5).

For readers who want to delve much more deeply and rigorously into Bayesian networks, Neapolitan (2003) provides a very good and 'solid' reference – although not an easy-going one: one important theorem is stated over one page, and proved over five!

Chapter 9

Bayesian Nets II: Constructing Probability Tables

9.1 Statement of the Problem

The discussion in the previous chapters makes clear that there are three conceptual steps in building a Bayesian net:

1. Identification of the relevant variables.

2. Specification of a set of causal relationships among them (subject to the Markov condition) – this step defines the topology of the Bayesian net.

3. Provision of the marginal and conditional probability tables.[1]

In this chapter we deal with the third topic, that is, we answer the questions: how can we build the conditional probability tables needed to obtain the joint probabilities? What information can we use for the task?

The tables contain marginal and conditional probabilities. As far as the marginal probabilities are concerned, the task is in practice far from trivial, but at least it is mathematically relatively simple: as long as we ensure that

$$0 \leq P(E_i) \leq 1 \quad \text{for any } i \tag{9.1}$$

we can at least rest assured that we have not introduced any logical impossibilities into our problem. Far more care will be required when we specify the conditional probabilities, because of the many possible logical pitfalls into which it is possible – indeed, easy – to fall. In this chapter I present a series of conditions and sanity checks that the risk manager

---

[1]For brevity, in this chapter I often call conditional probability tables the collection of the conditional *and* *marginal* probabilities associated with each node.

can – and should – perform 'by hand'. In the next chapter I will then show how to carry out more sophisticated and 'automatic' checks (and corrections) for the conditional probability tables using the Linear Programming technique.

If these latter checks are more sophisticated and 'automatic', why should the risk manager bother with the manually intensive ones? Because they provide a powerful indication of whether we have been thinking correctly about the problem at hand. Finding preliminary inconsistencies forces us to review our assumptions about how the world works, and to ask ourselves whether we have coherently translated this assumed knowledge about the world into probabilistic statements. *I cannot stress how important and how useful this part of the process is.* It is not an exaggeration to say that the risk manager may well learn more about the structure and vulnerabilities of the portfolio under her watch through this process of sanity checking than by looking at the final outcome.

So, let us look in some detail at how to assign the entries of the conditional probability table, starting from the marginal probabilities (Sections 9.2 and 9.3 present two different suggestions as to how this can be done), and then moving on to the conditional probabilities (Sections 9.5 and 9.6).

9.2   Marginal Probabilities – First Approach

In order to arrive at marginal probabilities, I recommend that each risk manager should begin by looking at a given asset class (e.g., equities, IR, ABSs, etc.), and identifying the 'vulnerabilities' of the portfolio. These may come from large concentrations, from very volatile positions (currencies that may depeg) or from a combination of the two. Ideally, the vulnerability should be due to a set of tightly linked and well-identifiable risk factors.

Once the portfolio vulnerabilities have been identified, for the next step there are four quantities to be specified:

- the holding period;
- the magnitude of the adverse move in the risk factor;
- the magnitude of loss incurred;
- the probability of an adverse move of a given magnitude over the chosen holding period.

Obviously, these four quantities cannot be assigned independently of each other. But, strictly speaking, not even two of the quantities above cannot be arbitrarily assigned. We will see below why this is the case.

Remember that we are dealing with Boolean variables ('events'), which can be true or false. So, we must assign a probability to each variable being true or false, that is, a probability of occurrence to each event. We can do this by identifying the event with a loss of a given magnitude. So, when we look at the problem from this angle, the event could be 'We lose $100m from our position in 10-year Treasuries'. The event is true if the loss is incurred. When we look at the problem in this way, the final goal is therefore to be able to generate, for each vulnerable position, a pair of numbers, the magnitude of the associated loss and its probability – as defined more precisely below.

9.2.1 Starting from a Fixed Probability

One possible way to proceed is as follows:

1. For each position choose a holding period. This should be linked to the 'liquidation period', i.e., to the time it would take to exit the position. This exit time is clearly linked to the size of the position, but it also depends on market conditions. Since we are looking at stress events, one can assume conditions of market distress. How severe? We will come back to this point (possibly in an iterative fashion), but for the moment we go with the flow. So, the risk manager should establish the approximate length of the liquidation period of the vulnerable position, given its size and assuming that the market is in a condition of stress. To avoid, as usual, spurious precision it is useful to group the holding periods into standard buckets: say, 2 days, a week, a fortnight, a month, a quarter, etc.[2]

2. The risk manager can then choose for each vulnerable position an order-of-magnitude probability, say, 10^{-1}, 10^{-2}, 10^{-3}, 10^{-4}, etc. It is reasonable, but not always necessarily the best choice, to choose the same approximate probability for all the vulnerable positions. Speaking of probability raises the question: Probability of what? This becomes clear when the size of the adverse move is brought into play.

3. The risk manager can then ask the question: by how much can the risk factor(s) that affect a given vulnerable position move in an adverse manner with a probability not lower than the chosen one? For instance: suppose the vulnerable position is a long position in the S&P and the probability level chosen is 10^{-3}. Then the question should be: what is the size of a fall in the S&P over the holding period such that the probability of *exceeding* that fall is 10^{-3}?

4. Given the size of the fall (derived from the probability level and the holding period) the loss can now be calculated (approximately or exactly, if by full revaluation). Note that, since we have estimated the minimum *magnitude* of the move for the given probability level, the loss associated with that move is a lower bound for the loss that could be sustained.[3] By definition this quantity is therefore very closely related to the value-at-risk statistic (VaR) at the appropriate confidence level for that position and the relevant risk factors. The estimation of the move in the risk factor need not (but can, if the risk manager thinks it is appropriate) be arrived at using a frequentist approach.

I said that a reasonable starting point is for the risk manager to choose the same probability level for all the moves associated with the portfolio vulnerabilities. Sometimes, however, this may not be a good idea. Why may a risk manager want to choose different levels of

---

[2]Different liquidation periods can be accommodated as long as one makes the assumption that the different traders are not allowed to 'reload the gun' once the simultaneous unwinding of all the risk positions has begun.

The final result of the calculation, i.e., the conditional expected loss, therefore implictly refers to the loss that can be expected to be incurred if all the traders began unwinding their positions at the first occurrence of the stress event (whichever this may be), and were not allowed to take on more risky positions ('reload the gun') until the position with the longest unwinding period has been liquidated.

[3]I am implicitly assuming linear risk positions. Severe non-linearities would require a more precise specification of the range of moves, and of the associated probabilities.

probability? Suppose that a vulnerable position is a short gamma position. At the chosen level of probability the move in the risk factor may be not large enough to produce a sizeable loss. But for a bigger move (associated, of course, with a lower probability of exceedance) the losses could become truly massive. In this situation, it would be useful to capture the lower-probability event.

The attentive reader will have spotted that the four steps outlined above imply a degree of circularity in the reasoning. We started by choosing a holding period, which we set equal to the liquidation period. To determine the liquidation period we looked, of course, at the size of the vulnerable position. But we also assumed 'stressed market conditions'. How stressed? We could not know that when we chose the holding period, because we had not worked out the magnitude of the move. If we fix the probability, the magnitude of the price move is determined, but only at this point can we tell how stressed the market condition is – and therefore what the liquidation period should be. Since a quantity such as the liquidation period cannot be known with any precision, in practice this rarely causes problems, but it is useful to carry out a self-consistency check here. If necessary, the probability level should be changed, so as to bring about a magnitude in the adverse move roughly in line with the length of the liquidation period. This is another reason why the final probabilities associated with the various vulnerable positions may not end up being all the same.

9.2.2   Starting from a Fixed Magnitude of the Move

Even if we continue to consider the occurrence of a given loss from a set of positions as 'the event', the approach just described is not the only possible one:

1. Step 1 (choice of a holding period) is exactly as above.

2. The risk manager chooses the magnitude(s) of the move(s) in the risk factor(s). A reasonable choice is a severe, large, but plausible move.

3. Since the risk manager now already knows the magnitude of the move (because she has just chosen it), she can already estimate the magnitude of the loss.

4. Finally the risk manager should try to estimate the probability of a move at least as large as the one chosen in step 2 over the liquidation (holding) period determined in Step 1.

This approach may seem more natural, but note that the mild circularity in the approach has not disappeared. We have chosen the holding period first, without knowing the probability of the adverse move. The two items should be at least roughly consistent. Again, a sanity check (or, if needed, an iterative process) may be useful.

9.3   Marginal Probabilities – Second Approach

The approach to assigning marginal probabilities that I have described above implicitly takes the loss itself as the event. Saying 'loss', however, is not enough. I must also specify from which (set of) positions this loss originates. It is for this reason that in the example I gave above I defined my event as 'We lose $100m *from our position in 10-year Treasuries*'.

There is a problem with this approach. Suppose that I am long 10-year Treasuries. Then the loss will be incurred if the 10-year point of the yield curve increases. But if my 'event' is the loss itself, I cannot distinguish between different causes that may have given rise to the same rise in the yield curve: perhaps it happened because Bernanke suddenly raised rates; or perhaps because China began selling US Treasuries. If we are (very) smart we can perhaps specify a marginal probability that 'knows about' all the possible causes that have given rise to the increase in the yield curve. But *when it comes to assigning the conditional probabilities* knowing whether the increase in rates was due to Bernanke or to China will make a big difference.

To circumvent this problem I propose below a set of definitions that can work more efficiently.

I start by taking the word 'event' as primitive – that is, I do not try to define this term. Two examples of an event could be: 'Bernanke raises rates by 100 basis points', or 'Moody downgrades the sovereign debt of Italy'. Then I define the following.

- *Probability of an event*: This is the probability of the event happening between now and time T (the *occurrence horizon*). We could take $T = 2$ days.

- *Risk positions*: These are the risk positions directly affected by the occurrence of the event. (Say, a position in 10-year Treasuries with a PV01 of $2m/bp.)

- *Unwinding horizon*: This is the time that it will take the trader(s) to exit the **risk positions** in an efficient manner given that the event has occurred during the occurrence horizon (i.e., at any time between time 0 and time T).

- *Risk factors*: These are the risk factors that affect the **risk positions**.

- *Moves in the risk factors*: these are the expected moves over the **unwinding horizon** in the risk factor(s) as a consequence of the occurrence of the event. For our example, we say that the event ('Bernanke raises rates by 100 basis points') will cause the 10-year yield to increase by 60 basis points.

- *Event-related loss*: This is the loss incurred because of the **moves in the risk factors**. In our case, the loss would be $120m ($2m/bp × 60bp).

In the definitions above, I use italic for words and expressions when first defined and bold when used as defined. So, the expression **moves in the risk factors** in the definition of event-related loss, means the *expected* moves over the **unwinding horizon** in the risk factor(s) as a consequence of the occurrence of the event.

Note the difference between the occurrence horizon and the unwinding horizon. The first is the 'surprise time' or the time between now and when I can begin to take action. It may be one day, or two or three days in the case of weekends. The second is the time it will take me to get out of the position 'in an efficient manner' given that the event has happened. The qualifier 'in an efficient manner' reflects the fact that no trader, even if determined to exit a position, will unwind it immediately at any cost, but will try to strike a compromise between exiting quickly and allowing the market to 'digest' her inventory.

Note also that, when I came to define the moves in the risk factors, I had to speak of expected moves. This is because I do not know by how much the 10-year point of the curve will move if Bernanke raises the short rate by 100 basis points.[4] In the example above, 60 basis points is my estimate of the expected increase in rates. Using the expected increase is reasonable, but not the only possible choice. If I were (very) brave, instead of 'the expected move' I could try to say something like 'the XXth percentile move in the 10-year point of the curve given that the event has happened'. However, this is something far more precise than I will ever feel able to express. If I wanted to be conservative, I could perhaps say something like 'a very adverse, but plausible, move in the 10-year point of the curve given that the event has happened'. This already sounds a bit better, but precision, as usual, is not the issue here.

9.4   Handling Events of Different Probability

The discussion above has highlighted that there are several reasons why we may want to associate probabilities of very different magnitude to the vulnerable positions we have identified. As a result of this, we need a way to handle events that, while being rare, can be of substantially different degrees of 'rarity'. To do this we can first categorize the marginal probabilities of each event into groups ('blocks') of roughly equal magnitude:

$$P(E_i) \simeq \eta * k^{m_i} \tag{9.2}$$

where i denotes the event and η is a 'small' reference probability, say, 10^{-2}.

Taking logs (in the chosen basis, k)

$$\log_k [P(E_i)] = \log[\eta] + m_i \tag{9.3}$$

A choice for the basis, k, for the logarithm of ten is reasonable: working in basis two (or using natural logarithms) would require too much knowledge about the marginal probabilities that we can reasonably expect to have for stress events. Basis five may be more reasonable, but we do not have a great intuition about increases in probability by a factor of five. In the future I will therefore always assume a basis of ten unless I say otherwise, but nothing hangs on the choice.

It is then useful to set

$$m_i \in [-M, -M+1, \ldots, -1, 0, 1, \ldots, M-1, M] \tag{9.4}$$

For practical applications (and base ten) a reasonable value for M is 1 or 2. So, with the first choice we partition the rare events into three groups, those of a reference small probability (for which m_i is 0), those with probability ten times larger (for which m_i is 1) and those with probabilities ten times smaller (for which m_i is -1). Similarly for $M = 2$.

So, to each event, E_i, we associate an exponent, m_i, which determines its (approximate) marginal probability, $P(E_i)$. What we are trying to do here is to group events into blocks of similar (and similarly small) probability. Both the widening of credit spreads by 300 bp and the default of a major bank counterparty are events of low probabilities (and, potentially,

---

[4]This is the drawback of not taking the loss as the event. On the other hand, when we took the loss as the event we had to speak of losses of, say, '$100m *or greater*'. As the attentive reader will notice, definitional problems can be moved around, but they rarely wholly disappear.

interesting stress events); but the default of a major bank counterparty is almost certainly much less likely than the widening of credit spreads. (Do you agree? Why – or why not?) These two events should therefore belong to different probability blocks.

When we move to conditional probabilities we shall see how this exponent grouping comes in very handy.

9.5 Conditional Probabilities: A Reasonable Starting Point

If we want a reasonable starting point in our construction of a conditional probability matrix, and we are not too sure where to begin, we can always remember that

$$\frac{P\left(E_i|E_j\right)}{P\left(E_j|E_i\right)} = \frac{P\left(E_i\right)}{P\left(E_j\right)} \tag{9.5}$$

Therefore, for all events in probability blocks i and j a reasonable starting point could be

$$\frac{P\left(E_i|E_j\right)}{P\left(E_j|E_i\right)} = 10^{(m_i - m_j)} \tag{9.6}$$

From the relationship above it is also obvious that the marginal and conditional probabilities cannot be assigned independently of each other. For n events there are n compatibility relationships

$$P\left(E_i\right) = \frac{P\left(E_i|E_j\right)}{P\left(E_j|E_i\right)} P\left(E_j\right) = 10^{(m_i - m_j)} P\left(E_j\right) \tag{9.7}$$

If this sanity check does not hold, we should rethink how we have estimated either our marginal or our conditional probabilities, or both.

To make progress recall the definition of the quantity x_i^k that I gave in Chapter 5, Sections 5.9 and 5.10:

$$P\left(E_i|E_j\right) \equiv P\left(E_i\right) x_i^j \tag{9.8}$$

This quantity gives by how much we can modify (increase or decrease) the probability of event E_i, given our knowledge that event E_j has happened.

Now, recall that we are dealing with stress events, and that their marginal probability is low to start with. This imposes serious constraints on the conditional probabilities. Let us look into this more precisely.

First of all, the most common mistake in assigning conditional probabilities is to express the intuitive idea that knowledge that event E_j has happened has no influence on our estimate of the occurrence of event E_j by assigning $P\left(E_i|E_j\right) = 0$. This mistake is common for risk managers who are accustomed to working with correlation matrix. But, of course, as we saw before saying that $P\left(E_i|E_j\right) = 0$ means that event E_i cannot occur, given that we know that event E_j has occurred. This is just the sort of incompatibility condition that we discussed in Chapter 5.

So, if we want to say that events E_i and E_j are independent we must set

$$P\left(E_i|E_j\right) \equiv P\left(E_i\right) \tag{9.9}$$

and therefore

$$x_i^j = 1 \tag{9.10}$$

If we want to say that knowledge that event E_j has happened *decreases* our estimate of the probability of occurrence of event E_i, then we have to set

$$x_i^j < 1 \tag{9.11}$$

And, of course, x_i^j can be reduced all the way to 0, which, as discussed above, corresponds to the case of incompatibility.

If we want to say that knowledge that event E_j has happened *increases* our estimate of the probability of occurrence of event E_i, then we have to set

$$x_i^j > 1 \tag{9.12}$$

By how much can we increase x_i^j? All probabilities (conditional or otherwise) must be smaller or equal to one. Therefore

$$P\left(E_i|E_j\right) \equiv P\left(E_i\right) x_i^j \leq 1 \Longrightarrow x_i^j \leq \frac{1}{\max\left[P(E_i), P(E_j)\right]} \tag{9.13}$$

So

$$0 \leq x_i^j \leq \frac{1}{\max\left[P(E_i), P(E_j)\right]} \tag{9.14}$$

As explained in Chapter 5, it is difficult to give a precise estimate of how much knowledge that event E_j has happened increases or decreases our estimate of the probability of occurrence of event E_i. It can therefore be useful to require that x_i^j should assume one of a limited range of possible values, say:

$$x_i^j \in \left[\varepsilon, 0.1, 1, 10, (1-\varepsilon)\frac{1}{\max\left[P(E_i), P(E_j)\right]}\right] \tag{9.15}$$

where ε is a very small, but strictly positive, quantity.[5] Note that, by doing so, we are refraining from imposing either absolute incompatibility or deterministic causation. The courageous risk manager can, of course, always set $\varepsilon = 0$.[6]

---

[5]In the denominator, we have $\max[P(E_i), P(E_j)]$ rather than $P(E_i)$ in order to preserve the symmetry of the matrix x_i^j (which is a mathematical requirement), and to ensure that neither conditional probability will be greater than one (also a mathematical requirement).

[6]In order to facilitate the cognitive task of the risk manager, she could be asked whether, in her opinion, the occurrence of event E_j (i) makes event E_i almost certain; (ii) has virtually no impact on the probability of the

This approach to setting conditional probabilities is extremely useful in avoiding logical pitfalls – and these pitfalls are particularly insidious when we deal with very small marginal probabilities.

There is another important advantage. The matrix of elements $P\left(E_i|E_j\right)$ is, of course, not symmetric. The risk manager must therefore assign $n^2 - n$ elements, linked by $\left(n^2 - n\right)/2$ Bayes condition. But the matrix of elements x_i^j is symmetric and the risk manager must only assign $\left(n^2 - n\right)/2$ elements. The quantities x_i^j are fewer in number, and cognitively much easier to assign – the latter property deriving from the fact that they automatically do the Bayesian book-keeping for us, and help in correcting for the baseline bias that I will discuss in Chapter 12 (in particular, in Section 12.4).

9.6 Conditional Probabilities: Checks and Constraints

In this section I assume that the marginal and conditional probabilities have already been estimated and assigned to the appropriate probability buckets as described above. I will also assume that we have chosen the precision in our probability estimates (the width of our log bucket) literally to be one order of magnitude, that is, a factor of ten. If you feel more courageous, and you feel you can specify marginal probabilities of very rare events much more precisely, first of all I would like to hear how you do it, but then there is nothing stopping you from substituting your chosen basis k for my humble ten.

What we want to achieve in the rest of this section is to provide as much help as possible in ensuring that the conditional probabilities we have assigned are not inconsistent. This help will come from the mathematical requirements we must impose if we want the numbers we assign to be *bona fide* potential probabilities, and, in some cases, from our supposed knowledge about the problem at hand (e.g., from our assumption about independence, etc.).

9.6.1 Necessary Conditions

Needless to say, for any two events, E_i and E_j, it must be that

$$0 \leq P\left(E_i|E_j\right) \leq 1 \tag{9.16}$$

This seems too obvious to be worth mentioning. But consider the following events and tentatively assigned probabilities:[7]

- event E_1: equity market crash by 20% or more;
- event E_2: widening of AA credit spreads by 100 bp or more;
- $P(E_1) = 0.09\%$;
- $P(E_2) = 0.05\%$;
- $P(E_2|E_1) = 70\%$.

---

occurrence of E_i; or (iii) makes the occurrence of event E_i almost impossible. Factors x_i^j of $(1 - \varepsilon) \frac{1}{\max[P(E_i), P(E_j)]}$, 1 or ε would be associated with options (i), (ii) or (iii), respectively.

[7]This example has been adapted from Moskowitz and Sarin (1983).

Prima facie these assignments may seem plausible: we may or may not agree with the risk manager's assessment, but there does not seem to be anything 'impossible' in the numbers provided. A moment's reflection, however, shows that we have already violated the 'obvious' constraint coming from Bayes' theorem (9.16): because

$$P(E_2|E_1)P(E_1) = P(E_1|E_2)P(E_2) \tag{9.17}$$

it must be that

$$P(E_1|E_2) = P(E_2|E_1)\frac{P(E_1)}{P(E_2)} = 0.7 * \frac{0.0009}{0.0005} = 1.26 \tag{9.18}$$

But this cannot be, because a conditional probability, *qua* probability, must be smaller or equal to 1. Therefore a useful entry-level check should be that

$$P(E_1|E_2) \leq \frac{P(E_2)}{P(E_1)} \tag{9.19}$$

This is useful, but with a little more effort, we can do better.

9.6.2   Triplet Conditions

We have events E_i for $i = 1, 2, \ldots, n$. The starting point is the usual, that is, some rearrangement of Bayes' theorem, this time in the following form:

$$\frac{P\left(E_i|E_j\right)}{P\left(E_j|E_i\right)} = \frac{P\left(E_i\right)}{P\left(E_j\right)} \tag{9.20}$$

Using the fact exploited above that all conditional probabilities must be non-negative and smaller or equal to one, we can easily determine the following constraint (**Constraint Triplets**) among the conditional and marginal probabilities:

$$P\left(E_i|E_j\right) = P\left(E_j|E_i\right)\frac{P\left(E_i\right)}{P\left(E_j\right)} = P\left(E_j|E_i\right)\frac{P\left(E_i\right)P\left(E_k\right)}{P\left(E_k\right)P\left(E_j\right)} \Longrightarrow$$

$$1 \geq P\left(E_j|E_i\right)\frac{P\left(E_i|E_k\right)}{P\left(E_k|E_i\right)}\frac{P\left(E_k|E_j\right)}{P\left(E_j|E_k\right)} \geq 0 \text{ for } i \neq j \neq k \tag{9.21}$$

where, again, the double inequality in the second line follows because the first term in the first line $(P\left(E_i|E_j\right))$ must be a *bona fide* probability.

We have six combinations of $P\left(E_i|E_j\right)$ for $i \neq j$. **Constraint Triplets** shows that, given the conditional probabilities of five combinations, the sixth $(P\left(E_i|E_j\right))$ is uniquely determined (and, of course, must be smaller than or equal to 1 and non-negative). A simple routine can easily be written that returns all the inconsistent triplets, and allows the risk manager to make changes accordingly.

We note in passing that setting $P\left(E_i|E_j\right) = P\left(E_j|E_i\right)$ would ensure that **Constraint Triplets** is automatically satisfied for any triplet. But this is in general not a good place to start – the probability of a general equity market crash given a widening in the credit spread of firm X can be very different from the probability of a widening in the credit spread of firm X given a general equity market crash.

9.6.3 Independence

The sanity checks introduced so far apply to any form of dependence among the underlying Boolean variables. We now want to see what additional conditions we can establish if we are prepared to say something about the causal links among the variables – or lack thereof. We want to see, in other words, what we can say about the conditional probabilities in the case of independence, conditional independence, deterministic causation and incompatibility.

If you think that events E_i and E_j are independent it follows that

$$P\left(E_i|E_j\right) = P\left(E_i\right) \quad \text{(independence)}$$

Then

$$P\left(E_i, E_j\right) = P\left(E_i\right) P\left(E_j\right) \simeq 10^{-\left(m_i+m_j\right)} \tag{9.22}$$

and

$$P\left(E_i|E_j\right) \simeq 10^{-m_i}, P\left(E_j|E_i\right) \simeq 10^{-m_j}$$

In the case of independence the risk manager should therefore make herself happy that the singly-conditioned probabilities are the same as the marginal probabilities, and that the joint probability, $P(E_i, E_j)$, is just given by the product of the two marginals.

9.6.4 Deterministic Causation

If you think that A deterministically causes B, then $P(B) \geq P(A)$. This must be true, because every time A happens B happens as well, but there may be other events that cause B. So, as a first check, one should make sure that the grouping into blocks is compatible with this. If not, then either our assumed causation or our initial grouping into blocks must be wrong. Needless to say, imposing deterministic causation is a very strong constraint, which should not be imposed lightly.

If we are really confident about our understanding of the causal links problem at hand, then in the case of deterministic causation

$$P\left(E_i|E_j\right) = 1 \tag{9.23}$$

So

$$P\left(E_j|E_i\right) = \frac{P\left(E_j\right)}{P\left(E_i\right)} \simeq 10^{\left(m_j-m_i\right)} \text{ with } m_i \geq m_j \tag{9.24}$$

This condition looks identical to Equation (9.22). Note, however, that we now have a restriction ($m_i \geq m_j$) on the relative magnitude of the exponents that was absent in the case of independence.

So, a good way to check the reasonableness of deterministic causal links is to look at the events as they have been grouped into blocks. An event E_i can be considered as a potential deterministic cause for event E_j only if $m_i \leq m_j$.

What else does deterministic causation imply about conditional probabilities? Consider again the Venn diagram in the case of causation when i causes j. It readily follows that

$$\frac{P\left(E_i \cap E_j\right)}{P\left(E_j\right)} \leq \frac{P\left(E_i \cap E_j\right)}{P\left(E_i\right)} \tag{9.25}$$

But therefore a necessary condition for causation (i causes j) is that

$$P\left(E_j|E_i\right) \leq P\left(E_i|E_j\right) \tag{9.26}$$

9.6.5   Incompatibility of Events

If you believe that E_i and E_j are incompatible, then

$$P\left(E_i|E_j\right) = P\left(E_j|E_i\right) = 0$$

Just like deterministic causation, incompatibility is a very strong statement. Again, you must feel very sure about your knowledge of how the world works to invoke incompatibility. I recommend that, to avoid closing doors that should be left gently ajar, it is always advisable to set

$$P\left(E_i|E_j\right) = P\left(E_j|E_i\right) = 10^{-K} \text{ with } K \gg 1 \tag{9.27}$$

If, however, you really want to impose the requirement that two events, E_i and E_j, should be mutually incompatible, there are severe constraints on the other conditional probabilities. First, let us make use of the identity

$$P\left(E_i \cup E_j|E_k\right) = P\left(E_i|E_k\right) + P\left(E_j|E_k\right) - P\left(E_i \cap E_j|E_k\right) \tag{9.28}$$

(where $\cup$ and $\cap$ indicate union and intersection, respectively).

Exercise 28 Prove the relationship $P\left(E_i \cup E_j|E_k\right) = P\left(E_i|E_k\right) + P\left(E_j|E_k\right) - P\left[E_i \cap E_j|E_k\right]$ making use of Venn diagrams.

Now, if $P\left(E_i|E_j\right) = P\left(E_j|E_i\right) = 0$, it follows that $P\left(E_i \cup E_j|E_k\right) = P\left(E_i|E_k\right) + P\left(E_j|E_k\right)$.

Exercise 29 Making use of Venn diagrams again, prove the relationship $P\left(E_i \cup E_j|E_k\right) = P\left(E_i|E_k\right) + P\left(E_j|E_k\right)$ for incompatible E_i and E_j.

For all other events E_k, $k \neq i$, j, from Equation (9.28) it must therefore hold that

$$P\left[E_i \cap E_j | E_k\right] = 0 \tag{9.29}$$

Therefore (**Constraint Zeros**)

$$P\left(E_i | E_k\right) + P\left(E_j | E_k\right) = P\left[E_i \cup E_j | E_k\right] \leq 1 \tag{9.30}$$

A simple routine can be written to identify violations of this inequality for any zero conditional probability in the conditional probability matrix that the risk manager may want to assign.

9.7 Internal Compatibility of Conditional Probabilities: The Need for a Systematic Approach

The sanity checks I have suggested in the previous section can 'cure' the most glaring incompatibilities and impossibilities. If we have assigned the conditional probabilities making use of the quantities x_i^j it is more likely that our starting point for the conditional probability matrix was not too bad to begin with. Even so, if the conditional probabilities we have assigned were not obtained from the statistical analysis of data, but came from our expert subjective judgement, it is virtually unavoidable that, even after the cleansing above, the resulting conditional probability matrix will still contain subtler embedded logical impossibilities. These subtler 'impossibilities' are virtually impossible to spot 'by the naked eye'.

The next chapter will therefore deal with a systematic method to 'correct' the conditional probability matrix supplied by the risk manager. In short, for a conditional probability matrix to be admissible, we will have to ensure that there exists a set of marginal probabilities from which these conditionals can all be simultaneously derived. When this is not the case the algorithm provided in the next chapter will return the conditional probability matrix 'closest' (in some sense to be defined) to the one chosen by the risk manager.

Note that it would be a mistake to dispense with the sanity checks described in this chapter, and fast forward directly to the systematic solution that I describe in Chapter 10. This 'automatic' procedure will, in fact, return the closest feasible solution to the proposed one, but 'closest' will only be truly 'close' to our starting point if this was reasonable and well thought-out in the first place.

Part III

Applications

Chapter 10

Obtaining a Coherent Solution I: Linear Programming

10.1 Plan of the Work Ahead

The two chapters in Part III show how to apply the concepts and techniques introduced in Part II to stress-testing problems.

In Chapter 9 I discussed a series of 'manual' sanity checks to ensure the consistency of the marginal and conditional probabilities assigned by the risk manager. By themselves, these checks do not in general guarantee that the set of assigned probabilities will be self-consistent, but they do serve two important purposes.

First, they ensure that the search for the consistent solution we undertake in this chapter will start from a plausible set of initial conditions. As a result, we can hope that the 'optimal' solution returned by the Linear Programming algorithm will be close to what the risk manager actually 'meant'.

Second, and more important, the sanity checks force the risk manager to question the assumptions made, and to reason more clearly about assumed dependencies. I cannot stress strongly enough the importance and usefulness of this part of the process.

In this chapter I assume that all this groundwork has been carried out, and I will present the first systematic solution to the programme started in the previous chapters – where by 'solution' I mean a set of internally consistent conditional probabilities as close as possible to the risk manager's intuition. I will also discuss what we can do with this information – that is, what information about the problem at hand we can extract from the solution.

In the next chapter I will then show what we can do if the risk manager feels able to provide the full set of marginal and conditional probabilities, that is, the conditional probability tables associated with each mode. These conditional probability tables can yield much richer fruits if we are prepared to add to them our tentative understanding of how the world works – that is, of the causal links among the chosen variables. See, in this respect, the discussion in Sections 4.3 and 4.4.

Which approach is better? It depends on how confident the risk manager feels about the probabilistic and causal infromation she must supply. At one end of the confidence spectrum the risk manager may think that the marginal probabilities are, for very rare events, too difficult to estimate, and that she can only venture a guess at

- singly-conditioned probabilities;
- the relative likelihood of the stand-alone events.

If that is the case, then the approach presented in this chapter is the suggested route. The main task faced by the risk manager will then be to ensure consistencies among the set of conditional probabilities provided.

At the opposite end of the confidence spectrum, the risk manager may feel confident (bold enough?) to provide

- the marginal probabilities of all the individual stress events (or at least their orders of magnitude);
- the associated n-conditioned probabilities;
- the causal links among the variables at play.

When the risk manager feels confident that she can provide this degree of information, the approach presented in Chapter 11 is much more powerful, and yields richer results. This approach is directly based on the Bayesian-nets technology (and on the bounding techniques described in Chapter 7).

How confident can a risk manager be? Clearly, it is not realistic to expect anybody to be able to provide even an informed guess for a quantity such as, say, $P(E_1 = x_1 | E_2 = x_2 \cap E_3 = x_3 \cap \ldots \cap E_n = x_n)$, with $x_i = T, F$, for n larger than, say, 3 (i.e., for more-than-doubly-conditioned probabilities). However, if we are prepared to restrict the set of possible Bayesian nets underlying the problem (i.e., if we are prepared to simplify the causal structure among the underlying variables), dramatic simplifications can result. When these simplifications are acceptable, the full joint probability structure can be determined. This will be an approximation to the 'true' and latent set of joint probabilities. If we have been clever, it will be a close approximation to the true joint probabilities chosen from the set of joint probabilities that can be derived by the simplified Bayesian net structure that we have allowed. I will use some concrete examples to show how this can be achieved.

Between these two extremes (total ignorance of marginal probabilities and full knowledge of the marginal, n-conditioned probabilities and causal links required by the Bayesian net structure that we have chosen), there lies a full spectrum of intermediate states of probabilistic knowledge. Sometimes – actually, quite often – the risk manager will feel able to assign most marginal probability, many singly-conditioned probabilities and perhaps a handful of doubly-conditioned probabilities. In this situation the bounds determined in Chapter 7 can be extremely useful.

It must be stressed that, as long as we are well aware of what we can and what we cannot know, all these different degrees of knowledge provide useful risk-management information. Richer information is not always necessarily better, though – especially if one forgets the assumptions that have gone into obtaining the results. Even the simple identification of the stand-alone stress scenarios and of the associated losses with no probabilistic information at all can serve a very important and useful role – say, of raising awareness. Admittedly, it may well be difficult to associate capital to this probability-free information, but awareness and qualitative appreciation of danger is a valuable part of managing risk.

If, on the other hand, we feel that we can build the required joint probabilities – and we are confident that, given the rarity of the events, they 'make sense' – we have the fullest possible probabilistic information about the stress events at hand. With this information we can estimate all sorts of risk statistics associated with these stress events (expected loss, variance of loss, higher moments of the loss distribution, Value at Risk, Conditional Expected Shortfall, you name it).

And, of course, if we believe that we know how to associate capital (regulatory or economic) to losses at a given percentile level, we can calculate internal or regulatory capital, estimate return after adjusting for tail risk (tail-risk-adjusted return) and do all kinds of marvellous things. This is particularly relevant in these post-subprime-crisis days, because some banks have begun to build their Economic Capital directly from analysis of stress events, rather than by reading impossibly high percentiles of profit-and-loss distributions obtained using frequentist methods.

If, in addition to joint probabilties, we can offer a possible set of causal links among the stand-alone events, our understanding will be greatly enhanced. Moving from an associative to a causal description allows us to 'understand' the problem in a much deeper and cognitively more resonant manner. It also allows us to deal with changes in the causal dependence much more easily and constructively. See again the dicussion in Section 4.4, and the example about the sprinkler and wet pavement in particular.

These are indeed marvellous things, but we should never get carried away and convince ourselves that we can know more than we actually can. As Keynes said: Sometimes, 'we simply don't know'.[1]

10.2 Coherent Solution with Conditional Probabilities Only

In this section I formulate the problem at hand (finding a set of self-consistent conditional probabilities) in a way that lends itself to be solved by Linear Programming. The reader can find a simple description of the Linear Programming technique in the Appendix in Chapter 15.

We assume that the risk manager has at least provided a 'cleansed' matrix of singly-conditional probabilities – where by 'cleansed' I mean that all the manual sanity checks have been carried out. This is the minimal requirement to obtain some useful quantitative output from the analysis. The approach presented below can also be used if the risk manager can provide some or all of the marginal probabilities and some of the more-highly conditioned

---

[1]Robertson (1936): see the quote that opens Chapter 1.

probabilities. If she can, correspondingly richer and more comprehensive output can be generated (see Sections 9.3 and 9.4).

In all these cases, our goal is then to ensure that the set of conditional (and, if applicable, marginal) probabilities provided are internally consistent. By this I mean that there should exist at least one set of joint probabilities from which the exogenously supplied conditional (or, if applicable, marginal) probabilities could have been derived.

The general methodology consists in checking the exogenously assigned probabilities for consistency, and until consistency is proven we allow the conditional probabilities to be moved within a widening range of values. The specific tool we employ for the task is the (Revised) Simplex Method applied to Linear Programming described in the Appendix. At each iteration the algorithm suggests a consistent solution, and at any time this solution can be accepted (even if it is outside the current range).

The formulation is as follows.[2] To each of the stress events we associate an indicator variable, $I_i, i = 1, 2, \ldots, N$, where $I_i = 1$ if event E_i occurs, and $I_i = 0$ otherwise. As we know, for two-valued Boolean random functions, there are 2^N mutually exclusive and exhaustive joint events corresponding to the distinct combinations of the set of indicators I_is. We signify any given combination of I_is by the vector $\boldsymbol{I}$, and the set of all $\boldsymbol{I}$s by $\mathcal{I}$. To each vector $\boldsymbol{I}$ (i.e., to each possible combination of occurrence or non-occurrence for the events E_i) we associate a probability $p[\boldsymbol{I}]$.

In order for any set of proposed conditional probabilities, $P\left(E_i|E_j\right)$, to be *consistent* there must exist (at least) one set of $p[\boldsymbol{I}]$ of joint probabilities with

$$\sum_{\boldsymbol{I} \in \mathcal{I}} p[\boldsymbol{I}] = 1 \tag{10.1}$$

$$1 \le p[\boldsymbol{I}] \ge 0 \tag{10.2}$$

and such that the corresponding conditional probabilities (for conditioning on a single event) are given by

$$P\left(E_i|E_j\right) = \frac{P\left(E_i \cap E_j\right)}{P\left(E_j\right)} = \frac{\sum \boldsymbol{I}:\{I_i=1, I_j=1\} \, p[\boldsymbol{I}]}{\sum \boldsymbol{I}:\{I_j=1\} \, p[\boldsymbol{I}]} \tag{10.3}$$

Similarly, any set of doubly-conditioned probabilities, $P\left(E_i|E_j, E_k\right)$, are said to be *consistent* if there exists (at least) one set of $p[\boldsymbol{I}]$ of joint probabilities satisfying the same conditions (10.1) and (10.2) and such that the corresponding conditional probabilities (for double-conditioning) are given by

$$P\left(E_i|E_j, E_k\right) = \frac{P\left(E_i \cap \left(E_j \cap E_k\right)\right)}{P\left(E_j \cap E_k\right)} = \frac{\sum \boldsymbol{I}:\{I_i=1, I_j=1.., I_k=1\} \, p[\boldsymbol{I}]}{\sum \boldsymbol{I}:\{I_j=1, I_k=1\} \, p[\boldsymbol{I}]} \tag{10.4}$$

Finally, we can also define marginal probabilities to be *consistent* if they can be derived from joint probabilities satisfying the same conditions (10.1) and (10.2) and such that they

---

[2]The following treatment is based on Kwiatkowski and Rebonato (2010).

can be expressed in terms of the joint probabilities $p[I]$ as follows:

$$P(E_i) = \sum_{I:\{I_i=1\}} p[I] \tag{10.5}$$

For the sake of clarity, it is useful to reproduce again the matrix shown in Section 6.2. For $n = 3$ the matrix has the following representation:

$$
\begin{array}{ccccc}
 & E_1 & E_2 & E_3 & \\
J_1 & 1 & 0 & 0 & p(1) \\
J_2 & 0 & 1 & 0 & p(2) \\
J_3 & 0 & 0 & 1 & p(3) \\
J_4 & 1 & 1 & 0 & p(4) \\
J_5 & 1 & 0 & 1 & p(5) \\
J_6 & 0 & 1 & 1 & p(6) \\
J_7 & 1 & 1 & 1 & p(7) \\
J_8 & 0 & 0 & 0 & p(8) \\
\end{array}
\tag{10.6}
$$

So, an expression such as $\sum_{I:\{I_2=1\}} p[I]$ indicates the sum of all the probabilities for which $I_2 = 1$, i.e., it gives $P(E_2)$. In our case this means $p(2) + p(4) + p(6) + p(7)$. An expression such as $\sum_{I:\{I_1=1,I_j=2\}} p[I]$ indicates the sum of all the probabilities for which both $I_1 = 1$ *and* $I_2 = 1$ (i.e., $P(E_1 \cap E_2)$). For the matrix above this means $p(4) + p(7)$. So, the conditional probability $P(E_1|E_2)$ is given by

$$P(E_1|E_2) = \frac{\sum_{I:\{I_1=1,I_j=2\}} p[I]}{\sum_{I:\{I_2=1\}} p[I]} = \frac{p(4) + p(7)}{p(2) + p(4) + p(6) + p(7)} \tag{10.7}$$

Let us go back to the optimization problem. Any proposed set of marginal and/or conditional probabilities proposed on the basis of expert subjective judgement by a risk manager is very unlikely to be internally consistent. We therefore allow the marginal and conditional probabilities to lie anywhere between upper and lower limits, $P^{\pm}(\cdot)$, as follows:

$$P^{\pm}(E_i) \text{ for the marginal probabilities} \tag{10.8}$$

$$P^{\pm}(E_i|E_j) \text{ for the conditional probabilities} \tag{10.9}$$

$$P^{\pm}(E_i|E_j, E_k) \text{ for the doubly-conditioned probabilities} \tag{10.10}$$

These upper and lower limits reflect a confidence tolerance, and can be specified by the risk manager. They will be used to introduce the inequality constraints needed for the Linear Programming approach we intend to employ. Let us look again at Equation (10.5):

$$P(E_i) = \sum_{I:\{I_i=1\}} p[I] \implies P(E_i) - \sum_{I:\{I_i=1\}} p[I] = 0 \tag{10.11}$$

From our definition of upper and lower limits, it therefore follows that, for each event E_i,

$$P^+ (E_i) - \sum_{\mathbf{I}:\{I_i=1\}} p[\mathbf{I}] \geq 0 \tag{10.12}$$

$$P^- (E_i) - \sum_{\mathbf{I}:\{I_i=1\}} p[\mathbf{I}] \leq 0 \tag{10.13}$$

What we are saying here is that, on the basis of our expert judgement, we have assigned to event E_i a marginal probability $P(E_i)$. We are not too sure about this value, however, and we would not be too unhappy if the marginal probability were anywhere between $P^-(E_i)$ and $P^+(E_i)$.

We can follow the same approach for the conditional probabilities. Look back at Equation (10.3):

$$P(E_i|E_j) = \frac{P(E_i \cap E_j)}{P(E_j)} = \frac{\sum_{\mathbf{I}:\{I_i=1,I_j=1\}} p[\mathbf{I}]}{\sum_{\mathbf{I}:\{I_j=1\}} p[\mathbf{I}]} \tag{10.14}$$

We can rearrange it as

$$P(E_i|E_j) \sum_{\mathbf{I}:\{I_j=1\}} p[\mathbf{I}] = \sum_{\mathbf{I}:\{I_i=1,I_j=1\}} p[\mathbf{I}] \tag{10.15}$$

Replacing the upper and lower limits, $P^\pm (E_i|E_j)$, for $P(E_i|E_j)$ we therefore have for each i and j, the two inequalities (linear constraints)

$$P^-(E_i|E_j) \sum_{\mathbf{I}:\{I_j=1\}} P[\mathbf{I}] - \sum_{\mathbf{I}:\{I_i=1,I_j=1\}} P[\mathbf{I}] \leq 0 \tag{10.16}$$

and

$$P^+(E_i|E_j) \sum_{\mathbf{I}:\{I_j=1\}} P[\mathbf{I}] - \sum_{\mathbf{I}:\{I_i=1,I_j=1\}} P[\mathbf{I}] \geq 0 \tag{10.17}$$

Finally, we can do the same with the doubly-conditioned probabilities. From

$$P(E_i|E_j, E_k) = \frac{\sum_{\mathbf{I}:\{I_i=1,I_j=1,I_k=1\}} p[\mathbf{I}]}{\sum_{\mathbf{I}:\{I_j=1,I_k=1\}} p[\mathbf{I}]} \tag{10.18}$$

we rearrange as

$$P(E_i|E_j, E_k) \sum_{\mathbf{I}:\{I_j=1,I_k=1\}} p[\mathbf{I}] = \sum_{\mathbf{I}:\{I_i=1,I_j=1,I_k=1\}} p[\mathbf{I}] \tag{10.19}$$

and obtain[3]

$$P^+\left(E_i|E_j,E_k\right)\sum_{\boldsymbol{I}:\{I_j=1,I_k=1\}}p[\boldsymbol{I}]-\sum_{\boldsymbol{I}:\{I_i=1,I_j=1,I_k=1\}}p[\boldsymbol{I}]\geq 0 \qquad (10.20)$$

$$P^-\left(E_i|E_j,E_k\right)\sum_{\boldsymbol{I}:\{I_j=1,I_k=1\}}p[\boldsymbol{I}]-\sum_{\boldsymbol{I}:\{I_i=1,I_j=1,I_k=1\}}p[\boldsymbol{I}]\leq 0 \qquad (10.21)$$

Again, the same interpretation applies: the risk manager may not be too sure of the precise value for the singly- or doubly-conditioned probabilities she has assigned, but she would not be too unhappy if they turned out to lie anywhere between $P^-\left(E_i|E_j\right)$ and $P^+\left(E_i|E_j\right)$ or between $P^-\left(E_i|E_j,E_k\right)$ and $P^+\left(E_i|E_j,E_k\right)$, for the singly- or doubly-conditioned probabilities, respectively.

Following the standard Linear Programming approach sketched in the Appendix, we can now define non-negative 'slack' variables, $\pi_i^{\pm}$, $\pi_{i|j}^{\pm}$ and $\pi_{i|j,k}^{\pm}$:

$$\pi_i^- = -P^-\left(E_i\right)+\sum_{\boldsymbol{I}:\{I_i=1\}}p[\boldsymbol{I}] \qquad (10.22)$$

$$\pi_i^+ = +P^+\left(E_i\right)-\sum_{\boldsymbol{I}:\{I_i=1\}}p[\boldsymbol{I}] \qquad (10.23)$$

$$\pi_{i|j}^- = -P^-\left(E_i|E_j\right)\sum_{\boldsymbol{I}:\{I_j=1\}}p[\boldsymbol{I}]+\sum_{\boldsymbol{I}:\{I_i=1,I_j=1\}}p[\boldsymbol{I}] \qquad (10.24)$$

$$\pi_{i|j}^+ = P^+\left(E_i|E_j\right)\sum_{\boldsymbol{I}:\{I_j=1\}}p[\boldsymbol{I}]-\sum_{\boldsymbol{I}:\{I_i=1,I_j=1\}}p[\boldsymbol{I}] \qquad (10.25)$$

$$\pi_{i|j,k}^- = -P^-\left(E_i|E_j,E_k\right)\sum_{\boldsymbol{I}:\{I_j=1,I_k=1\}}p[\boldsymbol{I}]+\sum_{\boldsymbol{I}:\{I_i=1,I_j=1,I_k=1\}}p[\boldsymbol{I}] \qquad (10.26)$$

$$\pi_{i|j,k}^+ = P^+\left(E_i|E_j,E_k\right)\sum_{\boldsymbol{I}:\{I_j=1,I_k=1\}}p[\boldsymbol{I}]-\sum_{\boldsymbol{I}:\{I_i=1,I_j=1,I_k=1\}}p[\boldsymbol{I}] \qquad (10.27)$$

Given our definitions, the slack variables are indeed all positive, as they should be:

$$\pi_i^{\pm},\pi_{i|j}^{\pm},\pi_{i|j,k}^{\pm}\geq 0 \text{ for any } i, j, k \qquad (10.28)$$

---

[3]The careful reader will have noticed that the risk manager is now also required to provide the quantity $\sum_{\boldsymbol{I}:\{I_j=1,I_k=1\}}p[\boldsymbol{I}]$, which is the *joint* probability of occurrence of *two* events. This seems to be asking for more than I have so far advertised. However, we are dealing with the joint probability of occurrence of two events, say $P(A,B)$, which can always be written as

$$P(A,B)=P(A|B)P(B)$$

Therefore the risk manager still does not have to provide anything more complex than singly-conditioned and marginal probabilities.

We refer to any set of joint probabilities $\{p[I]\}$ that obey Equations (10.1) and (10.2) as a '*feasible*' solution. We call any set of joint probabilities $\{p[I]\}$ that in addition obey the constraint Equations (10.12), (10.13), (10.16), (10.17), (10.20) and (10.21) as a '*coherent*' solution. If we can find a coherent solution then the constraints assigned by the risk manager are consistent, otherwise they are not.

In order to find a coherent solution, we use Phase 1 of the Revised Simplex Method (see, e.g., Press *et al.* (1996)) that I outline in the Appendix. This involves defining non-negative artificial variables to give an initial 'basic' solution,[4] and minimizing the sum – which we shall call z – of the artificial variables subject to the given constraints. If the minimum value of z – let us call it z_{min} – is greater than zero, then we have not found a coherent solution, that is, not all the constraint equations are satisfied. However, the solution we have found is still feasible, which means that the probabilities $\{p[I]\}$ are non-negative and add up to 1. When z_{min} is greater than zero our optimal solution will be, in some sense, as 'close' as we can get to a coherent solution. The risk manager can then either accept the resulting 'close' solution or widen the limits, $P^{\pm}(E_i)$, $P^{\pm}(E_i|E_j)$ and $P^{\pm}(E_i|E_j, E_k)$, within which the marginal and conditional probabilities are allowed to lie.

It is worth noting that, if no marginal probabilities are provided, any feasible solution gives rise to an infinite number of related solutions. Indeed, if we denote by $\mathbf{0}$ the vector I whose components are all zero, by $p[\mathbf{0}]$ the (joint) probability that none of the events happens, by $p[I]$ a generic vector of joint probabilities, and by $p_{opt}[I]$ a given feasible solution, then any solution such that

$$p[\mathbf{0}] = \frac{1+\alpha}{1+\alpha p_{opt}[\mathbf{0}]} p_{opt}[\mathbf{0}] \tag{10.29}$$

and

$$p[I] = \frac{1}{1+\alpha p_{opt}[\mathbf{0}]} p_{opt}[I] \quad \text{for } I \neq \mathbf{0} \tag{10.30}$$

is also feasible for $-1 \leq \alpha$. Scaling all the individual probabilities (except $p[\mathbf{0}]$) by the same proportion clearly does not affect the conditional probabilities. This means that the solution can be associated with unconditional probabilities that are arbitrarily small or large (provided, of course, that none of them is greater than 1).

Note also that, given any proposed solution with $p[I] \geq 0$ for any $I \in \mathcal{I}$, we can always find a *feasible* solution (i.e., the additional constraint $\sum_{I \in \mathcal{I}} p[I] = 1$ can always be satisfied) simply by dividing each $p[I]$ by the sum of the $p[I]$s, and this will not affect the conditional probabilities.

---

[4]Recall that a 'basic' solution is one in which all but M of the variables are set to zero (where M is the number of constraints – excluding the non-negativity constraints). At each iteration, each of the basic variables and the objective function (z in our case) are expressed as affine functions of the non-basic variables. See the worked-out example in Section 10.5.

10.3 The Methodology in Practice: First Pass

Before delving into the implementation of the Linear Programming approach, let me give a flavour of how I intend the approach to work. I will assume for the moment that all the conditional probabilities assigned in this section satisfy the internally consistency requirements, and are therefore *bona fide* probabilities.[5]

Suppose that we have n positions, $\pi_1, \pi_2, \ldots, \pi_n$, which have been identified as 'large' by the desk risk managers. Let $E_1, E_2, \ldots, E_n$, $i = 1, 2, \ldots, 2n$, denote the significant events that would give rise to large profits *or* losses arising from our positions $\{\pi_i\}$ at a given point in time. Let G_i and L_i, $i = 1, 2, \ldots n$, be the largest plausible profits and losses, respectively, associated with position π_i if event E_i occurs. (I am using G – as in 'Gain' – rather than P – for Profit – because I am trying to avoid confusion with P for probability.)[6] So, to fix ideas, position 1, π_1, could be a large long equity position in the S&P. There are two events associated with position 1, E_1 and E_2: E_1 could be a 1987-like equity market crash; E_2 could be a large market rally. The rise and fall need not be of the same magnitude. Associated with event E_1 there is a profit, G_1, and a loss, L_1. Both profit G_1 and loss L_1 are a function of the event E_1 (the equity market crash) and of the position π_1: $G_1 = G_1 (E_1, \pi_1)$, $L_1 = L_1 (E_1, \pi_1)$. Similarly, there is a profit, G_2, and a loss, L_2, associated with the equity rally.

I want to stress that these events encompass not only the large losses, but also the large possible gains arising from the most significant positions $\{\pi_i\}$. Of course, for a given position, the expected profit or loss need not be just the same number with the opposite sign. This can be because the moves in the underlying are not symmetric (equity markets 'crash' in different ways than they spike, volatilities do not fall in the same way as they suddenly rise, etc.,) or because the underlying position may be not linear (e.g., a short-gamma position). The notation used in the following assumes that, say, a yield curve steepening and a yield curve flattening are two distinct events. If our portfolio contains, say, a steepener position, then the loss for the steepener scenario would be zero, and the gain for flattening scenario would be zero. In short, given a large position, the associated events will, in general, be the largest plausible moves that give rise *to profits or losses*.

As mentioned in the introductory section, we assume that the risk manager *can* express an informed opinion about the probability, $P(E_j | E_i)$, of occurrence of event E_j conditional on event E_i having occurred. For instance, if event E_i were a major equity market crash, the event E_j associated with a *drop* in equity volatilities would have a very low probability; however, the event E_k associated with widening in credit spreads could have a significant probability. In the following, to avoid spurious precision, these conditional probabilities can initially be grouped into buckets, as suggested in Section 9.4.

---

[5]The treatment that follows requires a somewhat more complex set-up, in that I will deal with scenarios that give rise to large losses *and profits*. This is much more satisfactory, because we can better handle 'diversification' and 'proxy hedging'. Conceptually, there are few differences. In practice, however, the approach requires considerably more care, and the conditional probability tables are more complex. After this section I will never deal again with the case of profits and losses.

[6]Ideally, these should be the profits or losses that our portfolio could incur *over and above the hypothetical profits or losses that our VaR engine, run with the longest time series and volatility rescaling, produces*.

Therefore, given n large positions, there will be in general $2n$ events, with a profit, P_i, and a loss, G_i, associated with each.

Consider now the $[2n \times 1]$ matrix $\mathbf{y}$, defined by

$$\mathbf{y} = \mathbf{p} \cdot \mathbf{E}$$

$$= \begin{bmatrix} y_1 \\ y_2 \\ \cdots \\ \cdots \\ y_{2n-1} \\ y_{2n} \end{bmatrix}$$

$$= \begin{bmatrix} 0 & 0 & P(E_2|E_1) & P(E_2|E_1) & \cdots & P(E_{2n}|E_1) & P(E_{2n}|E_1) \\ P(E_1|E_2) & P(E_1|E_2) & 0 & 0 & \cdots & P(E_{2n}|E_2) & P(E_{2n}|E_2) \\ & & & & & & \\ & & & & & & \\ & & & & & 0 & 0 \end{bmatrix}$$

$$\times \begin{bmatrix} L_1 \\ G_1 \\ L_2 \\ G_2 \\ \\ L_n \\ G_n \end{bmatrix} \tag{10.31}$$

Consider, say, the second entry of the matrix $\mathbf{y}$. Given the definition above it is given by

$$y_2 = (L_1 + G_1)\, P(E_1|E_2) + 0 + (L_3 + G_3)$$
$$\times P(E_3|E_2) + \ldots (L_n + G_n)\, P(E_{2n}|E_2) \tag{10.32}$$

This can be interpreted as the (conditional) expectation of the profits and losses incurred by our portfolio *due to positions other than position 2* if the second scenario event materializes. The total stress loss, SL_2, if the second *event* scenario materializes is therefore given by the sum of y_2 and the *loss* associated with the second scenario:

$$SL_2 = L_2 + y_2 \tag{10.33}$$

As Equation (10.31) shows, the matrix equation above can be written more concisely as

$$\mathbf{y} = \mathbf{P} \cdot \mathbf{E}$$

$$
\begin{bmatrix}
y_1 \\
y_2 \\
\cdots \\
\cdots \\
y_{2n-1} \\
y_{2n}
\end{bmatrix}
$$

$$
=
\begin{bmatrix}
0 & P(E_2|E_1) & P(E_3|E_1) & \cdots & \cdots & P(E_{n-1}|E_1) & P(E_n|E_1) \\
P(E_1|E_2) & 0 & P(E_3|E_2) & \cdots & \cdots & P(E_{n-1}|E_2) & P(E_n|E_2) \\
 & & 0 & & & & \\
 & & & 0 & & & \\
 & & & & 0 & & \\
P(E_1|E_{n-1}) & & & & & 0 & P(E_n|E_{n-1}) \\
P(E_1|E_n) & P(E_2|E_n) & & & & P(E_{n-1}|E_n) & 0
\end{bmatrix}
$$

$$
\times
\begin{bmatrix}
L_1 + G_1 \\
L_2 + G_2 \\
\\
\\
L_n + G_n
\end{bmatrix}
\tag{10.34}
$$

A simple example can clarify the notation and the approach. Let event 1 be an equity market crash (S&P). (Event 2 can be an equity market rally, but we do not consider this in this example.) Let event 3 be a flattening of the US$ yield curve and event 4 a steepening of the US$ yield curve. We assume that we are long the S&P and have a yield curve steepener on. Given an equity market crash we have a conditional probability of a curve steepening of the US$ curve, $P(E_4|E_1)$, of 80%, and a conditional probability, $P(E_3|E_1)$, of a flattening of 20% (the two probabilities only happen to add up to 1 by chance).

Since we have a long equity position and a yield curve steepener we then have the following:

- a gain, G_4, and a loss, L_4, of, say, $100m and $0m, respectively, associated with event 4 (the steepening of the curve) – L_4 is 0 because there is no loss from our position (a steepener) if event 4 happens, i.e., if the curve indeed steepens;

- a gain, G_3, and a loss, L_3, of, say, $0m and $100m, respectively, associated with event 3 (the flattening of the curve) – it is G_3 that is now 0 because there is no gain from our position (a steepener) if event 3 happens, i.e., if the curve flattens;

- a stand-alone loss, L_1, of, say, $200m on the S&P position if the equity market crash occurs.

The conditional losses associated with event 1 (equity market crash) are given by

$$y_1 = P(E_3|E_1)L_3 + P(E_3|E_1)G_3 + P(E_4|E_1)L_4 + P(E_4|E_1)G_4$$

$$= P(E_3|E_1)L_3 + P(E_3|E_1)(0) + P(E_4|E_1)(0) + P(E_4|E_1)G_4 \qquad (10.35)$$

The conditional expected stress loss 1, SL_1, associated with the equity market crash is then given by

$$SL_1 = L_1 + (G_3 + L_3)\, P(E_3|E_1) + (G_4 + L_4)\, P(E_4|E_1)$$

$$= L_1 + (0 + L_3)\, P(E_3|E_1) + (G_4 + 0)\, P(E_4|E_1)$$

$$= -\$200m - \$100m * 0.2 + \$100m * 0.7 = -\$150m \qquad (10.36)$$

It must be stressed again that the profits and losses L_2, G_2, L_3 and G_3 do not depend on event 1 (the equity market crash), and are unconditional (marginal) quantities. The link with the equity market crash comes only via the conditional probabilities, $P(E_4|E_1)$ and $P(E_3|E_1)$.

As our intuition suggests, in the example above the steepening position mitigates the stand-alone loss in the naked equity position, reducing it from $200m to $150m.

10.4   The CPU Cost of the Approach

The Simplex solution described above was first prototyped in VBA; for 12 scenarios this was taking of the order of 5–10 minutes to run. Coding it in C++ made the routines run 10 to 20 times faster.

Preliminary analysis suggests that each additional scenario will increase the run time by a factor of about three; considering that the analysis is likely to be required infrequently (say, on a weekly basis), the computation time should not be a problem with up to, say, 15–20 scenarios. In fact we are more likely to run into memory-space problems first. In any case, the main difficulties when dealing with 15–20 scenarios are of a cognitive nature, that is, they lie in the specification of the required conditional probability tables. I would not recommend working with more than about ten scenarios.

10.5   Illustration of the Linear Programming Technique

I now move to illustrating the precise workings of the Linear Programming technique described above in cleansing and fixing an exogenously assigned conditional probability matrix. In order to illustrate the procedure in practice I present in this section the results of a very simple fictitious case study. I assume, in particular, that the risk manager has only assigned singly-conditioned probabilities.

We have four scenarios, A, B, C and D, and we suppose that the risk manager supplied the following conditional probabilities:[7]

$$
\begin{bmatrix}
 & A & B & C & D \\
A & 1 & 0.60 & 0.50 & 0.60 \\
B & 0.80 & 1 & & 0.22 & 0.20 \\
C & 0.50 & 0.20 & 1 & 0.00 \\
D & 0.40 & 0.40 & 0.00 & 1
\end{bmatrix}
\tag{10.37}
$$

where, for example, the number 0.50 in the first row represents $P(C|A)$.

We first observe that $P(C|A) + P(D|A) = 1.1$. But, from the matrix, C and D are mutually exclusive events ($P(C|D) = P(D|C) = 0$). Therefore we need to reduce either or both of $P(C|A)$ and $P(D|A)$ so that their sum is ≤ 1. In fact we would make the sum strictly less than 1 to avoid making the overly strong statement that if A occurs then C or D must occur.

Suppose that the risk manager therefore sets $P(C|A) = 0.4$ and $P(D|A) = 0.5$. If we now look at the triplet $\{A, B, D\}$, we have

$$
P(A|D) = P(D|A) \frac{P(A|B) \, P(B|D)}{P(B|A) \, P(D|B)} = 0.5 \frac{0.80 \, 0.40}{0.60 \, 0.20} = 1.333
\tag{10.38}
$$

So the five probabilities to the right of the first '=' sign are clearly inconsistent. To fix the problem, the risk manager could set $P(D|B) = 0.3$, for example, which gives $P(A|D) = 0.89$. Our revised matrix therefore becomes:

$$
\begin{bmatrix}
 & A & B & C & D \\
A & 1 & 0.60 & 0.40 & 0.50 \\
B & 0.80 & 1 & 0.22 & 0.30 \\
C & 0.50 & 0.20 & 1 & 0.00 \\
D & 0.89 & 0.40 & 0.00 & 1
\end{bmatrix}
\tag{10.39}
$$

which shows no obvious inconsistencies. Note, however, that to 'fix the problem' the risk manager has had to change substantially her original estimate of $P(A|D)$ (from 0.40 to 0.89). The plausibility of this change should be questioned. Was the original suggestion ill-thought-out? Or is the 'fix' forcing assumptions on the risk manager she is not comfortable with? We view this as an important and useful part of the process (the 'auditable decision process').

We now move to the next phase, to ensure consistency of the plausible and 'cleansed' matrix. Suppose that the risk manager allows each of the conditional probabilities[8] to lie

---

[7] The conditional-probability matrix presented here is not particularly realistic from a stress-testing perspective. (Do you agree? Why?) It has only been provided to illustrate the numerical aspects of the methodology. Note, in particular, the assumed incompatibility between events C and D.

[8] Except, of course, those that are 1 or 0.

within a range

$$P\left(E_i|E_j\right)_1 (1-\delta) \le P\left(E_i|E_j\right)_2 \le P\left(E_i|E_j\right)_1 + \delta\left(1 - P\left(E_i|E_j\right)_1\right) \tag{10.40}$$

where the $P\left(E_i|E_j\right)_1$s and $P\left(E_i|E_j\right)_2$s are taken from the revised matrix above (the subscripts 1 and 2 indicate the first or second iteration of the procedure, respectively). Note that at this stage we are not yet necessarily dealing with *bona fide*, internally consistent conditional probabilities. Taking $\delta = 0.01$ gives lower and upper bounds:

$$\begin{bmatrix} & \text{A} & \text{B} & \text{C} & \text{D} \\ \text{A} & 1 & 0.59 & 0.40 & 0.50 \\ \text{B} & 0.79 & 1 & 0.22 & 0.30 \\ \text{C} & 0.50 & 0.20 & 1 & 0.00 \\ \text{D} & 0.88 & 0.40 & 0.00 & 1 \end{bmatrix} \tag{10.41}$$

and

$$\begin{bmatrix} & \text{A} & \text{B} & \text{C} & \text{D} \\ \text{A} & 1 & 0.60 & 0.41 & 0.51 \\ \text{B} & 0.80 & 1 & 0.23 & 0.31 \\ \text{C} & 0.51 & 0.20 & 1 & 0.00 \\ \text{D} & 0.89 & 0.41 & 0.00 & 1 \end{bmatrix} \tag{10.42}$$

respectively.[9]

We now define the 16 indicator vectors and their corresponding probabilities:

$$\begin{bmatrix} \text{Indicator} & A & B & C & D & \text{Prob} \\ I_0 & 0 & 0 & 0 & 0 & p(0) \\ I_1 & 0 & 0 & 0 & 1 & p(1) \\ I_2 & 0 & 0 & 1 & 0 & p(2) \\ I_3 & 0 & 0 & 1 & 1 & p(3) \\ I_4 & 0 & 1 & 0 & 0 & p(4) \\ I_5 & 0 & 1 & 0 & 1 & p(5) \\ I_6 & 0 & 1 & 1 & 0 & p(6) \\ I_7 & 0 & 1 & 1 & 1 & p(7) \\ I_8 & 1 & 0 & 0 & 0 & p(8) \\ I_9 & 1 & 0 & 0 & 1 & p(9) \\ I_{10} & 1 & 0 & 1 & 0 & p(10) \\ I_{11} & 1 & 0 & 1 & 1 & p(11) \\ I_{12} & 1 & 1 & 0 & 0 & p(12) \\ I_{13} & 1 & 1 & 0 & 1 & p(13) \\ I_{14} & 1 & 1 & 1 & 0 & p(14) \\ I_{15} & 1 & 1 & 1 & 1 & p(15) \end{bmatrix} \tag{10.43}$$

---

[9]Note that the incompatibility constraint has remained 'hard'.

Recall that indicator variables represent the occurrence of combinations of scenarios. Thus, for example, the indicator variable I_3 represents the outcome that scenarios C and D occur and scenarios A and B do *not* occur, and $p(3)$ is the corresponding joint probability (to be solved for).

We have 12 constraints of the form:

$$P^- \left(E_i|E_j\right) \sum_{I:\{I_i=1\}} p[I] - \sum_{I:\{I_i=1,I_j=1\}} p[I] \leq 0 \tag{10.44}$$

and 12 of the form

$$P^+ \left(E_i|E_j\right) \sum_{I:\{I_i=1\}} p[I] - \sum_{I:\{I_i=1,I_j=1\}} p[I] \geq 0 \tag{10.45}$$

For example, corresponding to $P[D|A]$ we have

$$P[D|A] * \{p(8) + p(9) + p(10) + p(11) + p(12) + p(13) + p(14) + p(15)\}$$
$$- \{p(9) + p(11) + p(13) + p(15)\} \leq 0 \tag{10.46}$$

that is,

$$0.5 * \{p(8) + p(9) + p(10) + p(11) + p(12) + p(13) + p(14) + p(15)\}$$
$$- \{p(9) + p(11) + p(13) + p(15)\} \leq 0 \tag{10.47}$$

where the term 0.5 comes from $P[D|A] = 0.5$.

Recall that we deal with inequality constraints by introducing slack variables, and turning the inequality into equality constraints. We do this now by introducing the slack variable $\pi_{D|A}^-$, – see Equation (10.22):

$$\pi_{i|j}^- = -P^- \left(E_i|E_j\right) \sum_{I:\{I_j=1\}} P[I] + \sum_{I:\{I_i=1,I_j=1\}} P[I] \tag{10.48}$$

This gives

$$P[D|A] * \{p(8) + p(10) + p(12) + p(14) - p(9) - p(11) - p(13) - p(15)\}$$
$$+ \pi_{D|A}^- = 0 \tag{10.49}$$

that is,

$$0.5 * \{p(8) + p(10) + p(12) + p(14) - p(9) - p(11) - p(13) - p(15)\}$$
$$+ \pi_{D|A}^- = 0 \tag{10.50}$$

where $\pi_{D|A}^-$ is the 'slack' variable corresponding to inequality constraint (10.46).

Trivially, all the constraints, as formulated, can be satisfied by setting $p(\mathbf{0}) = 1$ (the probability of no scenarios occurring is one), and all other variables to zero. Clearly, however, in this case the conditional probabilities are not defined and we do not have an economically interesting solution. Therefore we introduce non-negative 'artificial' variables, $a_{X|Y}$, of the following kind:

$$a_{D|A} = 0.5 \left\{ P(8) + P(10) + P(12) + P(14) - P(9) - P(11) - P(13) - P(15) \right\}$$

$$+ \pi_{\overline{D|A}} \tag{10.51}$$

We create all the possible artificial variables $a_{X|Y}$, for $X, Y = A, B, C, D$. In order to get the algorithm started we initialize all of these to some arbitrarily small value, ε.

Our initial (infeasible) solution is given by setting all the artificial variables to ε, and all other variables to zero.

As explained above, we need now to express the artificial variables in terms of the currently zero variables.[10] This can be done by summing the right-hand sides of all the equations exemplified by Equation (10.51). We are finally in a position to use the Revised Simplex Algorithm to minimize this expression.

This gives the following solution:

$$
\begin{bmatrix}
\text{Indicator} & \mathbf{A} & \mathbf{B} & \mathbf{C} & \mathbf{D} & \mathbf{K} \\
I_2 & 0 & 0 & 1 & 0 & 1.606 \\
I_1 & 0 & 0 & 0 & 1 & 0.336 \\
I_{14} & 1 & 1 & 1 & 0 & 0.702 \\
I_9 & 1 & 0 & 0 & 1 & 0.865 \\
I_{13} & 1 & 1 & 0 & 1 & 0.946 \\
I_{12} & 1 & 1 & 0 & 0 & 0.537 \\
I_4 & 0 & 1 & 0 & 0 & 0.664 \\
I_{10} & 1 & 0 & 1 & 0 & 0.734 \\
\end{bmatrix}
\tag{10.52}
$$

where K is a quantity proportional to the joint probabilities and all other joint probabilities, except $p(\mathbf{0})$, have been set to zero. (Recall that in our starting conditional probability matrix we had set, perhaps unwisely, $P(C|D) = P(D|C) = 0$. This being the case, looking back at the table in Equation (10.43), one can see that the joint probabilities $p(3)$, $p(7)$, $p(11)$, $p(15)$ have to be zero.)

Exercise 30   Why?

---

[10]Recall that this is what is required for the Revised Simplex Algorithm: at each iteration we have a set of 'basic' (in general non-zero) variables, and 'non-basic' (zero-valued) variables. The value of each of the basic variables and the value of the 'objective function' (the expression to be optimized) are expressed as functions of the non-basic variables only. See, e.g., Press *et al.* (1996).

The corresponding solution in terms of conditional probabilities is

$$
\begin{bmatrix}
\text{Trial Solution} & \mathbf{A} & \mathbf{B} & \mathbf{C} & \mathbf{D} \\
\mathbf{A} & 1.00 & 0.58 & 0.38 & 0.48 \\
\mathbf{B} & 0.77 & 1.00 & 0.25 & 0.33 \\
\mathbf{C} & 0.47 & 0.23 & 1.00 & 0.00 \\
\mathbf{D} & 0.84 & 0.44 & 0.00 & 1.00
\end{bmatrix}
\tag{10.53}
$$

For ease of comparison I show below the conditional probability matrix from which we started:

$$
\begin{bmatrix}
\text{Initial Guess} & \mathbf{A} & \mathbf{B} & \mathbf{C} & \mathbf{D} \\
\mathbf{A} & 1 & 0.60 & 0.40 & 0.50 \\
\mathbf{B} & 0.80 & 1 & 0.22 & 0.30 \\
\mathbf{C} & 0.50 & 0.20 & 1 & 0.00 \\
\mathbf{D} & 0.89 & 0.40 & 0.00 & 1
\end{bmatrix}
\tag{10.54}
$$

Comparing these two tables we see that the largest violation of the constraints is for $P\,[A|D]$, where the above solution lies 0.04 below its lower limit. We could accept this solution, implicitly making ad hoc changes to the tolerance limits ($\delta = 0.01$) we had assigned at the start (i.e., in this case setting $\delta = 0.04$). Or we could increase δ from 0.01, while keeping it below 0.04, and re-optimize.[11]

10.6 What Can We Do with this Information?

After the manual cleansing 'sanity checks' suggested in Section 9.4 and the systematic procedure just presented, we finally have a logically-coherent matrix of conditional probabilities. It may not be quite the one we had assigned to start with, but it should be very close to it. What can we do with it?

10.6.1 Extracting Information with Conditional Probabilities Only

Even if the risk manager has not felt confident to provide any marginal probabilities, we can still obtain quantities of interest. Here are a few examples of what we can do.

To begin with, to each event, E_i, we can associate a conditional expected loss, $\overline{L}_i$:

$$
\overline{L}_i = L_i + \sum_{j \neq i} P(E_j|E_i)L_j
\tag{10.55}
$$

This is the loss we can expect, *given that event E_i has occurred*. It is made up of two components: the stand-alone loss from events E_i, L_i, that will occur with certainty if event

---

[11] Perhaps if we had set a less ambitious tolerance δ, say $\delta = 0.02$, we may find a solution closer to our initial guess than the one we just obtained.

E_i occurs, plus the sum from all the losses from the other events, L_j, each weighted by its conditional probability of occurrence.[12]

By looking at all the events in turn and comparing their conditional expected losses, we can ascertain which individual events are expected to be associated with the largest conditional expected losses. Arguably, these are the events on which the risk manager should focus her attention most closely. Limited as it may be, this information is simple, transparent and lends itself to questioning by traders and senior management. Something not to be sniffed at.

Note that we still cannot say anything about which *joint* events produce the largest expected losses, because of the indeterminacy in the joint probabilities that I highlighted above. The conditional expected loss conveys *more* information than the stand-alone loss, but *less* information than the loss associated with a joint event and the probability associated with that loss.

We can do more. To start with, if one wanted to link regulatory capital, RC, to the conditional expected losses, these largest losses would also be a natural starting point. A plausible suggestion could be

$$RC = \max \left\{ \overline{L}_i \right\} \tag{10.56}$$

A further simple piece of analysis that can be carried out once we have the set of expected conditional losses is the following. After running the analysis for several weeks, the risk manager can begin to record the number of times that the maximum conditional loss is associated with event $E_1, E_2, \ldots, E_n$. She can then build a simple histogram. If the same event, say E_k, were always, or predominantly, associated with the maximum conditional loss, this would suggest a portfolio with a very clear and persistent risk concentration. As the analysis is repeated week after week, it is also useful to track the time series of the top-most expected conditional losses.

There is more that we can do with the minimal input of the conditional probability matrix. Let us for simplicity assume now that, if event E_j does not occur, then the loss associated with that event will not be incurred at all ($L_j = 0$). Recall also that

$$P(E_j|E_i) + P(\widetilde{E}_j|E_i) = 1 \tag{10.57}$$

Now, consider events E_i and E_j. Conditional on event E_i having occurred, event E_j will therefore contribute a loss L_j with probability $P(E_j|E_i)$, and no loss with probability $P(\widetilde{E}_j|E_i)$. Of course, the contribution to the expected conditional loss from event E_j given that event E_i has occurred, $\overline{L}_{j|i}$, is then just

$$\overline{L}_{j|i} = P(E_j|E_i)L_j + P(\widetilde{E}_j|E_i) * 0 = P(E_j|E_i)L_j \tag{10.58}$$

as we saw before. We can therefore redefine

$$\overline{L}_i = L_i + \sum_{j \neq i} P(E_j|E_i)L_j = L_i + \sum_{j \neq i} \overline{L}_{j|i} \tag{10.59}$$

---

[12]The generalization to the case when offsetting profit-making positions are taken into account is straightforward.

And if we decide by convention to assign

$$P(E_j|E_j) = 1 \quad \forall j \tag{10.60}$$

then we can write this even more compactly as

$$\overline{L}_i = \sum_j \overline{L}_{j|i} \tag{10.61}$$

The variance of loss from event E_j conditional on event E_i having occurred, $var_{j|i}$, is then

$$
\begin{aligned}
var_{j|i} &= \left(L_j - \overline{L}_{j|i}\right)^2 P(E_j|E_i) + \left(0 - \overline{L}_{j|i}\right)^2 P(\tilde{E}_j|E_i) \\
&= \left(L_j - \overline{L}_{j|i}\right)^2 P(E_j|E_i) + \left(\overline{L}_{j|i}\right)^2 P(\tilde{E}_j|E_i) \\
&= \left(L_j - \overline{L}_{j|i}\right)^2 P(E_j|E_i) + \left(\overline{L}_{j|i}\right)^2 \left(1 - P(E_j|E_i)\right)
\end{aligned}
\tag{10.62}
$$

So, given the occurrence of event E_i, we can associate a conditional variance to each event $E_j \neq E_i$. For a given event E_i we have n such conditional variances, and so the conditional variance matrix can be arranged in an $n \times n$ matrix.

All of this sounds (and is) interesting and informative, but we must be careful to attribute the correct meaning to this quantity, and to understand clearly what this variance does and does *not* capture. We are dealing with two-valued Boolean random variables, which can either occur or not. Given that one event has occurred, there is therefore no variability whatsoever in the magnitude of the associated loss.[13] Also, we have not allowed for any uncertainty in the conditional probabilities. So, the variance just defined is only a function of the magnitude of the conditional loss associated with event E_i and of its conditional probability of occurrence given that the same event E_i has happened. All the uncertainty comes from whether the loss happens or not, and from the conditional probability of the loss.

This is an interesting quantity in itself, but probably not quite what we would like to have. In order to get a measure of uncertainty closer to what we are more likely to be interested in, we now have to bring in infromation about the marginal probabilities, $P(E_i)$.

10.6.2 Extracting Information with Conditional and Marginal Probabilities

As I mentioned at the beginning of the treatment, I recommend avoiding spurious precision by assigning conditional probabilities to coarse probability buckets. Also, it is much easier to work with the multiplicative factors x_i^k (see Sections 5.9, 5.10 and 9.3), rather than directly with the conditional probabilities. Multiplicative factors of 0 or $\frac{1}{P(E_i)}$ are left to the courageous, and for the reasons explained in Sections 5.9 and 9.3, I prefer to work with minimum and maximum factors of ε and $(1 - \varepsilon) \frac{1}{\max\{P(E_i), P(E_j)\}}$. Of course, if the marginal probabilities are given, each multiplicative factor x_i^k uniquely determines the

---

[13]Of course, in principle, we could remedy this by dealing with multi-valued Boolean variables (see, e.g., Moore (2001)). Given how difficult it is to assign the associated probabilities I have not pursued this route in this book.

associated probability $P(E_i|E_k)$. Therefore, once the x_i^k factors have been determined, one can equivalently talk of coarse conditional probability buckets.

For a given set of these coarse conditional probability buckets, the risk manager can then do the following:

- Take in turn each of the first-pass conditional probabilities assigned by the risk manager before the Linear Programming procedure described above.

- Randomly re-allocate each conditional probability to the same bucket or halfway between the assigned bucket and the bucket above or halfway between the assigned bucket and the bucket below with probability $\frac{1}{3}$.[14] So, for instance, if the multiplicative factor x_i^k had been assigned to be, say, 1, with probability $\frac{1}{3}$ it could be left unchanged, or moved to 5 or moved to 0.2.

- Now the usual cleansing of the conditional probabilities can be carried out (via the Linear Programming technique described above), and the conditional losses re-calculated.

- This process can be repeated many times and the highest conditional loss can be recorded for each iteration.

- A distribution of maximum conditional losses can finally be constructed.

An example of the distribution obtained using this procedure is given in Figure 10.1. Despite the nice-looking picture, there is nothing too 'scientific' about this distribution, because in obtaining it the multiplicative factors x_i^k were moved by a commonsensical but arbitrary amount (see the second bullet point above). Nonetheless, this heuristic procedure can give an idea of the sensitivity of the results to one of the most delicate inputs of the whole procedure, that is, the assignment of the conditional probabilities. What it does *not* address is the variation in the losses due to uncertainty in the occurrence of the different events. Can we say something about what we really care about?

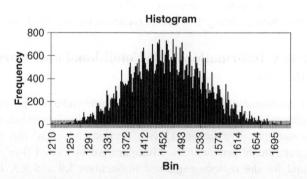

Figure 10.1   The dispersion of the maximum conditional expected loss with uncertainty in the input parameters.

---

[14]There is, of course, nothing magical about choosing exactly halfway. Perhaps a quarter of the way may work better. The choice, of course, depends on the coarseness of the original buckets (i.e., on the chosen basis of the logarithm).

To see what we can do, we go back to the quantities defined above:

$$\overline{L}_{j|i} = P(E_j|E_i)L_j \tag{10.63}$$

and

$$\overline{L}_i = \sum_j \overline{L}_{j|i} \tag{10.64}$$

If the risk manager feels that she can assign marginal probabilities, $P(E_i)$, to the various events E_i, then the total expected loss, $\overline{L}$, can be calculated as

$$\overline{L} = \sum_i \left[\sum_j P(E_j|E_i)L_j \right] P(E_i) = \sum_i \left[\sum_j \overline{L}_{j|i} \right] P(E_i) = \sum_i \overline{L}_i P(E_i) \tag{10.65}$$

This quantity is another possible candidate for regulatory capital, RC. The variance of the distribution can then be obtained in a straightforward manner.

There are, of course, many more useful things that one can do with the quantities that we have estimated. Constructing time series, for instance, of conditional expected losses, expected stress losses, variances and so on, is as simple as it is useful. I do not have to tell experienced risk managers what to do here – although I provide a few suggestions in Chapter 14.

If the risk manager feels confident enough to provide enough causal information to estimate (bounds for) the joint probabilities of stress events, then a much richer analysis is possible. I deal with this situation at the end of the next chapter.

Chapter 11

Obtaining a Coherent Solution II: Bayesian Nets

In this chapter I assume that the risk manager has provided the following:

- the structure of the Bayesian net (nodes, arcs and arrows);
- the associated conditional probability tables, i.e., the marginal and conditional probabilities for the various stress events, to the desired order.

I also assume that the entries of the conditional probability tables have already been cleansed via the sanity-checks-plus-Linear-Programming approach described in the previous chapter. Alternatively – or, rather, as a complement – the bounds obtained using the approach by Moskowitz and Sarin (1983) described in Chapter 7 may have been used.

Once the risk manager has at her disposal the required probability tables, the 'solution' of the problem (i.e., the derivation of the joint probabilities) becomes mechanical and is directly obtained via the Bayesian-nets technology, using the properties of Bayesian nets and of conditional and joint probabilities highlighted in Chapters 8 and 9. In this chapter we shall see how to do this in practice.

To make the approach feasible, some simplifications are required. In general, given n variables, the risk manager is supposed to be able to specify $(n - 1)$-conditioned probabilities. But it is not realistic to expect that the risk manager will be able to provide even an informed guess for all the required conditional probabilities for n larger than, say, 3 (i.e., for more-than-doubly-conditioned probabilities) – and even this is a big ask. As discussed, one possible way out of this impasse is to restrict the set of possible Bayesian nets underlying the problem. This ultimately means simplifying the underlying causal structure among the variables at hand, and should not therefore be undertaken lightly. When this 'structural pruning' can be done in a sensible way, however, dramatic simplifications can be derived and the full joint probability structure can be determined with relative ease.

Because of this pruning, the joint probabilities that we determine using this method will be an approximation to the joint probabilities that would have been obtained if God had whispered in our ears all the required conditional probabilities. The quality of the approximation will depend on how much of the underlying causal structure our ruthless pruning will have retained. Williamson (2005), as usual, provides a good discussion of these subtle points.

11.1   Solution with Marginal and *n*-conditioned Probabilities

In light of the above, we therefore assume that we have restricted the class of underlying Bayesian nets to, say, nets where each node has at most two parents. In the terminology of Chapter 8 (see Section 8.8.2 in particular), this set will be denoted by $\mathbb{S}_2$. In this case the marginal probability tables required to specify the net in its entirety consist of the marginal probabilities associated with each node and with at-most-doubly-conditioned probabilities.

In order to understand how the assumptions made can help us in obtaining the joint probabilities, let us consider a simple Bayesian net, such as the one depicted in Figure 11.1. We have four Boolean variables (four stress events), connected by the causal links we have specified in the figure.

To help our intuition, I am going to assign an interpretation to the four Boolean variables. So, event A could be an equity market crash, event B the default of a large bank counterparty, event C a large widening of credit spreads and event D a large increase in equity implied volatilities.

In our simple model of the world we assume that the rise in the implied volatilities of equities is directly 'caused' by the equity market crash, and by no other variable. We also assume that the widening of the credit spreads can be 'caused' either by the default of a major bank counterparty or by the equity market crash. Finally we have made the assumption that the default of the bank counterparty and the equity market crash are independent. This is debatable to say the least, but realism is not what I have strived for with this example, and the probabilities that I associate with the various events are totally 'made up'.

Exercise 31   How would you modify the Bayesian net in such a way that the default of a large counterparty is now assumed to cause an equity market crash, and the resulting net remains in $\mathbb{S}_2$?

The set-up I have chosen implies that events C and D are *conditionally* independent: once we know whether event A (the equity market crash) has happened or not, the increases in implied volatilities and the widening in credit spreads become independent, in the sense that knowledge that either has happened does not help us in predicting whether the other has occurred. I stress, however, that this is only true once I know whether the equity market crash has occurred or not.

Exercise 32   Assign a different interpretation to the events represented by the four nodes A, B, C and D, which is approximately compatible with the dependence structure in Figure 11.1.

We have four two-valued Boolean random variables. The associated joint probabilities are therefore $2^4 = 16$. If the risk manager wanted to assign them directly, instead of constructing them from simpler building blocks, not only would she have to specify 15 numbers, but

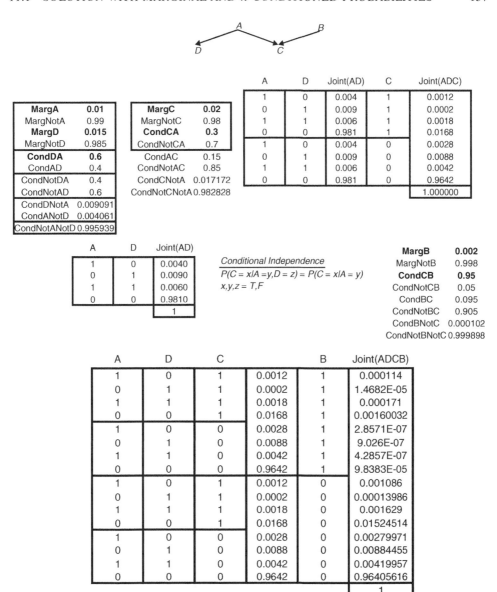

Figure 11.1 Construction of the conditional probability tables associated with the simple *A*, *B*, *C*, *D* net.

she would also have to dream up joint probabilities for pretty complex joint events, such as the probability of the equity market crash not happening and the default of a major bank counterparty happening and the widening in credit spreads happening and the increase in implied volatilities not happening.

I will show that, given the causal structure we have posited among the four variables (reflected by the topology of the associated Bayesian net), the task is not only simpler in terms of the number of quantities that have to be specified, but also cognitively feasible.

The task is still far from trivial, but a normal human being, armed with decent data and a plausible model of reality, can at least hope to come up with something that she could justify and defend. From the mere book-keeping point of view, the risk manager will have to specify seven quantities instead of 15.

It is useful to attack a tree starting from its last descendants. I will therefore start from node D (the increase in equity implied volatilities). First of all the risk manager will have to specify D's stand-alone marginal probability of occurrence, $P(D)$. In this case I have arbitrarily chosen this to be 0.015. In Figure 11.1 I have followed the convention that quantities assigned by the risk manager are in bold type, and all other (derived) quantities in normal (non-bold) type.

My first goal is to begin by producing a subset of the full set of joint probabilities, that is, the joint probabilities between event D and its parents – in our case, its only parent, event A (the equity market crash). So, I want to populate the following table:

$$
\begin{array}{cccc}
 & A & D & \text{Joint}(A, D) \\
J_1 & 1 & 0 & p(1) \\
J_2 & 0 & 1 & p(2) \\
J_3 & 1 & 1 & p(3) \\
J_4 & 0 & 0 & p(4)
\end{array}
\tag{11.1}
$$

Let us start from the easiest step: we know that, for any event D, $P(D) + P(\tilde{D}) = 1$, we have

$$
P(\tilde{D}) = 1 - P(D) = 1 - 0.015 = 0.985
\tag{11.2}
$$

In Figure 11.1, this quantity has been labelled, with hopefully self-explanatory notation, MargNotA. As it is a derived quantity, it is not in bold type.

The next quantity the risk manager is expected to supply is the conditional probability of D (the rise in implied volatilities) given A (the equity market crash). I have given this quantity, $P(D|A)$, the value of 0.60. It is shown in Figure 11.1 as the (bold typeface) quantity CondDA.

What about $P(A|D)$? We can easily derive this from the marginal probabilities, $P(A)$ and $P(D)$ – that we have already – from the exogenously assigned conditional probability, $P(D|A)$, and from Bayes' theorem. Let us build the easy quantities first:

$$
P(\tilde{A}) = 1 - P(A) = 1 - 0.01 = 0.99
\tag{11.3}
$$

Then, from

$$
P(D|A)P(A) = P(A|D)P(D)
\tag{11.4}
$$

we have

$$
P(A|D) = P(D|A)\frac{P(A)}{P(D)} = 0.60\frac{0.01}{0.015} = 0.4
\tag{11.5}
$$

In Figure 11.1 this is the non-bold quantity CondAD.

A simple but important observation: once the two marginal probabilities $P(A)$ and $P(D)$ have been assigned, from a mathematical point of view supplying $P(A|D)$ is totally equivalent to supplying $P(D|A)$, because the four quantities are linked by Bayes' theorem. Mathematical ease, however, is not the same as cognitive ease. Any risk manager will find it far easier and more 'natural' to assign the probability of equity implied volatility increasing given an equity market crash, as opposed to the probability of an equity market crash given that implied volatilities have risen. This is because the human mind works better in the causal than in the diagnostic mode (see also Chapter 12 on this point). For practical applications it is therefore essential to work in the causal direction as much as possible, and to let Bayes' theorem do the rest of the work for us. This is particularly true if the marginal probabilities of the two events are very different.

We are now going to use the relationship

$$P(A|D) + P(\tilde{A}|D) = 1 \tag{11.6}$$

which holds true for any A and D, to obtain

$$P(\tilde{A}|D) = 1 - P(A|D) = 0.6 \tag{11.7}$$

This is the (non-bold) quantity CondNotAD in Figure 11.1.

We can also build $P(\tilde{D}|A)$ immediately as

$$P(\tilde{D}|A) = 1 - P(D|A) = 0.4$$

What about $P(A|\tilde{D})$? Bayes' theorem helps us again:

$$P(\tilde{D}|A)P(A) = P(A|\tilde{D})P(\tilde{D}) \tag{11.8}$$

which implies

$$P(A|\tilde{D}) = P(\tilde{D}|A)\frac{P(A)}{P(\tilde{D})} = 0.4\frac{0.01}{0.985} \simeq 0.00406 \tag{11.9}$$

Exercise 33 Equation (11.9) states the following: given that implied volatilities have *not* increased sharply, $(\tilde{D})$, the probability that an equity market crash has occurred is very low indeed – less than half as large as the marginal (stand-alone) probability of the same crash. Are you happy with this derived conclusion? It seems reasonable to me. Does it seem reasonable to you? Why? If not, why not?

Finally we need $P(\tilde{A}|\tilde{D})$ which is easy: it comes from $P(A|\tilde{D}) + P(\tilde{A}|\tilde{D}) = 1$ and gives

$$P(\tilde{A}|\tilde{D}) = 1 - P(A|\tilde{D}) \simeq 0.99594 \tag{11.10}$$

This equation says that, given that implied volatilities have not risen, the fact that we have not had an equity market crash is a virtual certainty. Also, this conclusion passes my personal plausibility test.

Now we have all the ingredients to build our first sub-joint-probability matrix. Let us start from the first entry of the joint probability table, $P(A = T, D = F)$, which for simplicity of notation we write as $P(A, \tilde{D})$:

$$P(A, \tilde{D}) = P(A|\tilde{D})P(\tilde{D}) = 0.00406 * 0.985 = 0.004 \qquad (11.11)$$

All the other joint probabilities can be obtained using the formal relationship

$$P(A = x, D = y) = P(A = x|D = y)P(D = y) \qquad (11.12)$$

for $x, y = T, F$. Note that we have arranged the events in the joint probability following the ordering induced by the topology of our Bayesian net. So we have written $P(A = x, D = y)$ rather than $P(D = x, A = y)$. See the discussion in Section 8.3.

Thanks to this ordering we already have all the building blocks (i.e., the marginal probabilities $P(A)$, $P(\tilde{A})$, $P(D)$ and $P(\tilde{D})$ and the conditional probabilities $P(A|D)$, $P(D|A)$, $P(\tilde{A}|D)$, $P(\tilde{D}|A)$, $P(A|\tilde{D})$, $P(D|\tilde{A})$, $P(\tilde{A}|\tilde{D})$, $P(\tilde{D}|\tilde{A})$) needed for filling in all the elements required for the joint probability table:

$$
\begin{array}{cccc}
 & A & D & \text{Joint}(A, D) \\
J_1 & 1 & 0 & p(1) = 0.004 \\
J_2 & 0 & 1 & p(2) = 0.009 \\
J_3 & 1 & 1 & p(3) = 0.006 \\
J_4 & 0 & 0 & p(4) = 0.981
\end{array}
\qquad (11.13)
$$

Note that the probability of an equity market crash occurring and implied volatilities *not* rising (0.004) is much smaller than the stand-alone probability of an equity market crash (0.01). It is also smaller than the probability of both the equity market crash and the rise in implied volatility occurring (0.006). Sometimes, therefore, the probability of the occurrence of two very rare events can be higher than the probability of occurrence of just one of the two rare events. I am happy with this result – by which I mean that it makes intuitive sense to me. Are you happy as well? By the way, what should the conditional probability $P(D|A)$ have been for this result not to apply? And what would have this implied about the factor x_D^A?

As a next step we can now move to building the joint probability matrix between variables A, D and C:

$$
\begin{array}{cccccc}
 & A & D & \text{Joint}(A, D) & C & \text{Joint}(A, D, C) \\
J_1 & 1 & 0 & p(1) = 0.004 & 1 & p(1) \\
J_2 & 0 & 1 & p(2) = 0.009 & 1 & p(2) \\
J_3 & 0 & 1 & p(3) = 0.006 & 1 & p(3) \\
J_4 & 1 & 1 & p(4) = 0.981 & 1 & p(4) \\
J_5 & 1 & 0 & p(1) = 0.004 & 0 & p(5) \\
J_6 & 0 & 1 & p(2) = 0.009 & 0 & p(6) \\
J_7 & 1 & 1 & p(3) = 0.006 & 0 & p(7) \\
J_8 & 0 & 0 & p(4) = 0.981 & 0 & p(8)
\end{array}
\qquad (11.14)
$$

The strategy should by now be clear. We are going to need joint probabilities such as, for instance,

$$p(1) = P(A \cap \tilde{D} \cap C) = P(C \cap A \cap \tilde{D}) \tag{11.15}$$

where I have used the commutative property to obtain the last equality (see Section 8.5). We rewrite this as

$$P(C \cap A \cap \tilde{D}) = P(C|A \cap \tilde{D})P(A \cap \tilde{D}) \tag{11.16}$$

The term $P(A \cap \tilde{D})$ has already been obtained from the joint probability table between A and D. We just need the term $P(C|A \cap \tilde{D})$. But, given the causal links posited in our view of the world, and reflected in the topological structure of the Bayesian net we have drawn, we know that

$$P(C|A \cap \tilde{D}) = P(C|A) \tag{11.17}$$

Note that we are not saying that C (the widening in credit spreads) and D (the increase in implied volatilities) are independent – they are not! What we *are* saying is that, once we know A (the occurrence or otherwise of the equity market crash, which is the common 'cause' for C and D),[1] knowledge of C would not help us in predicting D, and *vice versa*.

To proceed, the risk manager has to provide two more quantities, the marginal probability, $P(C)$, of C happening (MargC in Figure 11.1) and the conditional probability $P(C|A)$. When these quantities are given, the next step is just a matter of applying Bayes' theorem, and the closure relationships (again, see Section 8.5)

$$P(X|Y) + P(\tilde{X}|Y) = 1 \tag{11.18}$$

$$P(X|Y \cap Z) + P(\tilde{X}|Y \cap Z) = 1 \tag{11.19}$$

in order to obtain all the remaining conditional probabilities we need, namely: $P(\tilde{C}|A)$, $P(A|C)$, $P(\tilde{A}|C)$, $P(C|\tilde{A})$ and $P(\tilde{C}|\tilde{A})$. Note that, in order to do so, we will have to invoke again the conditional independence conditions

$$P(C = x|A = y \cap D = z) = P(C = x|A = y) \tag{11.20}$$

for $x, y = T, F$.

Exercise 34   Derive $P(\tilde{C}|A)$, $P(A|C)$, $P(\tilde{A}|C)$, $P(C|\tilde{A})$ and $P(\tilde{C}|\tilde{A})$.

---

[1] Note carefully that we are not saying that A, the equity market crash, is the only cause for C, the widening in the credit spreads. In our simplified world, credit spreads can increase also because of the default of a major bank counterparty, event B.

When we have all the conditional probabilities we need, we are one step away from building the joint probabilities between A, D and C. We simply have to use the relationships

$$P(C = x \cap A = y \cap D = z) = P(C = x | A = y \cap D = z)P(A = y \cap D = z) \quad (11.21)$$

for $x, y, z = T, F$. Once we have done so, we can build the joint probability table shown in Figure 11.1, and labelled Joint(ADC). The numbers turn out to be as follows:

	A	D	Joint(A, D)	C	Joint(A, D, C)	
J_1	1	0	$p(1) = 0.004$	1	$p(1) = 0.0012$	
J_2	0	1	$p(2) = 0.009$	1	$p(2) = 0.0002$	
J_3	1	1	$p(3) = 0.006$	1	$p(3) = 0.0018$	
J_4	0	0	$p(4) = 0.981$	1	$p(4) = 0.0168$	(11.22)
J_5	1	0	$p(1) = 0.004$	0	$p(5) = 0.0028$	
J_6	0	1	$p(2) = 0.009$	0	$p(6) = 0.0088$	
J_7	1	1	$p(3) = 0.006$	0	$p(7) = 0.0042$	
J_8	0	0	$p(4) = 0.981$	0	$p(8) = 0.9642$	

Apart from adding up to 1 (which they do) and being all positive (which they are), do these numbers make sense? First of all, by far the most likely joint event, J_8, is that no stress event at all occurs. With a probability of 96.42% none of the stress events we have chosen will materialize. As we are dealing with rare events, this makes sense.

Note, however, that despite the rarity of the underlying events, the joint event, J_3, 'all events happen at the same time' (i.e., we have the failure of a major bank counterparty, and an equity market crash and an increase in implied volatilities) is not the most unlikely event, because it has a probability, $p(3)$, of 0.18%, which is greater, for instance, than the probability of joint event J_2 (there is an increase in implied volatilities and in spreads, but no equity market crash): $p(2) = 0.02\%$. This is both good and bad. The fact that the joint event, J_3, 'all events happen at the same time' does not have the lowest probability makes sense: we have implied, via our causal links and via the conditional probabilities we have assigned, either a reinforcing or a neutral influence of each variable on its descendants. In our example, when there is a dependence, the conditional probabilities, $P(X|Y)$, are always higher than the marginal probabilities, $P(X)$.

What we may not like as much is that the lowest probability joint event is J_2, 'we have an increase in implied volatilities and in credit spreads without an equity market crash'. What we have 'hard-wired' in our Bayesian net and in the probabilities we have assigned is the fact that having an increase in equity implied volatilities without an equity market crash is extremely unlikely. So, despite the fact that an equity market crash and a sharp increase in implied volatilities are rare events to start with, the occurrence of the crash without the increase in volatility is even rarer.

If you do not find this conclusion plausible, what would you have to change in the probability inputs to obtain an outcome more consonant with your intuition? This is an example of the analysis that should always be carried out when filling in conditional probability tables and examining the partial joint probabilities built along the way.

Let us go back to the building of the probabilities. Completing the full joint probability table for the four variables is now easy. We juxtapose two copies of the joint probability table labelled Joint(A, D, C) in Figure 11.1; we insert an extra column that has the first eight elements corresponding to event B (the default of the bank counterparty) happening, and the remaining eight entries corresponding to $P(\tilde{B})$.

Next we write

$$P(A = w, B = x, C = y, D = z) = P(B = w, A = x, D = y, C = z)$$

$$= P(B = w, A = x, D = y, C = z)$$

$$= P(B = w|A = x, D = y, C = z)P(A = x, D = y, C = z) \qquad (11.23)$$

for $w, x, y, z = T, F$. Then, given the structure of the Bayesian net we have built, we can write

$$P(B = w|A = x, D = y, C = z) = P(B = w|C = z) \qquad (11.24)$$

As a next step, the risk manager will have to assign the marginal probability of the default of a major bank counterparty ($P(B)$) and the conditional probability of credit spreads widening given the bank default, $P(C|B)$. Note that, logically, the risk manager could equivalently have assigned $P(B|C)$, but given the direction of the causal link, specifying one conditional probability is much more 'natural' than specifying the other. See the discussion in Section 4.4 and also the distinction drawn in Section 12.4 between causal and diagnostic logical relationships, and the associated biases. Note also that we have assigned a very high conditional probability to a widening of credit spreads given the default of a major bank counterparty. Given our experience of the events that followed the default of Lehman, this is a reasonable assumption. The conditional probability of a bank counterparty given a widening of credit spreads should, however, be much smaller – as it is – because, we hope, there should be many more 'causes' for a widening in spread than for the default of a major counterparty. Given Bayes' theorem, this can only come about if the marginal probability of B (the bank default) is much smaller than the marginal probability of credit spreads widening. This is reflected in the numbers I have chosen in Figure 11.1. See in this respect the discussion in Chapter 12 about representativeness and the neglect of the base-rate frequencies.

The last step then comes from multiplying the joint probabilities for A, D, C by the conditional probabilities, $P(B = w|C = z)$. This produces the 16 joint probabilities shown in Figure 11.1.

One may be tempted to say that we are done. Actually, the most interesting part of the exercise is only just beginning. We are now in a position, in fact, to interrogate the results and see whether they agree with our intuition. If they do not (barring any mistakes) the only causes for the discrepancy can be our faulty assignment of marginal probabilities our faulty assignment of conditional probabilities or our faulty intuition. For instance, it pays to compare these joint probabilities with the eight joint probabilities calculated for A, D and C. The probability that neither A nor D nor C happen, $P\left(\tilde{A}, \tilde{D}, \tilde{C}\right)$, is 0.96415. But the probability that neither A nor D nor C nor B happen, $P\left(\tilde{A}, \tilde{D}, \tilde{C}, \tilde{B}\right)$, is 0.96405. The two probabilities are almost identical. On the other hand, the probability of neither A nor D happening, $P\left(\tilde{A}, \tilde{D}\right)$, is 0.9810, considerably different from $P\left(\tilde{A}, \tilde{D}, \tilde{C}\right)$ or $P\left(\tilde{A}, \tilde{D}, \tilde{C}, \tilde{B}\right)$. Why is that the case? What in our probability assignments produces this result? Are we happy with what we have implicitly said about the way the world works?

The power of Bayesian nets comes from the ability it affords to mix powerful intuitive pieces of information (e.g., statements that there should be many more 'causes' for a widening in spread than for the default in a major counterparty, or that given the bank's default, a widening in credit spreads is almost a dead certainty) with logical book-keeping and 'automatic production' of conditional and joint probabilities for combinations of events about which we may have little intuition. This double reason – enhancement of intuition and logical book-keeping – is what makes Bayesian nets, in my opinion, so suitable for stress testing.

11.1.1   Generalizing the Results

The approach followed to 'solve for' the joint probabilities in the case depicted in Figure 11.1 gives a good flavour of the general strategy to tackle these problems. For pedagogical reasons the example just tackled is particularly apposite because we had to deal at most with singly-conditioned probabilities. This was despite the fact that we allowed for nets belonging to $\mathbb{S}_2$, i.e., with *two* parents. In general, these nets can give rise to the need to specify doubly-conditioned probabilities. Consider, for instance, the Bayesian net in Figure 11.2. Let us look at the last descendant, event E, and assume that the risk manager has assigned the marginal probability $P(E)$. What conditional probabilities will she have to assign? Let us try to follow the same approach as before. It is clear that now the lowest-level set of joint probabilities will involve three, not two, variables: D, C and E. After re-ordering, we will be left with an expressions of the following type:

$$P(E = x, C = y, D = z) = P(E = x|C = y, D = z)P(C = y, D = z) \qquad (11.25)$$

for $x, y, z = T, F$. We cannot invoke conditional independence to reduce the degree of conditioning any further. The last term in Equation (11.25) can be broken down, say, as

$$P(C = y, D = z) = P(C = y|D = z)P(D = z)$$

But there is no way to reduce the term $P(E = x|C = y, E = z)$ into some combination of singly-conditioned or marginal probabilities. Given what we have decided to say about the way the world works,[2] the risk manager will therefore have to specify conditional probabilities such as, for instance,

$$P(E|C, D) \qquad (11.26)$$

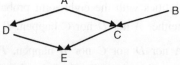

Figure 11.2   An example of a net where each node has at most two parents.

---

[2]Or, more precisely, I should say: given what we have been prepared to say about the simplest, yet reasonable, approximation about how the world works.

Then, as usual, we can use the closure relationship to write

$$P(\tilde{E}|C, D) = 1 - P(E|C, D) \tag{11.27}$$

One can then recall the extension of Bayes' theorem we discussed in Chapter 5: from

$$P(A|B)P(B) = P(B|A) P(A) \tag{11.28}$$

we obtain

$$P(A|B \cap C)P(B \cap C) = P(B|A \cap C) P(A \cap C) \tag{11.29}$$

Applied to Equation (11.26) this gives

$$P(E|C, D)P(C, D) = P(C|E, D) P(E, D) \tag{11.30}$$

and therefore, once the risk manager has specified $P(E|C, D)$, she can write

$$P(C|E, D) = P(E|C, D)\frac{P(C, D)}{P(E, D)} \tag{11.31}$$

with $P(C, D)$ and $P(E, D)$ decomposable as

$$P(C, D) = P(C|D)P(D) \tag{11.32}$$

$$P(E, D) = P(E|D)P(D) \tag{11.33}$$

The good news is that, given the limited topological complexity of $\mathbb{S}_2$ Bayesian nets (i.e., Bayesian nets with at most two parents), matters do not get any more complex. The risk manager may need a good amount of patience, but will not be required to provide estimates or guesses more complex than the ones we have encountered in this section. Trebly-conditioned conditional probabilities, for instance, will never be required.

There is more: as I showed in Chapter 7, even if the risk manager feels unable to provide doubly-conditioned probabilities, very useful bounds can still be obtained for the joint probabilities just by providing the marginals and (some of) the singly-conditioned probabilities. The analytical tool for obtaining this result is, again, Linear Programming. But, apart from the technical aspect, the tightness of the bounds on the joint probabilities provides invaluable help in the elicitation phase of the programme.

11.2 An 'Automatic' Prescription to Build Joint Probabilities

What we have done so far also gives a clear blueprint for 'automating' the procedure to build a set of joint probabilities. First we have to identify the dependence structure embedded in the Bayesian net we want to employ. Then we have to characterize its topological structure in a way that can be understood by a computer program. This can be accomplished via the g matrix. For a directed Bayesian network that links n Boolean two-valued random variables, this is an $n \times n$ matrix that contains 1s and 0s. The entries with 1s are those that correspond to causation links. Those with 0s signify that there is no link between the two variables. By convention, the diagonal is filled with 1s. So, for instance, for the Bayesian net in Figure 11.1, the g matrix has the following form:

$$g = \begin{bmatrix} & A & B & C & D \\ A & 1 & 0 & 0 & 0 \\ B & 0 & 1 & 0 & 0 \\ C & 1 & 1 & 1 & 0 \\ D & 1 & 0 & 0 & 1 \end{bmatrix} \tag{11.34}$$

I have also chosen the convention that the causal link goes from row entries to column entries. So a 1 in the cell (row $= C$, column $= A$) means that C 'causes' A – or, more precisely, that there is a directed edge (arrow) *from A to C*.[3] Note that, given the matrix g above, one could build the net in Figure 11.1: just draw on a piece of paper as many dots as variables; whenever you find a 1 in the matrix, draw a directed arrow between the two variables, remembering the column/row convention. Done.

Now our computer knows about the topological structure of the net we have chosen. If you want to be clever, you can note that, for $\mathbb{S}_2$ Bayesian nets, the matrix will be very sparse (i.e., it will be mainly populated by 0s). One could therefore store information in more efficient ways, but for the size of nets we are going to deal with, size should never be a problem.

Exercise 35   At most, how many non-zero elements will there be in an $[n \times n]$ g matrix obtained from a Bayesian net belonging to $\mathbb{S}_2$?

Exercise 36   Build the g matrix for the net in Figure 11.2.

The next step is to take as inputs the quantities that the risk manager must assign, that is, the marginal and conditional probabilities. The risk manager should always specify the marginal and conditional probabilities in the 'order' that makes more sense to her. So, for instance, typically $P(X)$ will be more natural to specify than $P(\tilde{X})$. And very often there is a natural direction of causality that makes either $P(A|B)$ or $P(B|A)$ more 'intuitive' to assign. For instance, specifying the conditional probability of equity implied volatilities increasing given an equity market crash can be easier than assigning the conditional probability of an equity market crash given an increase in implied volatilities. Of course, the two are linked via the respective marginal probabilities (and Bayes' theorem). See the diagnostic/causal distinction drawn in Section 12.4.

As a next step, one starts from the lowest descendants in the tree, and determines the joint probabilities for the associated variables, using the primitive and derived marginal and conditional probabilities for the variables at hand, much as we have done in the examples above.

---

[3]Obviously, if the network is non-directed, the g matrix is symmetrical. Having directed edges, which is necessary to speak of causation, breaks the symmetry.

Once the joint probabilities for all the lowest-level variables have been determined, one moves one step up the generations. The new joint probabilities (i.e., the joint probabilities at the next level up) will be determined using the lower-level joint probabilities and the marginal and conditional probabilities connecting the new and the old variables – making use, of course, of the central tool at our disposal to keep the problem manageable: conditional independence.

A simple book-keeping device for doing so is to repeat twice the 2^k lower-level joint probabilities determined at the previous level, and juxtapose next to them 2^k 1s and 2^k 0s, corresponding to the possible values of the indicator values of the new variable encountered at the higher level. This is exactly what we have done in Figure 11.1. Of course, if moving to the higher level brings in two more variables, then we will have to repeat *four* times the 2^k lower-level joint probabilities, and associate them with the appropriate combinations of 1s and 0s for the indicator functions of the two new variables. Since we are limiting ourselves to $\mathbb{S}_2$, this is as hard as it gets.

Proceeding this way we can mechanically work our way all the way to the root(s) of the tree, and determine all the joint probabilities that we need. The precise equations that have to be coded are given in Section 8.7.

I stress again that the difficulty is in the specification of the inputs to the problem, not in the construction of the joint probabilities. Even if the risk manager may feel a bit daunted by the construction task the first time around, the process is totally mechanical, and relatively ease to code, as long as one is not too concerned about numerical efficiency. As I recommend working with no more than about ten (well-chosen) stress events, storage, CPU time and computational efficiency are not of great concern. All the 'thinking time' should be devoted to assigning the marginal and conditional probabilities, in making critical use of the various sanity checks, and in scrutinizing carefully the intermediate conditional and joint probabilities. If something looks 'strange' in any of the intermediate or final outputs, our estimates were faulty, our intuition about how the world was supposed to work was faulty, or both. *This* is what the risk manager should worry about, *not* the mechanical book-keeping to obtain the various joint and marginal probabilities. The next chapter therefore deals with providing the risk manager with all the help she can get in the providing good, sensible inputs to the problem.

11.3 What Can We Do with this Information?

I suggested at the end of the previous chapter the type of analysis that can be carried out using conditional probabilities only. As discussed, it was useful, but limited.

We now assume that we have obtained the full joint distribution – as advertised, the probabilistic Holy Grail. What can we do with it?

Assume that we have captured all the important stress events, which is clearly unrealistic but we can use this assumption as a starting point. Also, we do not address the issue of how the statistical information about stress losses can be aggregated with the (typically much smaller) losses captured by techniques such as VaR.[4] The problem is not a small one, but

---

[4] A good idea is to define the losses associated with each event in the stress-testing exercise as the extra loss over and above the largest VaR loss generated by the same risk factor. If the risk factor is not captured by VaR at all – in regulatory parlance, if it is a Risk Not In VaR the extra loss is the full stress loss.

Easier said than done.

we can either be conservative and simply add (as the regulators are likely to require), or be optimistic and aggregate, perhaps via the square-root-of-sum-of-squares rule.

So, let us keep these caveats in mind, and see what we can do with the information we have obtained.

First of all we can associate a loss to each of the joint events. Of course, to do so, we will need some mapping from event space to profits or losses. This mapping can be as simple as multiplying a basis point move by a PV01,[5] or it may be a full revaluation. The details are immaterial for the purpose of this discussion.

Since we have the probability of each joint event, we can calculate the total expected loss, $\overline{L}$. It is just given by

$$\overline{L} = \sum_{j=1}^{2^n} L(J_j) p(j) \tag{11.35}$$

where n is the total number of stress events and the expression $L(J_i)$ emphasizes that the ith loss is a function of the joint realization J_i of elementary events.

Since we have the full distribution we can now calculate the variance, or any moment we may have confidence in, of the loss distribution. Note that this variance has a different (and richer) meaning than the variance I defined in the case of conditional expected losses. See the discussion in Section 10.6. It still does not address the question of variance of output losses coming from the uncertainty in the model parameters (e.g., subjective probabilities and the direction of causation). Again, an obvious adaptation of the heuristic technique discussed in Section 10.6 can be of help.

Needless to say, we still have the conditional expected loss given that any of the elementary events have occurred. But, if we want, now we can also calculate the conditional expected loss given that any *combination of* elementary events has happened.

We can also estimate the probability that none of our events have happened: we call this $P(\widetilde{E}_1 \cap \widetilde{E} \cap, \dots, \cap \widetilde{E}_n)$. Then $1 - P(\widetilde{E}_1, \widetilde{E}_2, \dots \widetilde{E}_n)$ is the probability that we will incur a loss at least as large as the smallest loss $L(J_i)$. This loss is by definition our stress-loss-percentile (stress VaR). We can then also integrate the tail losses beyond the VaR level to obtain a Conditional Expected Shortfall (CES) statistic.

11.3.1   Risk-Adjusting Returns

There is more than can be done. Very often investment decisions are made on the basis of the RAROC (risk-adjusted-return-on-capital) criterion,[6] expressed as a ratio of the expected return from a given initiative over the associated capital.[7] If the capital in question is the regulatory capital, then the definition is unambiguous. But if it is 'economic'

---

[5] Present Value of a Basis Point.

[6] There are deep corporate finance questions as to whether, and if so why, this rule should be employed. I elegantly sidestep these issues here, and pragmatically assume that a RAROC-type criterion is used in practice, whatever its theoretical attractiveness – or lack thereof.

[7] The expected return is to be understood as net of expected losses, costs and taxes. Note in passing that, as Matten (2000) points out, given the definition just provided one should speak of return on risk-adjusted capital (RORAC), rather than risk-adjusted return on capital (RAROC), because it is the denominator (the capital) that is risk-adjusted, not the numerator (the expected return). The distinction has more-than-semantic relevance, but I shall not pursue this topic.

capital – understood as the capital a firm would prudentially hold even in the absence of any regulatory constraints – then its calculation becomes more problematic. To the extent that capital should be risk-based, it should be some monotonic function of risk. To capture the idea of risk in the quantity that goes in the denominator, it has been common to use the VaR statistic:

$$RAROC_j \propto \frac{\left[Expected\ Return\right]_j}{VaR_j} \tag{11.36}$$

where the index j labels the particular business line, or the investment initiative. A conceptually more attractive alternative is

$$RAROC_j^{CES} \propto \frac{\left[Expected\ Return\right]_j}{CES_j} \tag{11.37}$$

However, both these approaches neglect the fact that truly tail events – such as liquidity, and, in general, events not contained in the data historical base – are poorly captured by VaR or CES, if at all. An analysis purely based on return-over-VaR 'efficiency' would therefore favour lines of business with leptokurtic profit-and-loss profiles – the fatter the tails for the same variance, the greater their apparent attractiveness. But plausible utility functions, and common sense, suggest that, for a given variance, we should prefer less fat-tailed distributions.

There is a further practical consideration that suggests that using VaR[8] in the denominator may not be such a good idea. When the trading-book capital used to be almost exclusively a function of the VaR, then, with some heroic distributional assumptions, this provided a simple alignment of 'economic' and regulatory capital for the trading book. After the financial crisis of 2007–2009 we live in a different world, and regulators are increasingly requiring that capital should also cover stress and other events not captured by VaR. Therefore including in the denominator a measure of stress risk not only makes the measure more intellectually appealing, but also better aligns this statistic with the likely capital charge. One can therefore complement the naive VaR measure above with a 'Stress RAROC' metric:

$$Stress\ RAROC_j \propto \frac{\left[Expected\ Return\right]_j}{\left[Stress\text{-}related\ risk\ statistic\right]_j} \tag{11.38}$$

where the term *Stress-related risk statistic* refers to a suitable proxy for stress losses associated with business line j.

Neither statistic (using VaR or stress as the denominator) tells the whole story, or contains 'the truth'. Should we be concerned more about 'normal' or 'tail' losses? How unlikely must a loss become before we stop worrying about it? Ultimately, our preferences are primary, and utility functions should be calibrated to revealed preferences, not the other

---

[8]By the way, when I say 'VaR', do I refer to the stand-alone or the marginal VaR? Conceptually, the marginal VaR seems to make more sense, but only to the extent that the business or investment mix coming from the *other* areas of activity is relatively stable, and 'structural'.

Furthermore, marginal calculations can be very noisy, especially if the new investment or business line is much smaller than the exisiting portfolio: the more so, the higher the percentile.

way around. However, we cannot express preferences about risky prospects ('lotteries') unless cognitively resonant points of the risk/reward profile are presented to us. So, if a given business line shows a more attractive ratio of expected return to 'risk' both when VaR and when expected stress losses are taken as a proxy for risk, then choosing between the two looks like a no-brainer. But if the order is reversed, our preferences should be carefully interrogated.

Finally, what is the *Stress-related risk statistic* I refer to above? There is no unique answer: the expected stress loss, the stress VaR, the stress CES and so on can all be taken to be suitable proxies. In the wake of recent events, regulators are trying to make the capital charge more truly risk-sensitive. If this were achieved by the inclusion of a capital component arising from subjective stress losses, there would be great appeal in employing for internal decision-making whatever measure the regulators choose. If, however, the capital were linked to, say, the 99.975th percentile of a one-year loss distribution, then there would probably arise a chasm between the regulatory charge and what institutions would be really looking at. See Rebonato (2007) for more on this point.

Part IV

Making It Work In Practice

Chapter 12

Overcoming Our Cognitive Biases

Conditional probabilities lie at the heart of the approach I have suggested in this book. The success or failure of what I propose therefore largely depends on how well we can provide good estimates of these quantities. This is not an easy task. Therefore, in this chapter I deal with some of the problems that stand in the way of coming up with reasonable conditional probabilities. These problems are of a cognitive nature, that is, they can be traced back to systematic errors human beings tend to make when dealing with probabilities in general, and with probabilities of remote events in particular.

There is little question that these systematic biases are real, and that human beings are imperfect Bayesian machines. *How* imperfect, as we shall see in the next section, is still up for debate. But, looking on the bright side, there is little to suggest that these biases are so 'hard-wired' that they cannot be overcome. Indeed, the first step to take in order to avoid falling prey of these cognitive shortcomings is being aware of their existence. This is therefore the first goal of this chapter.

Awareness of these biases is one thing, but we can hope for something more. Indeed, several studies suggest that we *can* learn to think better (in this context, that we can learn to 'think Bayesian').[1] I therefore discuss in some detail the origin of some of the most common biases (for instance, representativeness), with the hope that self-awareness combined with training can improve our ability to suggest reasonable conditional probabilities.

So, what is the problem? In the last few decades psychologists and behavioural finance scientists have highlighted important and systematic deviations in the reasoning process displayed by most human beings with respect to the normative standard provided by Bayesian rationality. These findings have had, and are having, a profound effect on the theory and practice of finance and economics, and are currently the subject of lively debate. They go straight to the core of the neo-classical set-up, questioning as they do the status of central theories such as the Efficient Market Hypothesis and the Rational Expectation Theory in economics, and the Rational Agent Model in political science. Bounded rationality is

---

[1] See, in particular, Nisbett (2009) and references therein, and Griffiths and Tenenbaum (2005).

the term often used to describe these systematic deviations from Bayesian rationality. For reasons that I explain in the next section I find the term potentially misleading, and I prefer to speak of cognitive biases. Understanding the difference between bounded rationality and cognitive deficiencies is important in order to appreciate what needs fixing and what does not. I therefore turn to this distinction in the next section.

12.1   Cognitive Shortcomings and Bounded Rationality

In the neo-classical theory the view of the economic agent as a rational Bayesian actor constitutes both the normative and the descriptive standard. I have discussed in Chapter 3 how inflexible the straight-jacket imposed by this view of rationality can be. All ortho-doxies, however, create dissenters, and indeed two distinct schools began to emerge almost half a century ago just as the neo-classical consensus was firming up. The first was the bounded rationality' school (Simon 1956, 1957 and Selten 1991, 1998). The second was the 'irrationality', 'behavioural finance' or 'cognitive biases' school pioneered by Kahneman, Tversky and others in the 1970s (see, e.g., Kahneman and Tversky (1972a, 1972b, 1973, 1979a, 1979b)). The two schools have a lot in common and are often confused, but there are very important differences between the two, which are of relevance to our discussion.[2]

Starting from the similarities: both schools point out that individuals do not employ the 'rational' Bayesian cognitive processes posited (either literally or in an as-if sense) by the neo-classical school. The behavioural finance school points to the systematic 'errors' or 'biases' (representativeness, anchoring, overconfidence, hot-hand fallacy, gambler's fallacy, etc.) stemming from the failure to employ the Bayesian methods of belief update. These arguments are very well known, and there is no need to dwell upon them here at length.[3]

The less-well-known bounded-rationality view also concedes that human beings do not analyse difficult problems or reach decisions by optimizing some target function or by using Bayesian methods. However, it differs from the behavioural school in claiming that human beings often employ 'fast and frugal' heuristics (in the form of rough-and-ready general rules) that produce results *often almost as good as if the full optimization approach had been employed*.

To understand how this comes about, I briefly examine three areas of disagreement between the two schools that are of relevance for our discussion: the first is the prevalence of these cognitive shortcomings; the second is the different emphasis on the social context; and the third refers to the adaptive value of the imperfect heuristics employed in the decision-making process.

---

[2]There is yet another interpretation of bounded rationality that developed into an opposite direction. This line of thought recognizes that gathering all the information required fully to analyse a problem is time consuming and entails a cost – to fix ideas, think of gathering information about buying a new home. In this school of thought (Stigler, 1961), the gathering of extra information – with presumably declining marginal benefit to the quality of the choice outcome – is stopped when the search costs exceed the benefits. The problem now becomes one of optimization under constraint (a stopping problem). Although appealing, the approach moves in the opposite direction to that of the current bounded-rationality school, in that it implies an even more complex optimization, and possibly an infinity of meta-optimizations that take into account incorporating in the cost-benefit analysis the cost of gathering information, of analysing the cost of gathering information, of analysing the cost of the cost of gathering information, etc. If anything, 'wholly unbounded rationality' would seem a better description of this modus operandi. I will not pursue this line of inquiry in the discussion that follows.

[3]See Section 12.6 for references on this topic.

12.1.1 How Pervasive are Cognitive Shortcomings?

The first point of disagreement between the two schools is the degree of pervasiveness of human cognitive deficiencies. Proponents of the bounded rationality school emphatically remind us that most of the time we do *not* make decisional mistakes, and point out that 'myriad ways in which human observers act as optimal Bayesian actors' (Knill and Pouget, 2004) have been observed. And, as Brighton and Gigerenzer (2008) remind us, '[t]he strength of this viewpoint – the implied ability of the cognitive system to "act Bayesian" – rests on the [wide] range of settings in which this finding holds…'. In a similar vein, Gigerenzer and Hoffrage (1995) argue that base-rate neglect can be perfectly rational 'when information is represented in terms of natural frequencies rather than probabilities'. So, as a partly tongue-in-cheek remark, we should perhaps ask ourselves whether we may not be victims of the representativeness heuristic ourselves when we (over)estimate the importance and pervasiveness of our cognitive failures in the face of a large body of evidence pointing to cognitive successes.

12.1.2 The Social Context

When it comes to judging the effectiveness of a way of reaching decisions, the bounded-rationality approach places strong emphasis on the context (environment) where the choice is made.[4] The metaphor often used is that of scissors, one blade of which is the cognitive limitations and the other the 'structure of the environment':

> …a great deal can be learned about rational decision making […] by taking account of the fact that the environments to which it must adapt possess properties that allow […] simplifications [of the problem at hand].
>
> Simon (1956)

As Gigerenzer and Selten (2002) point out … [s]tudying only one blade is not enough; it takes both for the scissors to cut…. So, spectacular cognitive failures due to the use of heuristics may only be such in a laboratory environment (often a 'set-up' by a clever experimenter to highlight and magnify the failure), but may be much smaller, or indeed disappear, in real-life situations. To see how this can happen in practice, take a look at the following example.

A friend of yours, Alice, wants to buy a new TV set.[5] She has dutifully read the consumer report in *Best-Buy TV*[6] and concluded that, given her budget and requirements, brand X is the best choice. Just before her purchase, however, she meets a friend, John, who, upon hearing about her choice, expresses strong reservations: 'I have bought this brand myself, and in three months I have had nothing but problems: first the remote control broke down;

---

[4]For instance, anchoring – i.e., being influenced in one's decision by an 'irrelevant' piece of pre-existing information – can have very different outcomes depending on whether the 'irrelevant information' is planted in the laboratory by an experimenter, or naturally occurs in the environment. In the latter case, it is much less likely to be truly irrelevant, and the adaptive value of being influenced by it may well be positive. See Gintis (2009), Chapter 3, for a related discussion.

[5]This example has been adapted from Schwartz (2004).

[6]I am not aware of the existence of any publication called *Best-Buy TV*. If any such publication exists, I am obviously not referring to it.

then the DVD connection stopped working; then it deleted the programmes I had recorded. And the colours are *sooo* flat ...'.

Logically, this one extra piece of information should alter minimally, if at all, Alice's resolve to buy brand X. After all, *Best-Buy TV* presumably conducted hundreds of tests under very different conditions, and the statistical weight of this body of evidence far outweighs the single, albeit first-hand, opinion of Alice's friend. In a laboratory setting, giving undue weights to John's opinion is therefore a statistical mistake, and if Alice changes her choice as a result, her decision will be labelled by the cognitive psychologist as having being biased by one of the many decisional biases, say, salience. In the real world, however, is Alice's decision not to buy brand X decision really so 'wrong' – or, perhaps, one should say, so maladaptive?

Now, *Best-Buy TV* may well present itself as an impartial tester of TV brands but how do we know that it is so impartial after all? Does a board member of X TV perhaps also sit on the board of the publishing company that controls *Best-Buy TV*? And does *Best-Buy TV* accept advertising of TV brands on its pages? If so, is brand X a major advertiser for *Best-Buy TV*? On the other hand, Alice has known John for ages as an honest, straight-talking friend, and he certainly does not work for TV makers Y. Unless Alice is prepared to do a lot of extra homework – e.g., to assess the actual impartiality of *Best-Buy TV*, or to ascertain whether John may now be working for TV makers Z – is her choice not to buy brand X after all so irrational? Is her distrust of a 'professional' rater necessarily so misplaced?

Moving from TVs to matters of more direct financial relevance, how many stocks were rated 'strong buy' by stock analysts just before the bursting of the tech bubble? How many AAA-rated CDOs defaulted within months of their stellar rating being granted? How 'irrational' would it have been to disregard the rating-based information on the basis of some piece of evidence – admittedly anecdotal and statically-insignificant – provided by someone who looked in detail at the structure of one CDO of ABSs?

12.1.3   Adaptiveness

This brings me to the third difference between the bounded-rationality and the cognitive-bias (behavioural–finance) schools. This difference stems from the evolutionary and adaptive perspective that is embraced by the bounded-rationality approach: the heuristics employed in reaching decisions may well be fast and frugal, this school says, but they must also be reasonably good for their evolutionary development to have occurred. If this were not the case, we would, after all, be an evolutionary paradox.

Bounded rationalists therefore place their emphasis on how *close* the outcomes produced by the fast and frugal heuristics actually are to the outcomes of the optimization process, not on how crass the mistakes are. So, the bounded-rationality school tends to see as

> an essential part in the architecture of the human mind [...] a collection of fast and frugal heuristics, each of which is well designed for solving a specific class of inference tasks. This adaptive toolbox contains strategies for estimation, comparison, and categorization, to name a few.
>
> Martignon (2002)

When it comes to comparing the performance of the fast and frugal adaptive toolbox with the Bayesian normative standard, Martignon (2002) finds that it is 'remarkably accurate, often outperforming multiple regression, the normative benchmark in the class of linear models. Even compared with Bayesian models, the differences in outcomes are seldom large'.

In a similar vein, Grifftiths and Tenenbaum (2005) report related results pointing out that predictions of non-experts can come remarkably close to the Bayesian normative standard in a surprisingly wide range of forecasting settings. Their findings are of particular relevance to our discussion because they focus on the implicit estimation of conditional probabilities.[7] It is also very relevant for us that, when failures in their experiments were observed, these could be explained by imperfect factual knowledge, rather than deficiency in reasoning. Griffiths and Tenenbaum (2005) show that *once better factual information was provided, a better conditional estimate was obtained*. This provides a first, simple suggestion to the risk manager faced with the task of assigning a difficult conditional probability: do your homework well. Learn, that is, the 'facts' about the problem at hand: question the causal links, and, yes, do look very carefully at the frequentist information at hand.

This point is reinforced by Jolls and Sunstein (2005), who point out that, given some legally relevant facts and evidence, subjects were first observed systematically to overesti- mate the probability of success in a trial. The reason for these overestimates can be readily traced to some of the cognitive biases (such as overconfidence) highlighted in the behavioural finance literature. The important observation, however, is that these estimates were substan- tially corrected by a number of 'cognitive exercises', for example, by suggesting that they take the other side's view into account.[8] So, here is another way to improve our probabilistic assessments: look at the problem from different angles (the different interpretative models of reality I discuss in Chapter 3).

The discussion above is important in the context of expert-judgement-based stress testing. It has two distinct implications: the first is that, pervasive as these cognitive deficiencies may be, it *is* to some extent possible to overcome them – for example, by providing better information or being aware of our tendency to fall into systematic mistakes. The second is that, as the bounded-rationality school points out, we may not be perfect Bayesian machines, but the probabilistic tasks before us are not beyond our cognitive reach: the 'fast and frugal

---

[7]Grifftiths and Tenenbaum (2005) ask their subjects to answer questions such as: a friend is reading to you a line from her favourite poem, and she tells you that it was line 5 of that poem. What would your guess be of the total length of the (unknown) poem? Or: if you met an 18-year-old man, what would your prediction be for his residual lifespan? Or, again, you walk into a kitchen and observe from the timer above the oven that a cake has been cooking for 35 minutes. What would you guess for the total baking time? Finally, suppose that someone told you that a Pharaoh who reigned in Egypt around 4000 BCE had been ruling for 11 years. What would you predict about the duration of his reign?

All these questions have a similar logical structure: they assume that you have some prior knowledge about a given topic: the typical length of reign of a Pharaoh, the life expectancy of a man, the typical baking time of a cake, etc. This, in Bayesian terms, is the prior. Then some evidence is provided about the specific problem at hand: e.g. the age (18) of the man, the time the cake has already been in the oven (40 minutes), etc. This is the 'evidence'. The subject is then required to revise the prior information on the basis of the evidence. To do so she will (implicitly) make use *of the conditional probability of each possible answer* given the evidence provided.

The high degree of success in answering this set of questions indicates not only that we can handle difficult probabilistic tasks, but also that we can be surprisingly good at estimating *conditional probabilities*.

[8]More precisely, Jolls and Sunstein (2005) refer to the work by Babcock *et al.* (1995) 'on the tendency of litigants to evaluate likely outcomes, as well as questions of fairness, in ways that systematically serve their own interests. [...] Babcock, Loewenstein and Issacharoff (1997) find, however, that in an experimental setting, this self-serving bias may be eradicated by requiring litigants to consider the weaknesses in their case or reasons that the judge might rule against them. In these circumstances, individuals in the plaintiff's and defendant's roles have similar views on likely trial outcomes and fair settlements.'

heuristics' that we employ in solving these problems are very often not so bad after all, even when a full analytical solution of the problem may not be possible or may be beyond our abilities.

If the best cure against these biases is awareness of their existence and of their exact nature, it is useful to look at them in some more detail. For this reason, I look at representativeness in the next section.

12.2   Representativeness

The simplest way to understand what the representativeness bias entails is through an example, which goes as follows.

Here is the description of a fictitious student, Tom W, taken from Shefrin (2008) who quotes and discusses original work from Kahneman and Tversky (1973):[9]

> *Tom W. is of high intelligence, although lacking in true creativity. He has a need for order and clarity, and for neat and tidy systems in which every detail finds its appropriate place. His writing is rather dull and mechanic, occasionally enlivened by somewhat corny puns and by flashes of imagination of the sci-fi type. He has a strong drive for competence. He seems to have little feeling and little sympathy for other people and does not enjoy interacting with others. Self-centred, he nonetheless has a deep moral sense.*

Consider now the following nine fields of academic specialization:

- business administration;
- computer science;
- engineering;
- humanities and education;
- law;
- library science;
- medicine;
- physical and life sciences;
- social science and social work.

As a first step some subjects[10] were asked to give their estimates of the relative frequency of students in these nine areas of specialization. This means that they were asked to give their estimates of the probability that a randomly chosen student belonged to any of the nine fields. These are the subjects' prior beliefs. We shall denote them by $P(F)$, where F stands for field (of specialization).

---

[9]Shefrin (2008), Chapter 2, page 19.

[10]The original study had a between-subject design. See Kahneman and Tversky (1973) for details – the exact experimental set-up matters little for our discussion. In my presentation, I have simplified the experiment in several respects.

Other subjects where then asked to state their opinion of how likely it was that the description (D) given above related to students in each of the nine fields. In Bayesian terms, this is just $P(D|F)$ – the probability of the description being relevant, given the field. So, when $F = Engineering$, $P(D|F)$ gives the probability 'that an engineering student shares the features in Tom's description'.[11] It provides, in other words, 'a measure of how representative Tom's description is of an engineering student'.[12] As for $P(D)$, of course, it gives the probability that a randomly chosen student should share Tom W's character description. The quantity $\frac{P(F)}{P(D)}$ then gives the ratio of engineering students who share Tom W's description. What can we say about $P(F|D)$, that is, about the probability that, given the description above, Tom is an engineering student? Before reading further, how would *you* answer this question?

Now, from Bayes' theorem we know that

$$P(F|D) = P(D|F)\frac{P(F)}{P(D)} \tag{12.1}$$

The subjects in Kahneman and Tversky's experiments estimated correctly that engineering students are 'rare' compared to other students. But they overestimated the probability that a student fitting the description above would be an engineering student. Why? Because they did not take into account in their estimate how rare engineering students are in the first place, and how this should be reflected in the ratio $\frac{P(F)}{P(D)}$.[13] Even if every single engineering student fitted Tom W's description (i.e., even if the term $P(D|F)$ were exactly equal to 1) – which is obviously an unrealistic generalization – the probability that a student fitting the description will be an engineering student ($P(F|D)$) would still be low because the fraction of engineering students ($P(F)$) is so low to start with. The reader may want to revisit the example about the deadly disease Wrong-Bayesitis discussed in Section 5.8.2. Also in that case it was representativeness that was likely to lead us astray.

The conclusion we can draw from this example is therefore the following. When one event is of much lower probability than the other, we often fail to make full use of this information, that is, we ignore the base-rate differences in probabilities between the two events. For this reason the representativeness bias is often also referred to as the base-rate bias.

Let us see how representativeness can lead us to provide a faulty assessment of a conditional probability in a financial stress-testing context. Suppose that we have to provide the probability, $P(BF|SW)$, of the failure of a major bank counterparty, BF, given a very large and sudden widening in credit spreads, SW. From Bayes' theorem we know that

$$P(BF|SW) = P(SW|BF)\frac{P(BF)}{P(SW)} \tag{12.2}$$

Once again, we can safely assume that, if a major bank fails, credit spreads will widen suddenly and massively – for the purpose of this argument we could even assume that

---

[11] Shefrin (2008), page 20.

[12] Shefrin (2008), page 21.

[13] It is worthwhile pointing out that the term $P(D)$ (how likely it is that a random student will fit Tom's description) does not change across different fields, and therefore, even if wrongly estimated, it would not affect the ratios of the across-field estimates.

the widening will occur with certainty: $P(SW|BF) = 1$. But the probability of a Lehman-style bank failure should (today, at least) be very, very low – much lower than a large and sudden widening in credit spreads. Therefore the ratio $\frac{P(BF)}{P(SW)}$ should also be very, very low, reflecting the fact that there are many more causes for a large and sudden widening in credit spreads than the failure of a major bank counterparty. As a consequence, the conditional probability $P(BF|SW)$ should be not too different from $\frac{P(BF)}{P(SW)}$:

$$P(BF|SW) \simeq \frac{P(BF)}{P(SW)} \tag{12.3}$$

So, the first message from this discussion is that, in order to provide good estimates of conditional probabilities, it is very useful to have an idea of the relative probabilities of the stand-alone events. We do not need the precise probabilities: just an understanding of which event is more likely is already of great help.

The second message is that we should be particularly careful when we deal with events of very different probabilities. The 'trick' at the root of the Wrong-Bayesitis paradox (see Section 5.8.2) lies exactly in the large difference in probability of the two 'rare' events, contracting the deadly illness and receiving a wrong positive test result. It is for this reason that assigning conditional probabilities by means of the multiplicative factors introduced in Sections 5.9 and 5.10 can be so useful. In my experience, when risk managers are asked to fill conditional probability matrices using the factors x_i^k, the resulting matrix tends to be much closer to being a coherent matrix[14] than if the conditional probabilities are directly assigned.

Lastly, the financial example of the default of a major bank and of the widening of credit spreads suggested that when we expect a causation-like link (and I am using the word 'causation' with circumspection), a good starting point for the conditional probability is the ratio of the two marginals, as shown in Equation (12.3). But we can do better than that. Causal links, as I have stressed throughout this book,[15] are extremely important and cognitively helpful. Consider Bayes' theorem again:

$$P(S)P(S|C) = P(C)P(C|S) \tag{12.4}$$

Give to the variable S the meaning 'the credit spreads of CMBSs have widened' and to C the meaning 'China has defaulted' as we did in Section 5.9. Now, would you rather assign $P(S|C)$ (the probability of CMBS spreads widening given that China has defaulted) or $P(C|S)$ (the probability that China has defaulted given that CMBS spreads have widened)? If the two marginal probabilities are given, from a mathematical point of view either task is just as simple (or difficult) as the other.[16] Not so from a cognitive point of view. Most people find that assigning $P(S|C)$ is much easier than estimating $P(C|S)$. This is because we can see a clear causal link between the default of China, the mayhem that would ensue, and the

---

[14]By coherent, I mean a conditional probability matrix that can be derived from a set of bona fide joint probabilities.

[15]See Sections 4.3 and 4.4 and Pearl (2009), Chapter 1.

[16]Also if we had frequentist information about the two events (which is obviously not the case with China defaulting), assessing from the data one conditional probability is just as easy as giving the other, but the fact would not change that we can 'work' with one piece of information more easily than with the other. Again, association is less cognitively powerful than causation.

widening of credit spreads. But we do not perceive (correctly, I believe) the widening of CMBS credit spreads as causing the default of China. At most, their widening may be an indication (a diagnosis) that China may have defaulted. For this reason, assigning $P(C|S)$ requires us to 'work against our cognitive grain'. I will touch on this point again later in this chapter when I deal with the causal and diagnostic interpretation of a conditional probability. But for the moment here is another suggestion to avoid cognitive errors: always assign conditional probabilities in the direction that you find more cognitively 'natural' – which is almost invariably the causal direction – and let Bayes' theorem do the rest of the work.[17]

12.3 Quantification of the Representativeness Bias

Behavioural finance is often accused of providing so many and so different explanations for human cognitive differences that virtually anything can be *ex post* explained, but very little *ex ante* predicted. In the case of representativeness, however, Bayes' theorem gives us a way to identify and *quantify* systematic deviations from Bayesian rationality due to representativeness. Consider once again

$$P(A|B) = P(B|A)\frac{P(A)}{P(B)} \tag{12.5}$$

and take logs of both sides:

$$\ln[P(A|B)] = \ln[P(B|A)] + \ln\left[\frac{P(A)}{P(B)}\right] \tag{12.6}$$

Trivially this can be rewritten

$$\ln[P(A|B)] = \alpha_0 \ln[P(B|A)] + \alpha_1 \ln\left[\frac{P(A)}{P(B)}\right] \tag{12.7}$$

with $\alpha_0 = 1$ and $\alpha_1 = 1$. Equation (12.7) gives the weights that a rational (Bayesian) agent should attribute to her log-prior[18] ($\ln\left[\frac{P(A)}{P(B)}\right]$) and to the log-likelihood function ($\ln[P(B|A)]$) in forming an opinion about the posterior. However, from experiments like the one reported above one can test whether either empirical coefficient turns out to be significantly different from 1. The result of this regression analysis lends itself to a ready interpretation. If a population of subjects gave too little importance to the base-line frequencies ($\ln\left[\frac{P(A)}{P(B)}\right]$ – representativeness again) this would show up in a coefficient α_1 smaller than 1. If, instead, the subjects gave too much importance to the likelihood function term ($\ln[P(B|A)]$), the coefficient α_0 would end up being significantly larger than 1. The test,

---

[17]As I will discuss, we find assigning causally-interpreted conditional probabilities perhaps too easy. This can give rise to another bias. See Section 12.4.

[18]The log of the prior is actually given by $\ln[P(A)]$, but the term $-\ln[P(B)]$ simply provides a constant offset that does not affect the conclusion. Indeed, Bayes' theorem is often written as

$$P(A|B) \propto P(B|A)P(A)$$

therefore, does not only tell us whether the estimates are Bayesian or not, but also what the root cause of the deviation is.

Although the actual experimental results have been more complex than sketched above (see Grether (1980)), the hypothesis of $\alpha_0 = \alpha_1 = 1$ has been rejected in many experiments. Representativeness in the sense explained above tends to be the most convincing explanation for the deviation from the Bayesian prescription.

12.4   Causal/Diagnostic and Positive/Negative Biases

Representativeness is not the only bias of relevance when subjectively estimating conditional probabilities. Moskowitz and Sarin (1983) look at the problem of elicitation of conditional probabilities in situations when 'the conditional probability of an event A given that some other event B is known to have occurred, $P(A|B)$, can only be assessed subjectively by an "expert"' (Moskowitz and Sarin, 1983, page 735). Their approach is of relevance to our study because they make clear that in their work conditional probability is a basic measurement that cannot be computed and has to be elicited from the subject'. These authors go on to claim that the systematic errors made even by experts in their subjective estimation of conditional probabilities 'result from systematic perceptual and cognitive biases in experts' responses. Moreover, even statistically mature experts are highly susceptible to these errors' (Moskowitz and Sarin, 1983, page 736).

What are these systematic errors due to? As we have seen, representativeness is an important, but not the only, cause for systematic biases. We can get an understanding of these additional biases by looking at a conditional probability $P(A|B)$ as a revision of the marginal probability $P(A)$ given knowledge that B has occurred. This is just the idea behind the factors x_A^B we introduced in Section 5.9. We know that conditional probabilities convey no information about causality or temporal sequence (see the discussion in Section 5.5). However, given our 'models of how the world works' we often tend to organize in our minds questions about conditional probabilities in terms of causation. There is nothing wrong with this: conditional probabilities do not pin down causation, but causation certainly affects conditional probabilities. Now, causes can work in two directions (a feature that, as we have seen, Bayesian networks exploit): when asked to estimate the conditional probability $P(A|B)$ we tend to think (perhaps unwarrantedly) that either B caused A or that A caused B. Using obvious terminology, with respect to the conditional probability $P(A|B)$ the first case is referred to as *causal* and the second as *diagnostic*. Tversky and Kahneman (1979) find that, if the subject's 'picture of the world' is such that she believes that B causes A, $(B \Longrightarrow A)$, then the elicited $P(A|B)$ turns out to be too high (in the testable sense discussed in Section 12.3) to be consistent with Bayes' theorem. The opposite is true if the relationship between A and B is perceived to be of the diagnostic type $(A \Longrightarrow B)$: 'A causal relation leads to a more substantial revision in conditional probability.' Furthermore '[i]ndividuals [...] find it easier to assess $P(A|B)$ if B is causal and have more confidence in their assessments'.[19]

In a similar vein, Tversky and Kahneman (1982) observe that 'we expect an asymmetry in inference regarding two variables whenever the first appears to explain the second better than the second explains the first'. Pursuing their argument, suppose that we define as

---

[19]Tversky and Kahneman (1979), pages 740–741, quoting results in Kahneman and Tversky (1973).

'tall' and 'fat' those individuals in a population who are above the 90th percentile of the weight and height distribution, respectively. Now, if asked to venture a guess, would you say that the probability of a person being fat given that we know she is tall is greater or smaller than the probability of a person being tall given that we know she is fat? Pause to think for a second. Now, if like most people who are asked the question you answered $P(fat|tall) > P(tall|fat)$, you have been a victim of the diagnostic/causal bias. Indeed, as the base-rate frequencies of tall and fat people in the population are by construction the same in this example, it must be that $P(fat|tall) = P(tall|fat)$.[20] The 'mistake' is due to the fact that we tend to think of being tall as a possible cause for being fat, but we do not think that being fat 'causes' a person to be tall.

To see the relevance of the diagnostic/causal bias, the reader should consider carefully again the example about China's default and the widening in CMBS spreads presented in Section 5.9. (I mean it!) As we think that the default of China 'causes' the widening of the spreads, we are likely to *overestimate* the conditional probability $P(CMBS|China)$ (when we reason in the causal direction) and *underestimate* the conditional probability $P(China|CMBS)$ (when we think in the diagnostic direction). That is why the symmetry constraint $x^{China}_{CMBS} = x^{CMBS}_{China}$ is of such help in overcoming the causal/diagnostic bias.

The representativeness and the causal/diagnostic biases are far from being the only pitfalls in making assessments of conditional probabilities. For instance, an overestimation of the conditional probability is also often observed when the relationship between the variables is perceived to be positive (increase in the marginal probability, $x^B_A > 1$) rather than negative (increase in the marginal probability, $x^B_A < 1$). So, for positive relationships the revision of the marginal probability tends to be too large and too small for negative relationships. Also in this case, awareness of the problem is the first remedy to fix our cognitive shortcomings.

A moment's thought suggests a link between the causal and the representativeness bias. Indeed, when we assume a strong causal link between A and B (in the sense that $B \implies A$), the quantity $P(A|B)$ will tend to 1 (see also the discussion in Sections 5.3 and 12.2). But then in the expression

$$P(B|A) = P(A|B)\frac{P(B)}{P(A)} \simeq \frac{P(B)}{P(A)} \tag{12.8}$$

what we are left with is only the ratio $\frac{P(B)}{P(A)}$. This is just the situation where neglect of the baseline probabilities ($P(A)$ and $P(B)$) can have a serious effect on our estimate of the conditional probability $P(B|A)$, the more so when $P(A)$ and $P(B)$ are very different – think of Wrong-Bayesitis again.

Finally, in the actual practice of risk management in general and of stress testing in particular, anchoring[21] is another cognitive bias that can stand in the way of a good assessment

---

[20]If this is not obvious to you, I am afraid you really should read Sections 5.6 to 5.9 again.

[21]Anchoring is described in the cognitive psychology literature as the tendency to be influenced by arbitrary 'reference points' that bear no relevance to the problem at hand.

As an example of anchoring, consider the following. In many countries, there are laws that require that any credit card statement should specify a minimum repayment amount. The idea behind the law is reasonable enough: it attempts to stop borrowers from just forgetting about what they owe, and accumulating amounts of debt that they will not be able to service. However, the same laws are not as prescriptive about how large the actual minimum repayment amount should be – and, as we have all certainly noticed, the repayment amounts suggested by the credit card companies are always a very small fraction of the debt incurred during the month.

This is no accident, as a study by Professor Neil Stewart, a psychologist at Nottingham University, suggests (Stewart, 2008). His intuition was that the suggested amount would turn out to be yet another of the many examples

of conditional probabilities. Anchoring works in this case when 'last week's estimate' of a conditional probability ends up influencing today's estimate, even if the market conditions may have changed, or new information has arrived in the meantime. In other words, the stale estimate can affect the current estimate just because 'it is there'.[22] Therefore, even if the availability of the latest estimates for the conditional probability matrices certainly makes the updating task less daunting and time-consuming, it is a good idea to restart 'with a clean slate' every time the construction of the matrix is undertaken.

As we have seen, the potential pitfalls are many. Luckily, Moskowitz and Sarin (1983) point out that, whatever the original causes of these cognitive biases, even if little or no instructions are given to experimental subjects, the availability and careful examination of the joint probabilities can significantly improve their initial estimates of conditional probabilities. This is particularly helpful for our applications, because the joint probability table is just the final output of the Bayesian-network approach recommended above. The reader is therefore invited to revise, once this output has been obtained, the original estimates of the conditional probabilities in the light of the joint probabilities. A simple example of this type of analysis was provided in Chapter 11.

12.5   Conclusions

The conclusions of this chapter are the following.

First, human beings are certainly not perfect Bayesian computing machines. In particular we often seem to make complex probabilistic assessment by means of 'fast and frugal heuristics' (in plain English, rules of thumb). However, these fast and frugal heuristics are frequently more effective than it would be reasonable to expect. Furthermore, lack of correct factual evidence, rather than an innate inability to 'think Bayesian', is often at the root of the probabilistic mistakes (see, in particular, the Pharaohs' example in Griffiths and Tenenbaum (2005)).

Second, the fact remains that there are still significant and systematic cognitive biases. There is no sure-proof way to overcome these biases, but some measures do help, such as the following:

- retaining an awareness of the nature of the bias;
- examining carefully all the information about the problem at hand, including, of course, the frequentist information;

---

of 'irrational anchoring': i.e., a spurious and logically irrelevant reference point that really has nothing to do with the choice at hand, yet tends to influence it in a predictable way.

To substantiate his hunch, Professor Stewart presented 413 subjects with the credit card bills for the same total amount of £435.67. The statements were identical in all respects apart from the fact that half specified a minimum repayment amount of £5.42 (little more than 1% of the outstanding amount owed), while the other half did not specify any amount at all.

Now, *per se*, the minimum repayment amount should have no influence on the decision of a rational borrower as to whether a larger amount should be repaid – and, if so, how much larger. Yet, Professor Stewart showed that, among the borrowers who did not pay their bill in full, those who had been presented with a repayment amount wanted to pay 43% less than those who had been shown any amount at all. As *The Economist* points out, '... in the real world, this would roughly double interest charges'. Not bad for a few lines' work.

[22] I am grateful to Dr Patrick deFontnouvelle for pointing this out during the course of a presentation I gave at the Federal Reserve Board of Boston in November 2009.

- cross-checking of the conditional probabilities against the joint probability matrix;

- paying explicit attention to the baseline frequencies;

- working in the causal rather than diagnostic 'direction';

- assigning the multiplicative factors x_i^k rather than the conditional probabilities directly.

These have all been shown to be useful in improving the 'undoctored' estimates.

Third, as studies in many areas of developmental and cognitive psychology show, what we can and cannot do – what we are good and bad at – is not always an intrinsic *datum*, but strongly depends on whether we believe, or are made to believe, that we are good or bad at these tasks. As the work by Professor Nisbet (2009) shows, this is true even for mathematical abilities. There is a danger, therefore, that dwelling too much on our cognitive deficiencies may become a self-fulfilling prophecy. We must always remember, after all, that if we were fundamentally unable to produce conditional estimates, our very existence would be an extraordinary evolutionary paradox.

12.6 Suggestions for Further Reading

The distinction between bounded rationality and the cognitive biases of the behavioural finance school is well discussed in Gigerenzer and Selten (20002) and references therein. In particular, an influential analysis of bounded rationality in terms of information costs dates back to Stigler (1961). Note, however, that in Stigler's analysis the economic agent not only remains unaffected by cognitive deficiencies, but also optimizes in her search for a preferred outcome (i.e., she does not use the fast and frugal heuristics posited by the bounded rationality school). The only difference with *Homo Economicus* is that Stigler's agent faces information costs, which (rationally) induce her to abandon the optimization process at a given point.

The literature on 'true' cognitive biases is enormous and has been accumulating for several decades. Much as it is still regarded as 'alternative', it must be remembered that Kahneman was awarded a Nobel Prize for his and Tversky's work. As a starting point, a good reference book is Kahneman, Slovic and Tversky (1982). A lighter and more engaging (but less precise) treatment can be found in Shefrin (2000). Kahneman and Tversky (2000) provide an excellent collection of perspectives on cognitive biases with a focus on decision-making and economic value. Chater and Oaksford (2008), and the contribution by Brighton and Gigerenzer it contains, provide a good Bayesian perspective of cognitive mechanisms.

Several papers quoted in Shefrin (2008) deal with the original studies on representativeness. They all make for very interesting reading. Grether (1980) deals with the quantification of the representativeness bias. All these papers deserve careful study to appreciate the nature of the problem. Shefirn (2008) also discusses at length heterogeneity of opinions among economic agents.

Chapter 13

Selecting and Combining Stress Scenarios

13.1 Bottom Up or Top Down?

Using the cleverest tricks to establish the marginal, conditional and even joint probabilities among events will do us very little good unless we have picked our stress scenarios in an intelligent way. There are two main schools of thought on how to do this: the bottom-up and the top-down approach.

The names are self explanatory: with the top-down approach, one selects broad 'macro' events of relevance to the economy (e.g., increase in unemployment), to the global geo-political landscape (e.g., tension between China and Taiwan), or of more general character (e.g., outbreak of a major epidemic). The links between these events and the positions on the books of the financial institution are then worked out, typically via positing interme-diate sub-events and using some model from events to losses: for instance, an increase in unemployment may cause a rise in mortgage delinquencies, which will reduce the value of mortgage-related assets via a pricing model. As a last step in the process, the associated losses (or, depending on the positions, possibly gains) are estimated.

The bottom-up approach starts instead from what I call the vulnerabilities of the portfolio, that is, from a detailed knowledge of 'where it hurts'. These vulnerabilities will generally arise either from concentrations (e.g., to names or sectors in the banking book), from large relative-value positions (long and short similar positions), or from high leverage – or, need-less to say, from combinations of the above. The portfolios are then stressed around their 'pressure points' to the desired level of severity.

13.2 Relative Strengths and Weaknesses of the Two Approaches

The top-down (or 'macro') approach has an immediate intuitive appeal, and a sort of 'West-Wing-like' glamour. Typically, behind the construction of the scenarios there is a structural model of what drives the economy – even better if there are several competing models. The top-down approach therefore builds directly into the formulation of the problem the causal links between the various macro drivers. In this respect, it lends itself very well to the Bayesian-net approach that I described in Parts II and III.

Despite its appeal, several practical problems begin to crop up as soon as one begins to put into practice a top-down approach. Let me review them in detail.

First of all, rarely do 'macro' events lead to unambiguously identifiable financial outcomes. As a consequence, the event tree can soon become very 'bushy'. A major financial crisis may weaken or strengthen the dollar depending on whether the 'market psychology' (or 'sentiment'[1]) of the moment sees the dollar as a haven currency, or the overvalued currency of an imports-addicted nation.

To give an idea of the practical difficulties associated with a top-down approach, one example springs to mind. In the summer of 2008, as the financial crisis was reaching its severest point and oil was hovering around $140/barrel, the possibility was mooted of a preemptive air strike by the Israeli air force against Iranian nuclear power plants (as if we didn't have enough problems at the time...). I was talking in those days with the head of trading of a commodities firm. I double-checked with him that such an air strike would send oil prices through the roof. His only-half-tongue-in-cheek answer was: 'An air strike will certainly do either of two things to oil prices: either they will go up a lot. Or they will plummet.'

The trader's thinking, of course, was that the air strike would either have a negative impact on the world oil supply or tip the economic sentiment resolutely towards doom and gloom, thereby depressing future projections of oil demand. The point of this anecdote is that even in this simplest of scenarios, the event tree begins to branch very soon (at the root); and almost any of the following branches carries a similar degree of uncertainty (what will the dollar do, for instance?). If our vulnerable positions are in oil (or if we are long dollars), handling this chain of dependencies may be easy enough. But what if our vulnerabilities are, say, in a large inventory of hybrid Adjustable Rate Mortgages (ARMs)? Before reaching the 'sub-event' that actually affects the vulnerable position in our books so many uncertain bifurcations in the event tree will have to be crossed that our confidence in being able to handle the associated probabilities can be rather shaken.

A second reason why a bottom-up approach may be better suited for positions held in the trading book is that relative-value trades can be extremely difficult to capture using macro scenarios. Think of a large butterfly position on a yield curve: say, paying the fixed rate in 9 years, receiving fixed in 10 years and paying fixed in 11 years in JGB (Japanese Government Bonds). (This position, by the way, is not fanciful, because around 1999–2000 the trading dynamics of the JGB futures contract were creating distortions exactly around this part of the Japanese yield curve; the distortions, in turn, were attracting the attention of relative-value traders who were taking leveraged bets that the resulting kink in the yield curve would revert to normality.) Which 'macro' scenario could possibly stress these particular positions? How do you go from 'Earthquake in Southern California' or from 'Unexpected rise in non-farm payroll' to the 'Japanese butterfly' – as the position was called at the time? How many steps does it take to get from A to B (or, perhaps, to Z)? *Is there a path connecting the macro event and the potential loss?*

---

[1] See, e.g., Akerlof and Shiller (2009), Shefrin (2008) and Skidelsky (2009) for the importance of sentiment ('animal spirits') on financial prices.

Here is a third problem with top-down approaches. If we want to assign marginal probabilities to the root events in a macro tree, we are sometimes faced with a task far more difficult than assigning marginal probabilities for financial price moves. I have stressed that a purely frequentist answer for the probability of a price move of a given (large) magnitude should always be regarded with healthy suspicion. But at least we have in the raw data a starting point, something to fall back on if everything else fails. How do we begin to assign even an order-of-magnitude probability to an event like 'Increased tension in the South China Sea'? In comparison, estimating an approximate probability for an event such as 'S&P falls by 20%' looks like child's play. In Keynesian language, we are dealing in the case of most geopolitical events with pure uncertainty, not with risk.

Sure enough, the problem does not magically disappear with the bottom-up approach. We still have to come up with marginal and conditional probabilities. The trick, however, is to choose our events as 'close' as possible to the pressure points of the portfolio, so that we can reach the significant losses we are interested in as small a number of steps as possible. Then the task of assigning the various probabilities can be made more manageable.

A fourth feature of macro approaches to stress testing that can limit their applicability for trading-book positions has to do with the holding period. When one specifies events like 'sharp rise in unemployment', 'onset of deflation', 'generalized fall in house prices', etc., one is referring to time periods ranging from a few months to a few years. For instance, the capital adequacy test run by the Federal Reserve Bank of New York early in 2009 for 'Fed-19 banks',[2] asked for cumulative losses over a two-year period given a base-line and an adverse scenario for unemployment, house prices and GDP growth. (See Hirtle, Schuermann and Stirch (2009) for an excellent example of a thoughtful exercise in stress testing at a macro level.) Such a time frame is very relevant to stress the structural or illiquid positions of a bank, but makes little sense for trading-book positions (assuming, of course, that what has been placed in the trading book belongs there...).

It is therefore fair to say that a top-down or macro approach can be well suited to stressing the resilience and survivability of a financial institution over time periods ranging from a few months to a few years, but does not readily lend itself to the analysis of trading-book positions.

Of course, there are also disadvantages with the bottom-up approach. The first is a certain degree of ad-hockery: since we start right from 'where it hurts' we may be missing the bigger picture. Trees loom very large in this approach, sometimes hiding the forest. For instance, some portfolio-related 'events' have common underlying causes that do not figure in our set of Boolean variables (say, a sudden and generalized deterioration in market liquidity, an increase in risk aversion or a widespread pulling-back from over-structured products). In principle the effect of these 'latent causes' could be captured by our conditional probability tables, but doing so can be difficult.

Also, when we employ a bottom-up approach, we are more likely to assign proximate rather than primary causes: we are closer to a reduced-form approach than to a fully-specified model. This can be good or bad, depending on how 'phenomenological' we want our approach to end up being.

So, when it comes to top-down or bottom-up, there is no such thing as an approach that works best under all circumstances. Questions of organizational resilience, analyses of the

---

[2]Why 19? The 'Fed-19 banks' were chosen as the banks that, at the point in time of the test, had a balance sheet of at least $100bn.

impact on profitability of regulatory or macro-economic events, studies of the performance under adverse conditions of buy-and-hold and banking-book portfolios are all probably better handled by a top-down approach. The shorter the holding period of the positions that are being stressed, the more compelling the case becomes for a bottom-up approach.

13.3   Possible Approaches to a Top-Down Analysis

If we decide that a top-down approach is our preferred route, we can do worse than looking carefully at what has been done for decades in areas such as foreign policy analysis and security planning. Much as I dislike the word 'paradigm', one useful approach goes under the name of creating strategic paradigms. For instance, in a security-planning context Davis and Sweeney (1999) identify several plausible, coherent geopolitical developments (which they call 'paradigms') and build their analyses around a number of *coherent* sets of events, rather than a series of isolated 'stresses'. Even if their focus is very different from that of a financial institution, it pays to look at their approach in some detail. Specifically, they analyse the following:

- *Paradigm A: Coalition of Opposing States*: the coalescence of a loose coalition of states opposed to the United States, led by a strong China and a weaker Russia (Davis and Sweeney, 1999, page 225).

- *Paradigm B: Multipolarity*: 'the United States does not face a bifurcated international system, but rather confronts a setting in which five or six great powers have emerged' (Davis and Sweeney, 1999, page 238).

- *Paradigm C: Weak Unipolarity*: 'the international system could develop in such a way that the United States remains the world's sole great power. This system would emerge [...] from the inability of other great-power contenders to develop the means or inclination to claim status as a major pole' (Davis and Sweeney, 1999, page 255).

- *Paradigm D: Chaos*: 'the United States is left as the sole superpower' and 'the major threat to global security comes from the breakdown of the state in several regions of the world' (Davis and Sweeney, 1999, page 274).

Why did I relate the approach by Davis and Sweeney (1999) in such detail? To underline the fact that, associated with each paradigm, there is a coherent story of how this posited development comes about, and of how it would affect different international players (Europe, China, the Middle East, etc.). Each paradigm therefore weaves together a set of linked interactions. Under the assumption underpinning each paradigm the question is asked of what the most likely response of each power block might be. Any of the available models, such as, say, the Rational Actor Model (see, e.g., Allison and Zelikov (1999)) or the institutional model (see, e.g., Davis and Sweeney (1999)), then provide an indication of what the response of the various players might be given the posited scenario.

In a financial setting, a paradigm is therefore made up of a story and model, not of a single event. 'Sharp rise in inflation', in this context is not a paradigm, but a stand-alone scenario. There are many states of the world in which a sharp rise of inflation may occur, and they may have very little in common. A sharp rise in inflation, for instance, can come about from an economy forging ahead on all cylinders in a situation of overloose monetary policy. But it may also arise as the consequence of overdone quantitative easing by central banks, carried out in order to pull an economy out of a deep recession. Clearly, the 'other events' (such as unemployment, corporate defaults, mortgage arrears, etc.) in the 'paradigm' will be very different in the two cases, at least in the short-to-medium term.

Once again, it is difficult to overemphasize the importance of simple structural models, imperfect as these may be.

13.4 Sanity Checks

Whichever approach is used, how do we make sure that we do not leave something obvious behind? When it comes to stress testing, there is no 'completeness theorem' to help us – there is no guarantee, that is, that we have not overlooked some major events. We can, however, employ a number of sanity checks.

The first and most obvious one is to compare the outcome of our stress analysis (i.e., the losses it suggests) against the worst losses our current portfolio would incur under the changes in risk factors 'contained' in the longest data series at our disposal. It is not necessarily the case that the loss produced by the most adverse historical change in risk factors (given today's portfolio) must be a lower bound for the subjective loss. Perhaps we are confident enough to argue that the conditions under which these most adverse historical changes occurred cannot possibly repeat themselves today. For instance, perhaps we can argue that the South-East Asia currency crisis of 1997–1998 cannot occur in, say, 2010 because the same countries are no longer relying on 'hot' foreign investment, and now sit on huge foreign reserves. Perhaps we can argue that a 1987-like equity market crash cannot occur because portfolio insurance is no longer as widespread. This is perfectly reasonable, since, after all, altering frequentist probabilities (or, indeed, possibility of occurrence) of events using subjective judgement is a two-way street: it can tell us that some events are more *or less* likely than they have been in the past (or, in the limit, impossible). It must be conceded, however, that from a prudential point of view only a very courageous risk manager would completely discard a chain of events that already happened in the past.

A second, weaker, sanity check is the following. We can compare the subjective loss we have produced with the largest historical loss actually incurred (with a possibly very different portfolio) by our financial institution. Here the warning sign is much weaker, and it is much easier to argue that we should not worry: for instance, if a bank exited a line of business after spectacular losses, those losses have very tangential relevance to today's conditions. The decision as to whether past losses are relevant to today's condition can become more nuanced if, for instance, we have today similar positions as when the loss was incurred, but we have put 'protection in place' (say, by buying CDSs or equity puts). Arguably, we could claim that, given this bought protection, the historical losses are no longer relevant. We would do well, however, to ask how confident we can be that the bought protection will still be there when we need it – as any purchaser of monoline protection knows all too well after *circa* 2007.

In short, also in this case there are no hard-and-fast rules, or unambiguous floors. However, bringing to light, analysing and comparing these reference losses with the subjective ones is a valuable and instructive process in itself. It is also a process that can provide a simple audit trail that elementary due diligence has been followed in arriving at the subjective losses. This is particularly important if the outcome of the subjective analysis is to be used for internal limits or for regulatory capital purposes.

Finally, we should always compare our subjective probabilities with the same quantities obtained using a purely frequentist approach. As I have said, in financial matters I consider subjective probabilities more reliable and useful. But I also believe that these subjective probabilities always rest on the twin pillars of data and models of reality. I have argued long enough that data by themselves are mute. However, models unsupported by data are vacuous. Frequentist data are not the ultimate answers, but it would be foolish to neglect them.

13.5   How to Combine Stresses – Handling the Dimensionality Curse

In this book I have argued that, to be of value, stress testing must be an exercise that combines in a coherent picture the various severe adverse events that can affect a book, a business or an institution. Simply producing a list of 'scary scenarios' is of limited use. Not surprisingly, when stress testing is simply the presentation of a number of unrelated adverse events, senior management are unlikely to engage and give it much attention. The words by Aragones, Blanco and Dowd (2001) and Berkowitz (1999) quoted in the opening pages of Chapter 1 give a clear explanation of why this is the case.

Weaving the various scenarios and stress events into a more coherent whole is therefore highly desirable. But, especially when one employs the bottom-up approach suggested above, one is still often faced with a very large number of events. Even if we limit our attention to a subset of the possible Bayesian nets that may conceivably connect them (say, to what we called in Section 8.8.1 the $\mathbb{S}_2$ subspace), the specification of the marginal and conditional probabilities can still become too difficult a task if the number of variables exceeds a dozen. For the avoidance of doubt, I must stress again that the difficulties I am referring to are not of computational nature – CPU is, these days, cheap and plentiful enough. What is time-demanding and cognitively challenging is the thoughtful, yet parsimonious, determination of the dependencies, and of the conditional probability tables (or matrices) that underpin the approach. The 'sanity checks' that I strongly advocate (such as the 'triplet constraint' described in Section 9.6.2) fulfil the important role of forcing the risk manager (and the trader, and, we hope, the senior manager) to think hard about how the different events 'hang together'. But they do not 'come cheap'. Having being involved in the process, I have found the exercise of creating, checking and revising the conditional probability tables and matrices one of the intellectually most demanding tasks a risk manager can undertake. There is little hope of carrying this out in a meaningful manner for more than about ten events. This being the case, how do we choose these events? How do we carry out the cruel 'pruning' without which the exercise is doomed to failure?

I can only offer some pragmatic suggestions here, which fall well short of a systematic approach to dimensionality reduction. I have nonetheless found them sufficiently useful in practice to deserve some attention. As the dimensionality problem tends to arise most frequently in the bottom-up approach, my treatment is tailored to this mode of operation.

Let us suppose that the activities of a bank are divided into business lines, which we will call in the following Equities (E), Foreign Exchange (FX), Commodities (C), Credit Trading (CT), Mortgages (M) and Fixed Income (FI). The risk manager responsible for, say, FI, will have determined – perhaps, but not necessarily, using the bottom-up approach – a handful of stressful events for the fixed-income book under her watch. Using the techniques described above (Linear Programming and Bayesian nets) she will also have determined the associated conditional expected losses, $L_i(FI)$, where the index i labels the FI-related events. Note that this can be accomplished even if the simple Linear Programming approach, which requires no marginal probabilities, has been followed. She can then rank the fixed-income-related conditional expected losses thus obtained from largest to smallest. At this stage no probabilistic statement about their occurrence has been made.

The other risk managers will have similarly determined, and ranked, their conditional expected losses, $L_{i_C}(C)$, $L_{i_E}(E)$, $L_{i_M}(M)$, $L_{i_{FX}}(FX)$ and $L_{i_{CT}}(CT)$. The indices $i_C, i_E, \ldots, i_{CT}$ label the losses from commodities, equities, ..., credit trading, and each index runs from 1 to the number, $n_C, n_E, \ldots, n_{CT}$, of vulnerabilities (and hence losses) in the various portfolios.

Once this is done, the losses from all the business lines can be put together and sorted from largest to smallest. The risk managers can then set a materiality cut-off, or more pragmatically, choose the maximum number of variables they feel they can handle. Suppose that n events (Boolean random variables) are selected, with $n \lesssim 10$. To each event (i.e., to the realization of each Boolean variable) there is associated a conditional expected loss that 'takes into account' the interaction of the other stress events in the same asset class. So, for instance, the event with the largest expected conditional loss could 'come from' the fixed-income area and it could correspond, say, to the steepening of the yield curve. Its associated expected conditional loss will of course also 'contain information' about the other *fixed-income-related* stress events (say, a widening of swap/government spreads, the narrowing of the OIS/LIBOR spread, etc.).

The risk manager can now begin to build the Bayesian network as described above using the n chosen events with the largest conditional losses as variables. The variable associated with each node will be the primary event associated with each of the top n losses. So, for instance, one event, coming from the fixed-income area, could be a yield curve steepening.

How shall the conditional probability table then be constructed? Since the losses are conditional expected losses, these are the losses that on average one can expect to make if the associated primary event (say, the yield curve steepening) occurs.

Let us collapse the full distribution of conditional losses associated with each primary event to a Dirac-δ distribution centred at its expectation. What we are saying is that, conditional on a given primary event happening, we will make the conditional loss associated with it with certainty.

This is crude but useful. In fact, if we are prepared to make this heroic assumption we can then associate to the expected conditional loss, $L_i(X)$ (where X denotes the generic business line), the same probability of occurrence as the event that gives rise to $L_i(X)$.

It bears repeating that with this approximation what one is saying is that, conditional on event E_{X_i} having occurred, the loss incurred will be $L_i(X)$ with certainty. I must stress, however, that this is *not* the loss due to the stand-alone occurrence of the associated stress event, but it is a loss that 'knows about' the interaction (concentration, diversification, etc.) with the other losses *in the same asset class*.

Of course, even if up to this point the risk managers had only provided conditional probabilities, to make progress the marginal probabilities for the primary events will now have to be supplied. The risk managers, however, will only have to supply, say, five to ten such estimates. The number of the conditional probability tables required by the pruned Bayesian net will also be correspondingly much, much smaller than if we had retained the losses from all the asset classes. And as for what is in the conditional probability tables themselves, the maximum order of conditioning, of course, will depend on the assumption about the 'connectivity', k, of the Bayesian net in the subset $\mathbb{S}_k$ that we want to build.

The advantage of this approach is substantial. If each risk manager has started from, say, eight stress scenarios for her own asset class, a brute-force approach with no 'pruning' would require about 50 marginal probabilities, and dozens of conditional probability tables. Questionable as the assumptions behind the approach described above might be, they can make the difference between being able to implement the approach in a real-life situation or not.

Of course, such a huge simplification does not come for free. There is, to start with, the collapse to a δ-distribution of the full possible distribution of conditional losses associated with a given stress event to worry about. More subtly, but, possibly more importantly, there is no guarantee that some stress event that was 'just below the cut-off' might not, if retained, have given rise to a more adverse interaction with other scenarios.

13.6   Combining the Macro and Bottom-Up Approaches

So far I have presented the bottom-up and the top-down approaches as incompatible. But this need not be the case. I present in this section an example of how they can be made to talk to each other.

Let us consider the case where we have identified five vulnerabilities for our portfolio:

- default of China;

- equity market crash;

- widening in spreads of CMBSs;

- generalized widening of credit spreads;

- sharp increase in short rates.

Suppose that we follow the prescription for building a Bayesian net outlined in Chapters 9 and 11. The first thing we have to do is to draw boxes with the names of the events on a sheet of paper. This is the easy bit. See Figure 13.1, where the different variables have been placed pretty much randomly, that is, without any thought as to the possible causal links we may end up drawing.

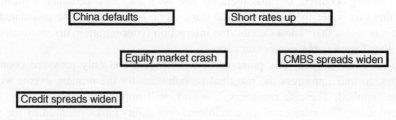

Figure 13.1   Building a Bayesian net: placing the variables.

Now we have to draw the arrows that connect the boxes. This is where the thinking begins.

The problem is that some events can be reasonably thought of as causes of others – say China's default would presumably 'cause' an equity market crash. But for some other events what causes what depends on how macro events in the real world are actually unfolding. For instance, an unexpected rise in short rates could cause a fall in equity prices. However, this may not be the case if the rise in rates came on the back of particularly good economic news – see, for instance, what happened to equity prices *worldwide* when the Australian Central Bank unexpectedly raised rates in October 2009.

It pays therefore to draw a small set of causal links (directed arrows) among the variables on the basis of a small number of macro scenarios. This means building a different Bayesian net for each of the underlying macro scenarios. The interesting feature of the approach is that the macro scenarios in question could be those chosen for a top-down stress-testing exercise for the firm as a whole. This approach therefore goes some way towards combining macro-driven with vulnerability-driven approaches to stress testing.

Let us see how this can work out in practice. In one macro scenario it is an Asian crisis that triggers mayhem in the markets. The variable associated with the event 'China default' could therefore be a primary ancestor in our Bayesian net. If this is the case, the widening in CMBS spreads and the generalized widening of credit spreads can probably be conflated into one single event. The sharp increase in short rates (which in this scenario is now very unlikely) would then probably be another primary variable (i.e., a variable without parents). The Bayesian net may therefore look something like Figure 13.2.

Another scenario could be driven by, say, a specific deterioration in the commercial real estate area. In this macro scenario it is unlikely that a rise in short rates could be due to 'good news'. So it is reasonable to posit a negative causal link between the rise in rates and equity prices. In this case a plausible Bayesian net could look something like Figure 13.3.

It is easy to see how the reasoning could be extended. The macro scenarios I have sketched for this baby example are, of course, over-stylized. In reality comprehensive 'paradigms' like the ones presented in Section 13.3 above should be carefully devised. As each 'paradigm' could be one of the firm-wide macro stress tests, we have a way to associate the 'banking book' losses coming from the top-down approach and the 'trading book' losses coming from the bottom-up approach.

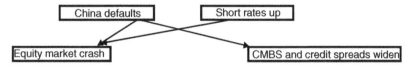

Figure 13.2 Building a Bayesian net: assigning the causal link among the variables.

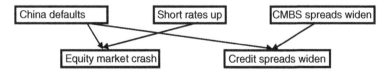

Figure 13.3 A Bayesian net reflecting the causal links discussed in the text.

Now that we have drawn the arrows (one set of arrows for each macro scenario), the next task is to fill in the conditional probability tables. Everything works as explained above, but needless to say, the entries in these tables are macro-scenario-dependent. For instance, the marginal probability of short rates rising could be very different in the case of an Asian crisis or of inflationary pressures appearing in Western economies.

The final result of this exercise would be a set of joint probabilities for each macro scenario. The analysis can then proceed as usual. We have to be careful, though: what we have obtained are now *sets* of joint probabilities, each conditional on one macro scenario coming true. Perhaps we may want to build a Bayesian net linking the macro scenarios, produce the associated conditional probability table and obtain a 'true' overall joint probability distribution. Appealing as this approach may be from a conceptual point of view, the practical difficulties in carrying out this exercise can make brave risk managers tremble with fear. I would suggest that just analysing the outputs from the various macro scenarios (with the attached probability of joint-event losses) is a very valuable exercise in itself. Going back to the capital adequacy stress test carried out by the Federal Reserve Bank in early 2009, this is exactly what it did: it produced a base-line and an adverse macro scenario, asked the banks to give their quantitative feedback for both scenarios and critically examined the results from the various banks originating from the two scenarios.[3]

If a way to associate capital to stress losses is what we are looking for, it does not take too much imagination to dream up some prudential worse-off rule.

---

[3] Incidentally, here is another similarity between the exercise carried out by the Federal Reserve Bank and the approach I recommend in this book: the 'adverse' scenario of the Fed was defined as a one-in-ten event (Schuermann, 2009, personal communication). Note the broad-brush, order-of-magnitude specification of the probability level, and the conscious effort to avoid spurious precision.

Chapter 14

Governance

14.1   The Institutional Aspects of Stress Testing

Stress testing does not take place in a vacuum. Even the best ideas about stress testing will come to little use unless the way it is carried out is consonant with the risk-management practices of the institutions that make use of it. To be effective, stress testing must lead to decisions and, when appropriate, to action. For this to occur, the overall stress-testing process must meet a large number of institutional requirements, such as the following:

- transparency and ease of use;

- challenge by non-specialists;

- checks for completeness;

- interactions among different specialists;

- auditability of the process and of the results;

- sensitivity of the outputs to the inputs and the underlying assumptions must be made transparent.

This list is far from exhaustive, but already gives an idea of the institutional complexity that a well-thought-out stress-testing programme entails. Let me explain what I mean by these one-liners in greater detail.

14.1.1   Transparency and Ease of Use

The outcomes of the stress-testing exercise must be presentable in a way that engages the attention of all its users, from expert risk managers and traders to non-specialist senior managers. The output of stress testing will typically serve different functions for different users: it can be used for information, for discussion, for risk control (e.g., via limits) and to inform action (e.g., reduction of positions or purchase of protection). As one moves up the decisional chain of a financial institution, the information provided must become progressively more synthetic, concise and easier to question at a qualitative level. When the risk manager communicates the results of the stress test to senior executives, the details of the construction of the conditional probability tables may have to be removed from sight like a piece of scaffolding that is removed once the building job is done. I say 'removed', but not discarded. At every step any user must be able to question and challenge the assumptions. Traders, for instance, may question a particular choice for a marginal or conditional probability (even if they may not phrase their challenge quite in these terms). When this happens, a risk manager had better have done her homework well if she wants to retain her credibility (see the next section).

14.1.2   Challenge by Non-specialists

One of the appealing features of the approach I propose is that non-specialists, and in particular, intelligent users with little or no quantitative background, can challenge the choices made along the way. A non-specialist should, for instance, be able to ask: 'Why did you assume that this event depends on these two events, not on these?' (By the way, 'for the sake of simplicity' is an excellent answer, as long as it is made clear that this is the case.) The same non-specialist should feel able, and encouraged by the way the results are presented, to ask: 'Why is the probability of credit spreads widening given an equity market crash 80%?' The input of a non-quantitative but experienced trader is in this respect invaluable.

The assumptions that underpin the approach presented in this book are more transparent than, say, the choice of the number of degrees of freedom in a t-Student distribution, or the exact type of copula function chosen. This is an advantage of the approach, and as such, it should be exploited.

14.1.3   Checks for Completeness

Most stress-testing approaches start from some criterion to decide whether a given candidate qualifies or not as a stress event to be analysed: for instance, the criterion may be based on the magnitude of the potential loss. No matter how thorough the risk manager strives to be, no list of possible stress events will ever be 'complete' – nor is it obvious what 'complete' could mean in this context. Nonetheless, the risk manager must ensure that she has not left something obvious by the wayside. This is far more common than one might think. Risk managers seem to be both constitutionally inclined and condemned always to prepare for yesterday's war. The endless arrays of Maginot lines built by risk managers (and regulators, bankers, etc.) in the financial theatres of operations are a testament both to Fortune's wickedness, and to the limitation of human imagination.

In order to try to contain the damage – and the embarrassment – some criteria should therefore be specified to ensure that major stress events have not been 'forgotten'. I mentioned several of these sanity checks in Section 13.4, but it is a good idea to go briefly over them again.

A good starting point is to consider the worst historical hypothetical loss[1] in the longest database at the risk manager's disposal, and compare it with the outcome from the stress testing exercise. The risk manager may well conclude that today's conditions are such that the historical loss cannot possibly repeat itself today, but the question of why this is the case should, at the very least, be asked.

Similarly, the largest losses incurred by a financial institution in the recent and not-so-recent past should be carefully examined, and the question asked whether they could occur tomorrow again. Perhaps the offending risk positions and concentrations have been cut; perhaps today's conditions are totally different; perhaps hedging positions have been put in place. But, just for peace of mind, all these 'perhaps' should be carefully examined.

Another valuable sanity check is simply asking traders and risk managers about potential losses and portfolio vulnerabilities in areas not under their daily professional watch. I have always found it amazing how penetrating traders' risk insight can be when they look not at their own but at their colleagues' positions.

Major historical blow-ups (from Metallgesellshaft to LTCM to Amaranth) should be carefully examined, especially when some of the strategies (from swap spread carry trades, to various cash/futures bases, to summer/winter gas spreads) have a tendency to be put in place, under different guises, over and over again: history does not repeat itself, but it certainly rhymes.

Many institutions routinely run stress scenarios against standardized stress events (such as: rigid move of all yield curves by 50 basis points, equity market crash by 30%, oil spike by 60%, etc.). These standardized stress events may not be particularly realistic (all yield curves have never moved in parallel by 50 basis points), and they may be unable to uncover the vulnerability of a complex portfolio, especially when this is peppered by highly leveraged relative-value positions. Despite all of this, the losses associated with these ready-made stresses should still be looked at and compared carefully with the output of the more realistic and sophisticated approach proposed above. There may be very good reasons why a more focused stress approach is 'superior', but these reasons must be identified and clearly articulated.

Finally, as discussed in the previous chapter, it would be foolish to dispense with the analysis of all the frequentist information the risk manager can gather.

Even when all of this checking has been done, still there is no guarantee that everything has been caught in the net of our stress-event identification procedure. However, if the risk manager has done her job properly, all these sanity checks should throw up either milder losses than the ones identified by the risk manager, or the same ones. Even in this case, the time spent carrying out the sanity checks will not have been wasted, because the outcomes can provide reassurance that a certain degree of 'due diligence' has been carried out in selecting the stress events. This can be of particular relevance when it comes to convincing a regulator or an audit committee that a robust and justifiable process has been followed.

14.1.4 Interactions among Different Specialists

For the process described in this book to work well, the interaction of professionals with very different skills and types of experience are required. Let me list a few:

---

[1]By hypothetical loss I mean a loss that would be incurred given today's positions if the combination of changes in risk factors that happened on one particular day in the past occurred today.

- The identification of relevant stress events will typically be carried out by traders and front-line risk managers. A strong understanding of market dynamics (understood as 'how the market works') is the most relevant skill here.

- The association of the magnitude of the loss with the probability level will have to be carried out by risk managers and quantitative analysts who have both a good understanding of statistical estimation techniques, and a strong grasp of how relevant past data may be to today's conditions.

- After this piece of analysis has been carried out, and the magnitude and type of the various losses has become apparent, the selection of the most salient stress events we want to retain and work with (what I called elsewhere the 'pruning' process) can take place. Risk managers with a good understanding of the capital and liquidity position of the institution they work for are best placed to carry out this task.

- Once we know what the relevant stress events are (or, rather, which ones we can handle given our cognitive and computational constraints) a parsimonious network of causal links among them must be established. Quantitative analysts, traders and front-office risk managers must interact here.

- The elicitation of the minimal set of marginal and conditional probabilities required to fill in the conditional probability tables requires careful analysis and discussion by the same parties.

- Obtaining the joint probabilities is, in a sense, a mechanical process, which could, in theory, be delegated to pure quantitative analysts. However, as I showed in Chapters 7 to 9, this is a very interactive process, during which the various derived probabilities (marginal via the completion property, conditional by repeated use of the Bayes' theorem, and joint by a combination of the above) should be questioned at each stage.

- Also the various 'sanity checks' (triplet conditions, etc.) should invite debate, questioning and a back-and-forth process of progressive adjustment.

- Finally we have the output. In a way, this is just the beginning of the process. Different ultimate users will look at the results in a different light. Traders may want to compare the outputs of this process with their qualitative understanding of their (and their colleagues') books. Risk managers will have a tool to check whether the positions taken on by the financial institution are congruent with the risk appetite articulated by the board. Of course, if limits or guidelines have been applied to the outcomes of the stress test, these must be monitored and enforced. Senior management must be presented with a synthetic and intuitive view of the results, possibly accompanied by an economic 'story' of how the stress losses may come about. In doing so, the detailed workings of the process, especially the most technical ones, will almost certainly be 'removed from sight'. It is important, at the same time, to convey an idea of which broad assumptions have gone into the analysis, and of the limitation of the approach. Given the intuitive appeal of the approach, it is possible that senior managers, and even board members, may be inclined to question some of the building blocks, such as: 'Why has this and not that causal link been chosen?', or 'Why has the probability of X happening given that Y has happened been assumed to be 40%?' For this debate to happen, information must be presented in an intuitively appealing and information-preserving manner.

The process is complex, and a lot of time must be devoted to it. Refreshingly, the 'time' in question is mainly thinking time, rather than CPU time. The important thing to point out is that there is only so much delegation of responsibilities to specialists and quants that can take place, if we want the process to remain effective.

This should come as no surprise. I believe that the output from a purely statistical approach such as VaR must be complemented by a tool, such as stress testing, which is different in nature but of similar breadth and import. If this is the case, it would be unreasonable to expect that a handful of clever people working quietly in a forgotten corner of the bank could provide all the answers required. If we think of the size of the capital expenditure budget and of the recurring payroll costs required to run the VaR programme for a bank, we cannot expect that a realistic alternative can be achieved at little cost and with negligible effort.

14.1.5   Auditability of the Process and of the Results

The stress-testing programme I have proposed in this book can have many applications, both internal and external to an institution. Regulators are still discussing exactly which form the capital add-ons beyond VaR will take, but they will certainly associate some form of stress testing to the new additional trading-book capital. At the time of writing, regulators are firmly leaving the responsibility of coming up with a workable stress-testing framework to the industry. Statistical (frequentist) approaches, especially when it comes to rare events, have many drawbacks (and these have been recognized by the regulators), but at least they have the advantage of an apparent ease of standardization. If the approach suggested in this book is going to be used to calculate some form of capital add-on the regulators must understandably be able to make themselves happy that the process is robust, and that a high-quality challenge by an independent function has occurred at every crucial stage of the process. The subjectivity of the probability inputs is one source of the strength of the approach and gives it the potential for being much more powerful than a traditional frequentist approach. The same subjectivity, however, can also be its weakness from the point of view of an external 'observer'. To allay the understandable scepticism of regulators, they must be reassured not so much of the 'correctness' of the inputs, but of the fact that they are unbiased, and that once chosen, they will not become subject to internal pressure by the front office. There are ways to ensure that this is the case, but the importance of this aspect cannot be overemphasized. I touched above on the need for transparency if the results are to be used effectively *within* an institution. An extra dimension of transparency must therefore be enforced if regulators are to endorse the process for capital purposes.

14.2   Lines of Criticism

There are several grounds on which the approach proposed in this book could be criticized. Having spoken to many risk managers, the main strands of criticism can be grouped under two broad rubrics: complexity and subjectivity. Given the particularly prominent role played by subjective expert judgement in the process I have described in this book, I will start from this aspect.

14.2.1   The Role of Subjective Inputs

> ...[t]he subjectivist states his judgements, whereas the objectivist sweeps them under
> the carpet by calling assumptions knowledge, and [...] basks in the glorious objectivity
> of science.
>
> Good (1973)

One of the recurrent objections that are raised to the approach I have presented is that 'it is too subjective'. Surprisingly, sometimes this objection is raised even by risk managers, who should be the 'experts' from whom the judgement is sought, and who, presumably, should feel empowered by an approach that calls for abilities not possessed by a 'shift-F9 monkey'.

It is true that the approach above calls for subjective judgement. Several clarifications are, however, in order.

First of all, every approach has a surprisingly large degree of subjectivity embedded into its execution. In this respect, the main difference between traditional techniques and the approach I propose here are the transparency and auditability of its subjective aspects, the ease with which its underlying assumptions can be understood, and the simplicity with which sensitivity analysis to its inputs can be carried out.

Let me start from my first claim, that is, that every approach to stress testing (and indeed to the quantification of risk) has an embedded element of subjectivity. Consider, for instance, the case of the VaR statistic calculated using a historical simulation approach. Surely, almost nothing has been left to the judgement of the risk manager. The answer is 'all in the data'. Or is it?

To begin with, how has the length of the data window been chosen? If, as frequently happens, we use a finite window with equal weights (say, of two years) we are implicitly saying that every single day in this two-year period 'counts' exactly as much as yesterday – where 'counts as much as yesterday' means here that it has exactly the same statistical relevance for the prediction of tomorrow's price moves. So, what happened exactly two years ago has the same 'salience' as what happened yesterday, but what happened two years and one day ago has no relevance at all. To understand the relevance of this very subjective (but rarely questioned) choice, the reader can reflect on the following: at the time of this writing the default of Lehman happened almost exactly one year ago. For those banks that, with the blessing of the regulators, calculate – and report! – their VaR on the basis of a one-year window, the institutional memory of the most dramatic financial event of the last 50 years will be lost next Monday. For those banks who instead use a two-year window (and also do so with the blessing of the regulators), the VaR analysed for internal risk management purposes and reported for external information will be affected by completely different events.

Surely, the solution here is to use non-constant weights. I am all in favour of using well-chosen weights. But the question is: what do we mean by 'well-chosen'? Is time proximity the only criterion of relevance? If not, then a subjective choice of which 'patches' of past history are relevant and which are not must surely be introduced. Even if past events are simply given exponentially decaying weights, how the decay constant is chosen can make an enormous (and opaque!) difference. The popular decay factor of 0.94, for instance, gives approximately half as much weight to events that happened 12 days ago as to yesterday's occurrence, and weighs events that happened 30 days ago little more than 15%.

Let us look at another topic that greatly affects 'objective' risk measures, yet is often swept under the carpet: the issue of mapping. Suppose that we are calculating VaR for a currency that has never de-pegged, but that we fear may do so in the near future. Clearly, the time series history for that particular currency will not give us a reasonable answer: a strict frequentist can only look at the available, de-pegging-free history, and shrug her shoulders. The standard response from less doctrinaire risk managers who still like their answers to come straight from distributions and percentiles is to 'map' the currency in question to the history of another 'similar' currency that *did* default. But what constitutes a *similar* currency? Is geographical proximity the main relevant criterion – that is, if the currency we are interested in is a South-East Asian should we necessarily look for another currency in this part of the world? Or is the state of current account balance of the country more relevant? More subtly: suppose that the particular currency we are interested in *did* de-peg in the past, say, during the 1997–1998 crisis, but is now running a massive current account surplus and has curbed the influx of hot investment money? Are we happy in using that patch of history for our guess about what might happen tomorrow, just because it is in our dataset?

The case of the currency de-pegging is, of course, a limiting one. But similar mapping choices are ubiquitous, because we cannot just have a time series for every single price, rate, volatility or risk factor. Of course, there is nothing wrong about this – these are just the hard choices that a reasonable risk manager or statistician will always have to make. It is the 'objectivity' pretence that is difficult to defend. Subjectivity plays an important role in all statistical analysis, and in statistical analysis applied to risk management more than anywhere else. The more productive approach is to acknowledge and make as transparent as possible the inevitable choices that invariably have to be made. Sunlight is also in this context the best disinfectant.

And there are far more subjective inputs that come into the determination of the so-called 'objective' risk measures – and that are routinely ignored or forgotten at disclosure time. To begin with, the choice of percentile in the case of the VaR or CES statistics is as arbitrary as it is important.[2] Once the percentile has been chosen, the method of calculation itself (Monte Carlo, historical simulation, variance-covariance, etc.) can also affect the results greatly. If more sophisticated techniques such as Extreme Value Theory or Copula Theory are used, the precise choice of the copula or of the tail behaviour and their precise parametrization can make enormous differences, especially when it comes to estimating the probability of very rare events. And, of course, this list is not exhaustive.

In short, the general point is threefold: subjectivity is unavoidable; in statistical risk analysis, the effect of subjective choices is always larger than you would like to think; it is better to have 'transparent' and 'auditable' subjectivity than invisible model choices embedded deep down in the core of the calculation or process.

14.2.2 The Complexity of the Stress-testing Process

The second most frequent objection that I hear about the approach I have proposed in this book is that it is too complex. There is no denying that it cannot be made to work in an

---

[2]Bank analysts tend to compare the 'objective' VaR inputs of banks who report VaR at different percentile levels by scaling up or down using the theoretical ratio of the corresponding percentiles in the case of the Gaussian distribution. This is reasonable, because the analysts cannot, of course, know the true tail behaviour of the profit-and-loss distribution of the various banks. However, this simple procedure can easily understate by 25–40% the estimate of the VaR at the 99 percentile if the reported number was evaluated at the 95 percentile.

afternoon, or in a week. It requires coordination among different functions (see my discussion in Section 14.1.4 above); it makes high demands on the thinking time of the risk managers; and it requires familiarity with quantitative techniques (such as Linear Programming and Bayesian networks), which are unlikely to be in the standard toolkit of the average risk manager.[3]

All of this is true. But, as I argued above, it would be truly extraordinary if we could overcome all the shortcomings the traditional statistical approach to risk quantification with a simple fix that can be added on as an afterthought at little effort and less cost. Solutions to (or improvements on) complex problems rarely are simple and even more rarely come cheap.

Despite the relatively high level of commitment and resources required by the full implementation of the stress-testing programme I have suggested in this book, there is one redeeming feature: every stage of the process brings about incremental improvements to our understanding of the risk position of a firm. Even the entry-level identification of portfolio vulnerabilities, with no probabilistic assessment whatsoever, has great value. So has the assignment of events to probability buckets (however we may choose to do so); the choice of the conditional probabilities; the teasing out of the causal link among the various events; the pruning of the Bayesian net; the analysis of the stand-alone expected conditional losses; etc. I do believe that these features in themselves (which I collectively refer to as the 'polyvalence' of the stress-testing programme I have proposed) can make it a worthwhile investment of resources.

In closing, I do not expect for a second that what I have proposed in this book is the definitive answer to the stress-testing problem, let alone to the current challenges of financial risk management. I just hope that it can provide material for discussion and improvements, and suggest a possible path to exit Berkowitz's statistical purgatory in which stress testing has so far been mired.

---

[3]By the way, these techniques may be less familiar, but they are far simpler, and require far less mathematical sophistication, than, say, stochastic calculus or measure theory.

Appendix

A Simple Introduction to Linear Programming

A.1 Plan of the Appendix

The task dealt with in the chapters in Part III is to obtain a set of self-consistent conditional probabilities as close as possible to the exogenous specification for the same quantities provided by the risk manager. One attractive way to ensure consistency is via Linear Programming. Since this technique is perhaps not as well known in the risk management community as, say, stochastic calculus or Extreme Value Theory, I present in this Appendix a brief and concise introduction. The main ideas behind the Linear Programming approach are very simple, but one of the main obstacles lies in the notation and terminology, which I will therefore try to present as clearly as possible with the specific application at hand clearly in mind.

A.2 Linear Programming – A Refresher

Linear Programming deals with constrained optimization problems[1] when

- the objective function, f (i.e., the function to be maximized or minimized), is linear in the control variables, $x_1, x_2, \ldots, x_n$; and
- the constraints among the control variables are linear inequalities.

The inequality constraints therefore restrict by (hyper)-planes the domain of the control variables.

---

[1]The treatment presented in this section closely mirrors Kreiszig (1993), Chapter 12.

205

The best way to understand the ideas behind Linear Programming and to introduce the terminology is to consider a concrete example. The following numerical example is taken directly from Kreiszig (1993).

Let the function to be maximized be given by

$$f(x_1, x_2) = 29x_1 + 45x_2 \tag{A.1}$$

and let the linear inequalities be

$$2x_1 + 8x_2 \leq 60 \tag{A.2}$$
$$4x_1 + 4x_2 \leq 60 \tag{A.3}$$
$$x_1 \geq 0 \tag{A.4}$$
$$x_2 \geq 0 \tag{A.5}$$

Let us focus on the first inequality (Equation (A.2)), which we can rewrite as

$$60 - 2x_1 - 8x_2 \geq 0 \tag{A.6}$$

So, if we define x_3 to be the quantity

$$x_3 = 60 - 2x_1 - 8x_2 \geq 0 \tag{A.7}$$

by construction it must be non-negative. It serves the purpose of turning an inequality such as Equation (A.2) into an equality:

$$2x_1 + 8x_2 + x_3 = 60 \tag{A.8}$$

plus a positivity constraint:

$$x_3 \geq 0 \tag{A.9}$$

A variable such as x_3 is called a *slack variable*.

Repeating the same procedure for constraint (A.3), and introducing slack variable x_4, we can write

$$2x_1 + 8x_2 + x_3 = 60 \tag{A.10}$$
$$4x_1 + 4x_2 + x_4 = 60 \tag{A.11}$$
$$x_1 \geq 0 \tag{A.12}$$
$$x_2 \geq 0 \tag{A.13}$$
$$x_3 \geq 0 \tag{A.14}$$
$$x_4 \geq 0 \tag{A.15}$$

with

$$x_4 = 60 - 4x_1 - 4x_2 \tag{A.16}$$

More generally, consider an objective function, f,

$$f = f(c_1 x_1 + c_2 x_2 + \cdots + c_n x_n) \tag{A.17}$$

that must be maximized subject to the constraints

$$a_{11}x_1 + \cdots + a_{1n}x_n = b_1 \tag{A.18}$$
$$a_{21}x_1 + \cdots + a_{2n}x_n = b_2$$
$$\cdots$$
$$a_{m1}x_1 + \cdots + a_{mn}x_n = b_m$$
$$x_i \geq 0$$

for $i = 1, 2, \ldots, n$. (Note that the index n includes the slack variables, for which the coefficients c in the argument of the function f are zero, and m is the number of 'original' constraints – that is, the number of constraints excluding the positivity constraints.) Then we can give the following definitions.

Definition 1 A solution (i.e., an n-tuple $x_1, x_2, \ldots, x_n$) that satisfies constraints (A.18) is called a feasible solution.

Definition 2 An optimal solution is a feasible solution that maximizes function f.

Definition 3 A basic feasible solution is a feasible solution for which at least $n - m$ of the variables $x_1, x_2, \ldots, x_n$ are 0.

Note that we have defined a basic feasible solution as a solution which satisfies the constraints, which maximizes f and for which at least $n - m$ of the variables are 0. We are not saying that all solutions that satisfy the constraints and maximize the function f are basic. The following fundamental theorem of Linear Programming, however, reassures ourselves of the following:

Theorem 1 Given the Linear Programming problem in Equations (A.17) and (A.18), some optimal solution is also a basic feasible solution.

The power of the theorem lies in the following observation. In general, a Linear Programming problem may have many optimal solutions (i.e., n-tuples $x_1, x_2, \ldots, x_n$ that maximize f and satisfy the constraints), but they may not all be basic feasible solutions. The fundamental theorem assures us that, even if we restrict our search to the basic solutions, we will never miss an optimal solution.

Restricting the search to basic feasible solutions simplifies the task, but it still remains far from trivial. There is a not-so-small cottage industry devoted to providing search methodologies of different complexity and efficiency. For our purposes the Simplex Method (introduced as far back as 1948) will serve us well enough.

A.3   The Simplex Method

The Simplex Method proceeds iteratively, by identifying a basic feasible solution to start with (we know that the optimal solution will belong to this set), and then performing three operations for each step:

1. We check whether the basic feasible solution is optimal (i.e., satisfies the constraints and maximizes the target function, f). If it does, we stop.

2. If it does not, we find a better basic feasible solution.

3. We transition to that better solution and go back to 1.

Let us see in detail how this works, by considering again the super-simple problem we looked at before: maximize

$$f(x_1, x_2) = 29x_1 + 45x_2 \tag{A.19}$$

subject to

$$2x_1 + 8x_2 + x_3 = 60 \tag{A.20}$$

$$4x_1 + 4x_2 + x_4 = 60 \tag{A.21}$$

$$x_1 \geq 0 \tag{A.22}$$

$$x_2 \geq 0 \tag{A.23}$$

$$x_3 \geq 0 \tag{A.24}$$

$$x_4 \geq 0 \tag{A.25}$$

with

$$x_3 = 60 - 2x_1 - 8x_2 \tag{A.26}$$

$$x_4 = 60 - 4x_1 - 4x_2 \tag{A.27}$$

To carry out the first step (i.e., finding a basic feasible solution) we divide the four variables, x_1, x_2, x_3, x_4, into two groups by selecting $m = 2$ variables as basic variables. Then, by definition of basic feasible solution, the other two variables must be zero at the basic feasible solution. We shall call these latter variables *non-basic variables*.[2]

---

[2]Some texts refer to these variables as right-hand variables. It is not a very good idea to identify some variables on the basis of an arbitrary decision of where we are going to position them on the page. I will not therefore follow this convention, but the reader should be aware of the terminology when reading other books on the subject.

For our problem we start by arbitrarily choosing x_3 and x_4 as basic variables. With some foresight we had already solved for them in Equations (A.26) and (A.27), otherwise we would have to do so now.

As a next step we set to zero the non-basic variables, x_1 and x_2. When we do so, we find from Equations (A.26) and (A.27):

$$x_3 = 60 \qquad\qquad\qquad\qquad (A.28)$$

$$x_4 = 60 \qquad\qquad\qquad\qquad (A.29)$$

As both x_3 and x_4 are greater or equal to zero, the solution we have found is indeed a feasible solution (i.e., the constraints are satisfied). Since we have chosen the basic variables arbitrarily, this will not always be the case. If our choice of basic variables had given a negative value once we had solved for either of them, we would have had to choose different basic variables to start the procedure.

We now test for optimality, that is, we check whether the constraint-satisfying solution we have found also maximizes f. Let us look at the objective function as a function of the non-basic variables:

$$f(x_1, x_2) = 29x_1 + 45x_2 \qquad\qquad\qquad (A.30)$$

(the basic variables are at zero). Note that the two coefficients are positive. Therefore the solution is not optimal because I could increase the value of the objective function by increasing both x_1 and x_2. This is allowed, because the constraints are simply $x_1 \geq 0, x_2 \geq 0$.

But this also tells us when we should stop in our search for an optimal solution: we are done when the coefficients of the objective function are all negative or zero. Then we know that we are at an optimal solution, because we cannot increase the objective function by increasing the nonbasic variables (remember that they must be non-negative). We can therefore express the following condition for optimality: a basic feasible solution is an optimal solution if the coefficients of the non-basic variables in the objective function are negative or zero.

We now move to the second step: finding a better basic feasible solution. We have to try another basic feasible solution, that is, we must go to a point where another variable x_i is zero. Remember why we are doing this: because, thanks to the fundamental theorem above, we know that some optimal solution is also a *basic* feasible solution. We can, in other words, restrict our search to basic solutions. Unfortunately the first basic solution we tried was not an optimal one. We must perform what is called an exchange of variables. We proceed as follows.

We want to carry out the switch of basic/non-basic variables that will give us the biggest 'bang for the buck', i.e., that will allow us to increase the target function as much as possible. We start by choosing a non-basic variable, x_{NB}, that has a positive coefficient. For our problem, this could be x_1:

$$x_{NB} = x_1 \qquad\qquad\qquad\qquad (A.31)$$

We set the other non-basic variables (in our case x_2) at zero. We determine the largest increase, Δx_{NB}, in x_{NB} that leaves all the previous basic variables (i.e., x_3 and x_4) non-negative. We call Δf the corresponding increase in the objective function, f. So, in our case we start from

$$x_3 = 60 - 2x_1 - 8x_2 \qquad\qquad (A.32)$$

$$x_4 = 60 - 4x_1 - 4x_2 \qquad\qquad (A.33)$$

We set the basic variables (i.e., x_3 and x_4) to zero to give

$$0 = 60 - 2x_1 - 8x_2 \qquad\qquad (A.34)$$

$$0 = 60 - 4x_1 - 4x_2 \qquad\qquad (A.35)$$

Since we have chosen $x_{NB} = x_1$, we set to zero the other non-basic variable:

$$0 = 60 - 2x_1 \qquad\qquad (A.36)$$

$$0 = 60 - 4x_1 \qquad\qquad (A.37)$$

Then, from $0 = 60 - 2x_1$ we get

$$\Delta x_1 = 30 \implies \Delta f = 29\Delta x_1 = 870 \qquad\qquad (A.38)$$

So, $\Delta x_1 = 30$ is the maximum increase we can give to x_1 because of the constraint imposed by Equation $0 = 60 - 2x_1$.

Similarly, from $0 = 60 - 4x_1$ we get

$$\Delta x_1 = 15 \implies \Delta f = 29\Delta x_1 = 435 \qquad\qquad (A.39)$$

We see that the objective function would increase more if we gave to x_1 the increment $\Delta x_1 = 30$, but if we did so, the quantity $60 - 4x_1$ would become negative. Therefore the maximum increment we can give to x_1 is $\Delta x_1 = 15$. The following equation prevents any increase in x_1 greater than $\Delta x_1 = 15$:

$$x_4 = 60 - \underline{4x_1} - 4x_2 \qquad\qquad (A.40)$$

We therefore underline the variable x_1 in Equation (A.40).

We must do the same for the other non-basic variable with a positive coefficient, that is, in our case, with x_2. This gives

$$x_{NB} = x_2 \qquad\qquad (A.41)$$

We set the other non-basic variables (now x_1) at zero. Then

$$x_3 = 60 - 2x_1 - 8x_2 \qquad\qquad (A.42)$$

$$x_4 = 60 - 4x_1 - 4x_2 \qquad\qquad (A.43)$$

Setting the basic variables and the other non-basic variable to zero now gives

$$0 = 60 - 8x_2 \tag{A.44}$$

$$0 = 60 - 4x_2 \tag{A.45}$$

Therefore, $\Delta x_2 = 7.5$ from Equation (A.44) and $\Delta x_2 = 15$ from Equation (A.44). This gives in one case

$$\Delta x_2 = 7.5 \implies \Delta f = 45\Delta x_2 = 337.5 \tag{A.46}$$

and in the other

$$\Delta x_2 = 15 \implies \Delta f = 45\Delta x_2 = 675 \tag{A.47}$$

Therefore, much as we would like to be able to increase the objective function all the way up to 675, we are 'blocked' by

$$x_3 = 60 - 2x_1 - \underline{8x_2} \tag{A.48}$$

Consider now the two equations with underlined variables:

$$x_3 = 60 - 2x_1 - \underline{8x_2} \quad \Delta f = 337.5 \tag{A.49}$$

$$x_4 = 60 - \underline{4x_1} - 4x_2 \quad \Delta f = 435 \tag{A.50}$$

We want to exchange the role of one basic and one non-basic variable. Which non-basic variable should we choose? The one that gave the greatest increment to Δf. Since $\Delta f = 435$ for Equation (A.50) and $\Delta f = 337.5$ for Equation (A.49), our switch will be between x_1 (which now becomes basic) and x_4. Solving for x_1 in Equation (A.50) and substituting in Equation (A.49) we get

$$x_1 = 15 - x_2 - \frac{1}{4}x_4 \tag{A.51}$$

$$x_3 = 30 - 6x_2 + \frac{1}{2}x_4 \tag{A.52}$$

The same three operations are now performed again with the new set of basic and non-basic variables. If the reader is patient enough, she will find that the new basic solution is still non-optimal, because not all the coefficients are negative. But she will also observe that now only one coefficient will be positive, and therefore there will be no need to make a choice of which variables should be switched between being basic and non-basic.

The switch procedure continues until all the coefficients are negative, at which point the basic solution will be an optimal basic solution. By the fundamental theorem above, we are done.

Obviously, I do not recommend carrying out this three-step-tango by hand for more than three variables. There are readily available pieces of source code that can be adapted for the purpose (see, e.g., Press *et al.* (1992)), but it is always useful to have an idea of what is inside the black box. Providing this idea was the purpose behind this Appendix.

References

Akerlof, G. A. and Shiller, R. J. (2009) *Animal Spirits – How Human Psychology Drives the Economy, and Why It Matters for Global Capitalism*, Princeton University Press, Princeton, NJ and Oxford.

Alexander, C. and Sheedy, E. (2008) *Model-Based Stress Tests: Linking Stress Tests to VaR for Market Risk*, MAFC Research Paper No. 33, Macquire University, Applied Finance Centre.

Allison, G. and Zelikow, P. (1999) *Essence of Decision*, 2nd edn, Addison Wesley Longman, New York.

Aragones, J. R., Blanco, C. and Dowd, K. (2001) Incorporating Stress Testing Into Market Risk Modelling, *Insitutional Investor*, Spring, 44–49.

Babcock, L., Loewenstein, G., Issacharoff, S. and Camerer, C. (1995) Biased Judgments of Fairness in Bargaining, *American Economic Review*, **85**, 1337–1343.

Babcock, L., Loewenstein, G. and Issacharoff, S. (1997) Creating Convergence: Debiasing Biased Litigants, *Law and Social Inquiry*, **22**, 913–925.

Berkowitz, J. (1999) A Coherent Framework for Stress-Testing, *Journal of Risk*, **2**(2), 5–15.

BIS (Bank of International Settlements) (2009) Principles for Sound Stress Testing Practices and Supervision, consultative paper, January 2009 (latest version, May 2009).

Bookstaber, R. (2008) *A Demon of Our Own Design*, John Wiley & Sons, Ltd, Chichester, UK.

Brighton, H. and Gigerenzer, G. (2008) Bayesian Brains and Cognitive Mechanisms: Harmony or Dissonance? in *The Probabilistic Mind – Prospects for Bayesian Cognitive Science*, N. Chater and M. Oaksford (eds), Oxford Univeristy Press, Oxford, UK, Chapter 9.

Casebeer, W. D. (2008) *The Stories Markets Tell – Affordances for Ethical Behaviour In Free Exchange*, in *Moral Markets – The Critical Role of Values in the Economy*, P. J. Zak (ed.) Princeton University Press, Princeton, NJ and Oxford, Chapter 1.

Chamley, C. P. (2004) *Rational Herds: Economic Models of Social Learning*, Cambridge University Press, Cambridge, UK.

Chater, N. and Oaksford, M. (eds) (2008) *The Probabilistic Mind – Prospects for Bayesian Cognitive Science*, Oxford Univeristy Press, Oxford.

Cohen, W. D. (2009) *House of Cards – How Wall Street Gamblers Broke Capitalism*, Allen Lane, London.

Davidson, P. (2009) *John Maynard Keynes*, Palgrave Macmillan, Houndmills, Hampshire, UK.

Davis, J. K. and Sweeney, M. J. (1999) *Strategic Paradigms 2025: US Security Planning for a New Era*, Institute for Foreign Policy Analysis, Cambridge, MA.

Dumas, B. (2008) Endorsement on back cover of Shefrin (2008).

Evans, G. W. and Honkapohja, S. (2005) An Interview with Thomas G Sargent, *Macroeconomic Dynamics*, **9**, 561–583.

Fauconnier, G. and Turner, M. (2002) *The Way We Think: Conceptual Blending and the Mind's Hidden Complexities*, Basic Books, New York.

Friedman, M. and Jacobson Schartz, A. (1963 [2008]) *The Great Contraction, 1929–1933*, Princeton University Press, Princeton, New Jersey.

Frydman, R. and Goldberg M. D. (2007) *Imperfect Knowledge Economics: Exchange Rates and Risk*, Princeton University Press, Princeton, NJ.

Frydman, R. and Goldberg, M. D. (2009) *Financial Markets and the State: Long Swings, Risk and the Scope of Regulation*, *Capitalism and Society*, **4**(2), available at: http://www.bepress.com/cas/vol4/iss2/art2, accessed 20 November 2009, Berkeley Electronic Press.

Gigerenzer, G. and Hoffrage, U. (1995) How to Improve Bayesian Reasoning Without Instructions. Frequency Formats, *Psychological Review*, **102**, 684–704.

Gigerenzer, G. and Selten, R. (2002) *Rethinking Rationality*, in *Bounded Rationality – The Adaptive Toolbox*, G. Gigerenzer and R, Selten (eds), MIT Press, Cambridge, MA.

Gigerenzer, G. and Selten, R. (eds) (2002) *Bounded Rationality – The Adaptive Toolbox*, MIT Press, Cambridge, MA.

Good, I. J. (1973) The probabilistic explication of evidence, surprise, causality, explanation, and utility, in *Foundations of Statistical Inference*, V. P. Godambe and D. A. Sprott (eds), Holt, Rinehart and Winston, Toronto.

Granger, C. W. J. (1969) Investigating Causal Relations by Econometric Models and Cross-Spectral Methods, *Econometrica*, **37**(3), 424–438.

Greenspan, A. (2008) Congressional Testimony, 23 October 2008.

Greenspan, A. (2009) We Need a Better Cushion Against Risk, *Financial Times*, p. 11, 27 March.

Greer, W. N. (2000) *Ethics and Uncertainty*, Elgar, Cheltenham, UK.

Grether, D. (1980) Bayes Rule as a Descriptive Model: The Representativeness Heuristic, *Quarterly Journal of Economics*, **95**, 537–557.

Griffiths, T. L. and Tenenbaum, J. B. (2005) Optimal Predictions in Everyday Cognition, *Psychological Science*, **17**(9), 767–773.

Guarino, A. and Cipriani, M. (2008) Herd Behaviour in Financial Markets: An Experiment with Financial Market Professionals. IMF Working Paper 08/141, International Monetary Fund.

Gintis, H. (2009) *The Bounds of Reason: Game Theory and the Unification of the Behavioral Sciences*, Princeton University Press, Princeton, NY.

Hirtle, B., Schuermann, T. and Stiroh, K. (2009) Macroprudential Supervision of Financial Institutions: Lessons from the SCAP, Federal Reserve Bank of New York Staff Reports, Staff Report no. 409, November 2009, available at http://newyorkfed.org/research/staff_reports/sr409.html (accessed 5 February 2009).

Hacker, S. R. and Hatemi-J, A. (2006) Tests for Causality between Integrated Variables Using Asymptotic and Bootstrap Distributions: Theory and Applications, *Applied Economics*, **38**(13), 1489–1500.

Hacking, I. (2001) *An Introduction to Inductive Logic and Probability*, Cambridge University Press, Cambridge, UK.

Jaynes, E. T. (2003) *Probability Theory: The Logic of Science*, Cambridge University Press, Cambridge, UK.

Jolls, C. and Sunstein, C. (2005) *Debiasing Through Law*, University of Chicago, John M Olin School of Law and Economics Working Paper No. 225, second series.

Kahneman, D., Slovic, P. and Tversky, A. (eds) (1982) *Judgement under Uncertainty: Heuristics and Biases*, Cambridge University Press, Cambridge, UK.

Kahneman, D. and Tversky, A. (1972a) On Prediction and Judgement, *ORI Research Monograph*, **12**(4).

Kahneman, D. and Tversky, A. (1972b) Subjective Probability: A Judgement of Representativeness, *Cognitive Psychology*, **3**, 430–454.

Kahneman, D. and Tversky, A. (1973) On the Psychology of Prediction, *Psychological Review*, **80**, 237–251.

Kahneman, D. and Tversky, A. (1979a) Intuitive Prediction: Biases and Corrective Procedures, *TIMS Studies in Management Science*, **12**, 313–327.

Kahneman, D. and Tversky, A. (1979b) Prospect Theory: An Analysis of Decision Under Risk, *Econometrica*, **47**, 263–291.

Kahneman, D. and Tversky, A. (eds) (2000) *Choices, Values, and Frames*, Cambridge University Press, Cambridge, UK.

Knill, D. C. and Pouget, A. (2004) The Bayesian Brain: The Role of Uncertainty in Neural Coding and Computation, *Trends in Neuroscience*, **27**(12), 712–719.

Knight, F. N. (1921) *Risk, Uncertainty and Profit*, Houghton Mifflin, New York.

Kreiszig, E. (1993) *Advanced Engineering Mathematics*, 7th edn, John Wiley and Sons, Ltd, Chichester, UK.

Kwiatkowski, J. and Rebonato, R. (2010). A Coherent Aggregation Framework for Stress Testing and Scenario Analysis, submitted to *Applied Mathematical Finance*.

Lakoff, G. and Johnson, M. (1980) *Metaphors We Live By*, University of Chicago Press, Chicago, IL.

Lucas, R. E. (1977) Understanding Business Cycles, in *Stabilization of the Domestic and International Economy*, K. Brunner and A. H. Meltzer (eds), Carnegie Mellon Conference on Public Policy, 5, North-Holland, Amsterdam.

Luce, D. R. and Raiffa, H. (1957) *Games and Decisions*, Dover Publications, New York.

Malvergne, Y. and Sornette, D. (2006) *Extreme Financial Risk: From Dependence to Risk Management*, Springer Verlag, New York.

Martignon, L. (2002) Comparing Fast and Frugal Heuristics and Optimal Models, in *Bounded Rationality – The Adaptive Toolbox*, G. Gigerenzer and R. Selten (eds), MIT Press, Cambridge, MA.

Matten, C. (2000) *Managing Bank Capital: Capital Allocation and Performance Measurement*, 2nd edn, John Wiley and Sons, Ltd, Chichester, UK.

McKenzie, K. (2006) *An Engine, not a Camera*, MIT Press, Cambridge, MA.

McNeil, A., Frey, R. and Embrechts, P. (2005) *Quantitative Risk Management*, Princeton University Press, Princeton, NJ.

Miller, J. H. and Page, S. E. (2007) *Complex Adaptive Systems – An Introduction to Computational Models of Social Life*, Princeton University Press, Princeton, NJ.

Moore A. (2001) *Bayes Nets for Representing and Reasoning About Uncertainty*, Carnegie Mellon University, http://www.autonlab.org/tutorials/bayesnet09.pdf, last accessed 18 August 2009.

Moskowitz, H. and Sarin, R. K. (1983) Improving the Consistency of Conditional Probability Assessment for Forecasting and Decision Making, *Management Science*, **29**(6), 735–749.

Muth, J. F. (1961) Rational Expectations and the Theory of Price Movements, *Econometrica*, **29**, 315–335, quoted in Frydman, R. and Goldberg, M. D. (2007) *Imperfect Knowledge Economics: Exchange Rates and Risk*, Princeton University Press, Princeton, NJ.

Neapolitan, R. E. (2003) *Learning Bayesian Networks*, Prentice Hall, Upper Saddle River, NJ.

Nelsen, R. B. (1999) *An Introduction to Copulas*, Lecture Notes in Statistics, Springer Verlag, New York.

Nisbett, R. (2009) *Intelligence and How to Get It – Why Schools and Cultures Count*, W.W. Norton, New York and London.

Ozdenoren, E. and Yuan, K. (2008), Feedback Effects and Asset Prices, *Journal of Finance*, **LXIII**(4), 1939–1975.

Pearl, J, (2009), *Causality*, 2nd edn, Cambridge University Press, Cambridge, UK.

Poirier, D. (1995), *Intermediate Statistics and Econometrics*, MIT Press, Cambridge, MA.

Press, W. H., Teukolski, S. A., Vetterling, W. T. and Flannery, B. P. (1992) *Numerical Recipes in Fortran 77 – The Art of Scientific Computing*, 2nd edn, Cambridge University Press, Cambridge, UK.

Rebonato, R. (2007) *The Plight of the Fortune Tellers – Why We Must Manage Financial Risk Differently*, Princeton University Press, Princeton, NJ.

Rebonato, R. (2009) What Models Do We Need for Risk Management?, in *QFinance – The Ultimate Resource*, Bloomsbury, London, 228–231.

Rebonato, R. (2010) Post-Crisis Financial Risk Management: Some Suggestions, *Journal of Risk Management in Financial Institutions*, **3**(2), 1–8.

Robertson, D. H. (1936) Some Notes on Mr. Keynes' General Theory of Employment, *The Quarterly Journal of Economics*, **51**(1), 168–191.

Sargent, T. J. (2005), interviewed in Evans and Honkapohja (2005).

Schwartz, B. (2004) *The Paradox of Choice*, Harper Collins, New York.

Schuermann, T. (2009) Personal Communication.

Selten, R. (1991) Evolution, Learning and Economic Behaviour, *Games and Economic Behaviour*, **3**, 3–24.

Selten, R. (1998) Features of Experimentally Observed Bounded Rationality, *European Economic Review*, **42**, 413–436.

Shamrakov, L. (2006) *Joint Dynamics of Credit Spreads and Equity Prices*, MSc Thesis, Oxford University.

Shefrin, H. (2000) *Beyond Greed and Fear – Understanding Behvioural Finance and the Psychology of Investing*, Harvard Business School Press, Harvard, MA.

Shefrin, H. (2008) *A Behavioural Approach to Asset Pricing*, 2nd edn, Academic Press, Oxford, UK.

Shelling, T. (1978) *Micromotives and Macrobehaviour*, Norton, New York and London.

Shleifer A. (2000) *Inefficient Markets – An Introduction to Behavioural Finance*, Clarendon Lectures in Economics, Oxford University Press, Oxford, UK.

Simon, H. A. (1956) Rational Choice and the Structure of Environments, *Psychological Review*, **63**, 129–138.

Simon, H. A. (1957) *Models of Man*, John Wiley & Sons Inc., New York.

Skidelsky, R. (2009) *Keynes – The Return of the Master*, Public Affairs, Perseus Books, New York.

Sorge, M. (2004) *Stress-Testing Financial Systems: An Overview of Current Methodologies*, Monetary and Economics Department, BIS Working Paper No. 165, December 2004, 1–41.

Soros, G. (1987) *The Alchemy of Finance*, John Wiley & Sons Inc., New York.

Soros, G. (2008) *The New Paradigm for Financial Markets: The Credit Crisis of 2008 and What It Means*, Public Affairs, New York.

Stewart, N. (2008) quoted in *The Economist*, 13 December 2008, 'Credit Cards – A Nudge in the Wrong Direction', 88.

Stigler, G. J. (1961) The Economics of Information, *Journal of Political Economy*, **69**, 191–214.

Stirzacker D. (1999) *Probability and Random Variables – A Beginner's Guide*, Cambridge University Press, Cambridge, UK.

Tversky, A. and Kahneman, D. (1979) Causal Schemata in Judgments under Uncertainty, in *Progress in Social Psychology*, M. Fishbein (ed.), Lawrence Erlbaum Associates, Hillsdale, Chapter 8.

Tversky, A. and Kahneman, D. (1982) Evidential Impact of Base Rates, in *Judgement under Uncertainty: Heuristics and Biases*, D. Kahneman, P. Slovic, and A. Tversky (eds), Cambridge University Press, Cambridge, UK, Chapter 10.

Tzani, R. and Polychronakos, A. P. (2008) Correlation Breakdown, Copula Credit Models and Arbitrage, *GARP Risk Review*, **December**, 27–37.

Williams, D. (2001) *Weighing the Odds – A Course in Probability and Statistics*, Cambridge University Press, Cambridge, UK.

Williamson, J. (2005) *Bayesian Nets and Causality – Philosophical and Computational Foundations*, Oxford University Press, Oxford, UK.

Index

ABSs 118, 176
acyclical directed graphs
  see also Bayesian networks
  concepts 49, 99–115
  terminology 99–101
adaptiveness concepts, bounded rationality
  176–8, 184–5
adjustable-rate mortgages (ARMs) 188
advanced quantitative foundations 5–6, 47,
  71–91
agents 9–10, 18, 21–2, 23–30, 173–4, 185
  see also asset managers; banks; pension fund
    trustees; traders
  coordination thesis 18, 25–7, 29–30
  principal/agent relationships 24–6, 30
  traders 18, 23–7
  types 26
Akerlof, G.A. 188
algorithms, Bayesian networks 111–15
Allison, G. 20, 23, 190
Amaranth 199
ancestors, graph concepts 99–115, 158–70,
  194–6
anchoring bias
  concepts 174–5, 183–4
  definition 183–4
appendix 205–12
applications 1–5, 9, 27–30, 39, 41, 49, 53, 57,
  90, 94, 98, 99, 101, 113–15, 131–70
Aragones, J.R. 1, 2, 4–5, 192
arbitrage 24, 30
arcs/edges, graph concepts 99–115, 155–70,
  194–6
Aristotle 42
ARMs *see* adjustable-rate mortgages
arrows
  see also Bayesian networks
  graph concepts 99–115, 155–70, 194–6
asset classes 118–29, 193–4
asset managers 26, 30
association
  causation 63–5

concepts 5, 37, 39–43, 63–5, 93–8, 100–15,
  118–29, 151–3, 180–1, 187–96
  critique 39–40
audits, stress tests 197, 199, 201, 203
Australian Central Bank 195
axioms, concepts 51–3

'backwards' contexts 40–2
banking-book portfolios 190
banks 10–11, 16–17, 24–6, 33–4, 49, 53–4,
  56–7, 58–9, 121–3, 135, 150–3, 156–70,
  179–81, 189–96, 201
  dimensionality problems 192–4
  failures 24–6, 33–4, 49, 53–4, 56–7, 58–9,
    121–3, 156–70, 179–81, 191, 194–6
  regulatory capital 10–11, 16–17, 24, 26, 135,
    150–3, 167–70, 189–90, 196, 201
  typical activities 192–3
base-rate bias *see* representativeness bias
basic variables, linear programming concepts
  114–15, 140, 148, 207–12
Bayes' Theorem 4, 22, 32–43, 57–62, 63–9, 71,
  83–91, 101–15, 126–9, 158–70, 173–85,
  200
  see also conditional probabilities; joint
    probabilities; subjective probabilities
  concepts 57–62, 63–9, 83, 101–15, 126–9,
    158–9, 163–7, 200
  definition 57–8, 63
Bayesian networks
  see also conditional probability tables;
    two-valued Boolean variables
  algorithms 111–15
  bottom-up approaches to stress scenarios
    188–96
  breaking-down-the-joint rule 107–11, 112–15
  closure rule 108–11, 161–5
  coherent solutions 155–70
  commutativity rule 108–11, 161–70
  concepts 4, 5, 6, 39, 41, 49–50, 53, 57, 69,
    73–91, 94, 98, 99–115, 117–29, 134–5,
    155–70, 182, 188–96, 204

Printed and bound by CPI Group (UK) Ltd, Croydon, CR0 4YY

16/04/2025

14658509-0001